Tracing Dominican Identity

Tracing Dominican Identity
The Writings of Pedro Henríquez Ureña

Juan R. Valdez

TRACING DOMINICAN IDENTITY
Copyright © Juan R. Valdez, 2011.

All rights reserved.

First published in 2011 by PALGRAVE MACMILLAN® in the
United States - a division of St. Martin's Press LLC, 175 Fifth Avenue,
New York, NY 10010.

Where this book is distributed in the UK, Europe and the rest of the World,
this is by Palgrave Macmillan, a division of Macmillan Publishers Limited,
registered in England, company number 785998, of Houndmills,
Basingstoke, Hampshire RG21 6XS.

Palgrave Macmillan is the global academic imprint of the above companies
and has companies and representatives throughout the world.

Palgrave® and Macmillan® are registered trademarks in the United States,
the United Kingdom, Europe and other countries.

ISBN: 978–0–230–10937–7

Library of Congress Cataloging-in-Publication Data

Valdez, Juan R.
  Tracing Dominican identity : the writings of Pedro Henríquez Ureña /
Juan R. Valdez.
    p. cm.
  Includes bibliographical references.
  ISBN 978–0–230–10937–7 (alk. paper)
  1. Henríquez Ureña, Pedro, 1884–1946—Criticism and interpretation.
  2. Henríquez Ureña, Pedro, 1884–1946—Knowledge—Spanish language.
  3. Henríquez Ureña, Pedro, 1884–1946—Knowledge—Dominican
  Republic.   4. National characteristics, Dominican, in literature.
  5. Dominican Republic—In literature.   6. Spanish language—
  Dominican Republic.   7. Language and culture—Dominican
  Republic.   I. Title.
  PQ7409.H4Z94 2011
  868'.6209—dc22   2010029868

Design by Integra Software Services

First edition: February 2011

10 9 8 7 6 5 4 3 2 1

Printed in the United States of America.

En memoria de mi querida madre, Melba Núñez

Contents

Acknowledgments	ix
Introduction	1
1 Pedro Henríquez Ureña: The Making of a Latinamericanist	7
2 Linguistic Ideologies and the History of Linguistic Ideas	33
3 Nationalism and Hispanoamericanism in the Dominican Republic and Latin America	63
4 Pedro Henríquez Ureña in Hispanic Linguistics	95
5 Pedro Henríquez Ureña and the Whitening of Dominican Identity	131
Conclusion	165
Notes	169
References	201
Index	223

Acknowledgments

I was able to begin and complete this book with the encouragement and support of a select group of individuals and academic institutions. My debt to José Del Valle includes his crucial guidance and tireless encouragement throughout my career as a doctoral student and since the beginning of this research project at the City University of New York's Graduate Center. His unique approach to the sociology of language and the political history of Spanish as well as his generosity and personal charisma have been an inspiration for this present work. I am most grateful for his friendship. Ricardo Otheguy helped to lay the foundation for my advanced sociolinguistic studies and also motivated my work on Pedro Henríquez Ureña with profoundly critical questions, constantly reminding me of the importance of rigorous research. Like *Don* Pedro, I also thank *los maestros y los sabios*, those wise teachers who inspired me and helped to create the right conditions for learning and exploring linguistic, political, and personal phenomena: Bonnie Urciuoli, Carol Rupprecht, Isaías Lerner, Eugenio Suárez Galbán, Rick Werner, Ana Celia Zentella, and Guadalupe Valdés. Julio Ramos was kind enough to read the manuscript and offered me the benefit of his insights and erudition. I wish to thank the anonymous reader of the manuscript, whose enthusiasm and critical comments helped to further advance this project and Robyn Curtis of Palgrave Macmillan for facilitating and moving things forward. CUNY's Doctoral Student Research Grant Program and the Centro de Estudios Puertorriqueños provided funds for initial research and participation in key conferences. Thanks to my friends and family, who at some point provided some form of assistance, camaraderie, or helpful hint, especially: Louis, the coolest cat in Berkeley; Marco Aponte; Laura Villa; Rafay Salim; Herbert Seignoret; Fernando Valerio-Holguín; Danny Mendez; Amir Farooq; Paul Nissler; Gregory M. Hodge; Antonio Giménez; Franklin Figueroa; Wendy Valdez; Ana Hall Valdez; Jonathan Valdez; and Landers Hall. Finally, this work could not have been completed without the loving support, input, wit, feedback, criticism, patience, smile, laughter, charm, and wonderful company of Katherine, *siempre, ¡mi sol de abril!*

Introduction

Invocations such as "In the beginning God created the Heavens and the Earth" or "Once upon a time" exercise a majestic power over memory and imagination. Beginnings and stories about beginnings are hard to resist, as the cultural critic Edward Said pointed out, because they establish priorities and convey greater explanatory power than other forms of analysis and explorations of history.[1] The Spanish word *principios* is synonymous with "beginnings," "first notions," and "established theoretical and moral criteria" and eloquently expresses these functions. A beginning is a set of principles that guides the effort to establish an unquestionable foundation for human behavior, social institutions, tradition, culture, and language. Guided by a sense of loss (of precious heritage, oral traditions, idiosyncrasies, or birthright), inquiry into the past becomes part of a process of restoration during which a great deal of work is done to recapture a language that best expresses our identity and indicates the definite place to which we belong in this world.

Certain transformations occur in the process of establishing beginnings and rooting ourselves. As a teenager in a South Bronx immigrant community, I remember trading my chemistry classes for *merengue* parties, trodden sneakers for pointy dress shoes, a short crop haircut for "Jheri" curls, homegrown humility for *tigueraje* (street savvy), and my recently acquired conversational English for the latest Dominican slang, all for the sake of solidifying my Dominicanness. This was much to the chagrin of one concerned and mortified teacher, who, for a minute, saw me going down the slippery slope of high school truancy and delinquency. As almost happened in my case, the present and the future can often be damaged or betrayed by a reconstruction of the past.

Arcadio Díaz Quiñones (2006) reminds us that, for the Latin American intellectual Pedro Henríquez Ureña, beginnings were vital. His work on the Spanish language and Latin American culture aimed to recreate a clear and historiographically solid foundation for Latin American societies. For example, Henríquez Ureña designated Christopher Columbus's *Diary* as the first expression of Dominican letters: "Columbus's Diary, selected and preserved by Fray Bartolomé de Las Casas, contains the pages with which we rightfully open up our literary history. The praise for our island combined with his general description of the Antilles created the defining image of America for Europeans."[2] The implication is clear: history begins at the designated point and not before.

Henríquez Ureña's views on Dominican beginnings converge with a classic historiographical theory in Dominican scholarship to which we can tentatively refer as "the theory of firstness." This theory proposes that most Dominican social phenomena can be explained with reference to the first permanent European settlement in the New World and its subsequent development. It goes something like this: the Dominican Republic was the site of the first colonial village, the first cathedral, the first convent, the first university, and so on. This theory goes beyond simply utilizing history and memory in order to understand the present; it seeks instead to reconfigure the present and the future on the basis of the model offered by a reconstructed and uncontested past. Traditionally, Dominican intellectuals have systematically applied this theory to a wide range of phenomena, including the status and history of Spanish in the Dominican Republic. For example, Emilio Rodríguez Demorizi (1975) wrote:

> According to Columbus, with Anacaona, Caonabo, and Enriquillo, *the smooth and polished tongue, the world's sweetest*, disappeared. And just like vanishing stars, whose fading light seems to dissipate during dawn's first glimmer—to use Zorrilla de San Martín's beautiful expression—so did the primitive languages of America vanish before the splendid beginning of the Spanish language which had already become a national body... It was precisely at that time that the Spanish language was becoming organized, developing norms, trading instability for precision, making a larger transition from the Middle Ages to the splendid Renaissance... From that moment on, Spanish became the only language in the island, before which only a few indigenous names in our toponymy, barely worth mentioning, and a few scarce African words remain.[3]

In other words, Dominican history began with the absence of indigenous elements and in the splendid presence of Spanish. Both Rodríguez Demorizi (1975) and Manuel Núñez (1990 and 2004) begin their reflections on the status of Dominican Spanish by alluding to the Spaniards' rather effortless conquest over the indigenous groups, in particular their attempt to maintain "linguistic order." In varying fashion, both authors utilize the "firstness" theory to argue that, in the Dominican Republic, Spanish is, above all, a homogeneous entity that both diachronically and synchronically reflects the nature, past and present, of the nation.

These authors belong to the Dominican scholarly tradition that has produced a number of foundational texts about language, race, and identity that significantly contributed to the homogenizing ideologies of Dominican national identity (García 1878, Lugo 1952, Peña Batlle 1968, Sánchez Valverde 1785). They argue that Spanish was imposed quickly, thus creating a linguistically homogeneous colony. For example, in narrating the monumental history of Spanish and the Dominican nation, then President Joaquín Balaguer (1991) stated:

> It must be affirmed that the survival of Hispaniola, Columbus's favorite, is a miracle that can only be explained by the strong vitality of our race and the persistent place which we occupy within the Spanish language, the foundation of our national being during the colony, still today, the principal basis of our development as an independent nation.[4]

Almost invariably, Dominican intellectuals and politicians identify the start of their nation's history with the arrival of the Spanish language. In other words, with Spanish, the Spaniards planted the seeds of the Dominican nation. Its quick spread and dominance established the homogeneity that would characterize the country throughout its history to the present time.

In contrast with the simplifying and commonly held belief that the Dominican Republic is a monolingual Spanish-speaking country, recent linguistic research has produced a more nuanced view of this territory as a complex speech community with a number of vibrant contact zones (Alba 2004, Jiménez Sabater 1975, Núñez Cedeño 1980, Toribio 2005). Yet, as I will show in Chapter 1, scholars do not give sufficient attention to the fact that the study of linguistic phenomena in the Dominican Republic must undergo a postcolonial framing. Considering the origin and evolution of these contact zones, we must shine a new light on the inflexible philological images of the past that prevail in Dominican scholarship and the Dominican imaginary.

In this endeavor, it will be crucial to understand exactly how representations of language and linguistic history are related, to a large degree, to a dynamic process that involves perceiving or creating similarity. From Plato to Charles Sanders Peirce, this phenomenon has occupied philosophers and writers for centuries. Scholars who study different aspects of this phenomenon call it *iconicity*. For semioticians, iconicity refers to the construction and interpretation of signs motivated by some degree of similarity, or by a perceived connection between words and the world, between language and reality. *Iconists* insist that language, to a large degree, is a reflection of reality. Naturally, for those who hold these views, language should also reflect the order of things in society. In Chapter 2, we elaborate and expand this concept under the label *iconization*, taking into account its ideological component, in order to understand the extralinguistic meaning that is created as a result of these semiotic processes and how it is related to issues of power. Here, I provide a number of essential reference points without which we could not identify the mechanisms nor understand the functions of language ideologies. This chapter lays out, on the basis of a perceived connection between speech patterns and racial or ethnic attributes of Dominican identity, the theoretical ground to analyze how Henríquez Ureña's linguistic texts constitute a representation of Dominican Spanish.[5]

In dealing with linguistic texts or representations of language in which identity and history intersect, it is essential to adopt an interdisciplinary approach. As Chapters 3 and 4 will make clear, representations of language cannot be fully understood without delineating the particular intellectual context and climate of opinion in which they emerge. This kind of analytical work requires an interdisciplinary effort that goes beyond my primary formalist training in the field of linguistics and delves into other diverse yet related fields of knowledge that include history, sociology, and anthropology. The purpose of this book is to approach Pedro Henríquez Ureña's linguistic work on Dominican Spanish by situating it in the intellectual climate and political context in which it emerged. Of particular interest is the role that Hispanism has played as a formative force in both the politics of identity in the Spanish-speaking world and the field of language studies. Throughout, I advance the argument that, in Henríquez Ureña's linguistic writings, Spanish stands as an object of discourse in which issues related to the nation's identity and racial composition are debated. Specifically, in Chapter 5, I analyze the two main semiotic strategies (*iconization* and *erasure*) that surface throughout Henríquez Ureña's description of Spanish in the Dominican Republic and the manner in which they are related to the construction of Dominican national identity, a linguistic project of the state, and the strategic sociopolitical formation some (Calvet 2005, Errington 2008) have called imperial or colonial.

While Pedro Henríquez Ureña remains a unifying figure for latinamericanists, his writings often drive a wedge between students of his work. Inevitably, opposition surfaces around the superficial question of whether his silence on the subject of Afro-Dominicans reveals racism. We, instead, will confront Henríquez Ureña's writings on Spanish and Latin American identities with more probing questions such as, Does this particular approach to culture and history, which constantly highlights and gives priority to the colonial beginnings of New World societies, emerge from fear of the untidy and changing circumstances of Latin American societies during the first half of the twentieth century? How often is the scrutiny of beginnings motivated by a need to reconsider the present order of things or driven by fear of an uncertain future? Initially, at least, we cannot escape a reflection on our subject's own beginnings as an intellectual and a linguist before we proceed to scrutinize and interrogate his texts.

I

Pedro Henríquez Ureña: The Making of a Latinamericanist

Many outstanding scholars and talented writers have examined Pedro Henríquez Ureña's (1884–1946) writings, leaving us with a fixed image of his life and work. Yet, we still do not have a clear intellectual and political profile of him. He is undoubtedly a pivotal figure in the study of the Hispanic world, especially for students of Latinamericanism. Pedro Henríquez Ureña's name is closely linked with the critical concept of Latin America. He is a key figure in the intellectual history of the Dominican Republic and in Latin American history as a whole. Essayist, critic, philologist, linguist, historian, humanist, and educator, Henríquez Ureña taught and worked in the United States, Mexico, Argentina, Spain, and the Dominican Republic.

For the Latin American intelligentsia of previous and current generations, Henríquez Ureña's singular contribution can be summed up in his own words: "we will undertake critical work, assigning each country to its corresponding place in the grand concert of scientific and artistic production, and according to each Nation, the influence of each writer. This shall be our enterprise."[1] Henríquez Ureña's work primarily endeavored to convene and organize the necessary intellectual resources and discourses, "a system of knowledge," for the cultural and scientific advancement of Latin American countries. His intentions, methods, strategies, and call to action on behalf of and for the benefit of Latin American countries resonated with many of his contemporaries, including Alfonso Reyes, José Vasconcelos, and Antonio Caso, and were closely followed or scrutinized by succeeding generations of Latinamericanists such as Enrique Anderson Imbert, José Arrom, Diony Durán, Jean Franco, Roberto González Echevarría, and Rafael Gutiérrez Girardot. Following Henríquez Ureña's own genealogical approach, but hopefully avoiding its pitfalls, we can—by briefly examining his origins, development, and impact as well as scholarly interpretations of his life and work—get a sense of why and how he influenced these generations of scholars.

Literature and patriotism (inherited from his mother, Salomé Ureña) and science and worldly cosmopolitanism (mediated by his father, Francisco Henríquez y Carvajal) are four elements that are relevant to understanding Henríquez Ureña's intellectual development. The distinguished Henríquez and Ureña families' rise to social prominence coincided with the beginning of historically significant social changes. Once united, the Henríquez Ureñas became one of the most intellectually elite, culturally prominent, and celebrated families in Santo Domingo. Pedro's father Francisco Henríquez y Carvajal (1859–1935), a doctor, lawyer, essayist, and diplomat, became the country's provisional President (1916–1917) after a long and active participation in Dominican politics. Even before Francisco achieved fame in Dominican scientific, intellectual, and political circles, his wife Salomé Ureña (1850–1897) was already a celebrated national poet. Later, as a disciple of Eugenio María de Hostos (1839–1903), she became a pioneering educator. Hostos, a Latin American social philosopher, educator, and writer, who we will discuss shortly, was an immensely influential person in Dominican history and had a particularly great impact on the thinking of several of the Henríquez Ureña generations. Henríquez Ureña's intellectual lineage also included his maternal grandfather, Nicolás Ureña de Mendoza (1822–1875), lawyer, politician, and poet, who founded the newspaper *El Progreso* (1853). His uncle, Federico Henríquez y Carvajal, publisher and writer, became famous for his pro-Cuban and Puerto Rican independence campaigns and friendships with the Cuban independence leader José Martí (1853–1895) and Martí's Puerto Rican counterpart, Ramón E. Betances (1827–1898). Federico was the editor of *Letras y Ciencias* (1892–1899), a leading publication in Santo Domingo that was essential reading material for young Pedro and his siblings.[2] Many diverse influences shaped the intellectual pedigree of this family.

In Santo Domingo during the 1880s, the Henríquez Ureña home was the hub of political and intellectual activity. Henríquez Ureña's parents were actively involved in their children's intellectual development. Their mistrust of Dominican parochial schools persuaded them, avowed positivists, to confine the children's education to their home environment, which already housed the Instituto de Señoritas (1891), Salomé's school for women and a teacher training center.[3] Benefiting from his mother's effective instructional methods and also his own diligent application and inquisitiveness, young Pedro quickly learned to read and took his home studies very seriously. His mother, amazed at the child's exceptional educational development, facilitated some of his first literary activities. From the beginning, Salomé became young Pedro's "spiritual guide," whom he "consulted every minute."[4] According to his biographers (Mateo 2001, Piña-Contreras 2001), the 12 years he spent next to her had a direct and decisive influence in Henríquez Ureña's personal and academic development. The son wrote in one of his letters: "only one woman could have been my mother."[5]

His father, on the other hand, would have a more indirect influence. His brother Max Henríquez Ureña (1885–1968), who became an important intellectual in his own right, wrote: "from the first moment, Pedro and I understood that he was a guide and a mentor of great authority. His commanding voice made a deep impression on us."[6] Although a very busy person and absent from their home for many years at a time, their father, "the man of science," imparted specific instructions as to the content and methods of his children's education and would send them the most up-to-date science books from Paris. After Salomé's death in 1897, despite young Pedro's constant inclination toward literary studies, Francisco Henríquez y Carvajal was very adamant that Pedro study science. This insistence resulted in a personal conflict between father and son, which would eventually resolve itself thanks to Pedro's taste for erudition. Together, mother and father as well as the other distinguished members of the family, planted the seeds of a broad-ranging intellect, but, more importantly, passed down values and ideas inherited from the Enlightenment ideology that was characteristic of the foundational phase of Latin American societies.

The Henríquez Ureña home often hosted readings, discussions, and debates. For young Pedro, there were plenty of role models, some of whom became his intellectual interlocutors.[7] As their interest in literary affairs grew, Pedro and his brother Max began to produce publications of their own, including a newspaper called *La Patria* (1896).[8] This rudimentary literary journal about Dominican poetry and literary criticism received praise from some of their parents' distinguished guests and marked the beginning of Henríquez Ureña's illustrious intellectual career.

Henríquez Ureña's career began in Santo Domingo at the turn of the century. He was recognized as the most talented of young Dominican intellectuals not only by his peers but also the established intelligentsia. According to the Dominican sociologist and chronicler Enrique Deschamps (1906):

> This [previous] generation was succeeded by a select group of young intellectuals... among them we will find some that are not just merely promising but already effective agents in the enhancement of national culture. Pedro

Henríquez Ureña, one of the youngest, presides over this select group. He has been ordained by his peers and others as a critic and a writer.[9]

Following this intellectual coronation, Henríquez Ureña visited New York with his father, who was there to negotiate the terms of his country's national debt. After the negotiations concluded, Henríquez Ureña stayed in New York (1901–1904), to be joined later by Max. Life in New York brought him in contact with an assortment of Latin American immigrants, expatriates, intellectuals, and artists, as well as North American families, North American modernity, educational and cultural institutions, the English language, and Panamericanism (the political vision of a united American continent under the tutelage of the United States). In his memoirs and in documents collected by Alfredo Roggiano (1961), we learn that the intellectual fervor of the city was quite stimulating for the young Henríquez Ureña. Roggiano notes, for example, that listening to Yeats discussing Irish modernism moved Henríquez Ureña to inquire about similar currents in Spanish poetry.

The engaging days of intellectual activity and cultural discovery turned unpleasant when, because of political turmoil in the Dominican Republic and a subsequent change of fortune, Henríquez Ureña's father could no longer support him or his brother and they had to find work.[10] Without ceasing to read or write, Henríquez Ureña continued to fully experience life in New York and suspiciously observe the process of "americanization" to which the increasing number of Dominican and other Latin American immigrants were subjected. These formative experiences colored his early writings and determined the direction of some of his later scholarly investigations.

When living conditions in New York became too harsh, and at the behest of his father, Henríquez Ureña briefly traveled to Cuba (1905), where the rest of the family now lived in exile and where he published his first book, *Ensayos críticos*, in 1905, a collection that includes essays on Dominican poets, Hostos, and Rodó, as well as D'Annunzio, Wilde, and Shaw. According to Guillermo Piña-Contreras (2001), this publication signals Henríquez Ureña's temporary exodus from the family's prevailing sphere of influence.[11] Ten years later, Henríquez Ureña would briefly return to the Northeast United States as a foreign correspondent for the Cuban newspaper *Heraldo de Cuba* and a contributor to the New York Spanish weekly, *Las Novedades*. In this new post, he closely followed the cultural and political events in Washington, D.C. and New York. His descriptions of these events reveal a keen awareness of the political and cultural differences that defined American North-South relations. For example, in his account of Woodrow Wilson's keynote speech at the Panamerican conference in

1915, Henríquez Ureña contrasts the U.S. president's progressive speech regarding the continental spiritual and material cooperation with some of the Latin American delegates' suspicious reception.[12] In these chronicles we learn about some of the economic, social, and political circumstances under which a number of important players came together to discuss and celebrate Hispanic culture, such as Archer Huntington, founder of the Hispanic Society, who headed the group that Henríquez Ureña described as "North American lovers of Hispanic culture."[13] In short, these intense linguistic and cultural contacts in the United States were significant influences in Henríquez Ureña's overall vision and interpretation of Hispanic-American culture.

While in the United States, Henríquez Ureña forged excellent relations with North American Hispanists such as J. D. M. Ford, who recommended him for a lectureship at the University of Minnesota. Ford recounted details of his recommendation in a note full of admiration and respect for Henríquez Ureña:

> When the Mexican tyrant and moron, Carranza, drove out the staff of the University of Mexico, Pedro turned to me, and I was fortunate to learn of an opportunity for him at the University of Minnesota. He was accepted there immediately and not only gave a good account himself as [a] teacher, but proceeded energetically to the acquisition of the degree of Doctor of Philosophy.[14]

His excellent scholarship and pedagogical effectiveness earned him the high regard of his colleagues and students and caught the attention of the local press. *The Minnesota Daily* published the following comments:

> The Spanish classes have an unusually large attendance this year. The first few days, even standing room was scarce. Mr. Henríquez found it necessary to highly praise the Italian language. He told his pupils that for those [intending] to go into business, Spanish was the language to study; for those taking Medical, Dental or English work, Italian had the greatest advantages. In spite of all his efforts, no one was willing to change.[15]

Henríquez Ureña's record as a teacher and scholar is impressive. Among his most important contributions, officials at the University of Minnesota highlighted the following: Henríquez Ureña's discovery of a new type of *versos endecásilabos* (11-syllable verse) in classical Spanish poetry, establishing the facts regarding the oldest book published by a writer born in the New World, creating the first complete bibliography of the works of Sor Juana Inés de la Cruz for the *Revue Hispanique,* and writing the first history of colonial culture in Santo Domingo.[16] Henríquez Ureña was a crucial resource in the advancement of Hispanic-American scholarship in the United States. His crowning achievement as a scholar in the United States came when he was appointed to the Charles Eliot Norton lectureship at Harvard University. Ford, again, gives an account of the origins of this prestigious honor: "Not long ago when the Committee on the Charles Eliot Norton foundation at Harvard was looking for an annual lecturer, I had the privilege of calling attention to Pedro. His fame was such that he commended himself to all concerned and he was appointed."[17] Newspapers in the United States and Latin America highlighted the fact that for the first time Harvard had selected someone from the Spanish-speaking world for this prestigious lectureship.[18] The series of Harvard lectures resulted in his most well-known work, *Literary Currents in Hispanic America* (1945). In his memoirs, Henríquez Ureña declared that he had come to the United States in order to absorb the influence of a superior civilization, but, in fact, he was quite influential himself. Thanks to his brilliant contributions, more U.S. universities began to open their doors to students and teachers from Latin America. Henríquez Ureña helped to advance a more interesting and dynamic dialogue on Hispanoamericanism and promote a contact zone where North and South could inquire about each other. This improvement was not achieved, however, without raising a series of critical questions and suspicions regarding the political foundations of the relationship between Latin American and North American societies.

Mexico was another country where Henríquez Ureña's talents contributed to an intellectual renewal. Henríquez Ureña first arrived there in early 1906. After a brief stay in the city of Veracruz, he settled in Mexico City, where he worked as a newspaper editor and began to establish relations with the Mexican intelligentsia, consisting of young and promising writers and artists. His intellectual acumen and activities quickly earned him the respect and affection of his peers and the nickname "Socrates." Among the group of young Mexican intellectuals, he instantly connected with Alfonso Reyes (1889–1959), a promising writer and budding philologist, who became his most cherished colleague and a lifelong friend. The genealogy and scope of this fraternal and intellectual friendship can be traced in their epistolary and essays about one another. The Mexican cultural critic Victor Barrera Enderle (2006) wrote an essay on how the friendship and association between Henríquez Ureña and Reyes unlocked a network of intellectual relationships that had a direct impact on the Mexican community and the larger Latin American context.

One of the most intensely productive stages of Henríquez Ureña's career, from 1906 to 1914, coincided with a period of cultural and political upheaval in Mexico. Henríquez Ureña joined the group of young Mexican intellectuals involved in a movement that became known as the

"Cultural Revolution," which was the preamble to the Mexican Revolution (1910–1920). The militaristic overtones of Henríquez Ureña's description of the period reveal how high the stakes were for this new group of intellectuals:

> While war ravaged the country and even groups of intellectually inclined men were becoming soldiers, our disorganized effort to spiritually renovate the culture was gaining ground. The fruits of our philosophical, literary and aesthetic revolution were gradually taking shape.[19]

These intellectuals were affiliated through the Ateneo de la Juventud de México (Atheneum of Mexican Youth, 1909), an intellectual society that, surrounded by the revolutionary violence and ideological fervor, sought to dismantle the Cientificos's[20] institutional network and its monopoly on education and culture in Mexico. The Ateneo's founding members included Alfonso Reyes, Antonio Caso (1883–1946), José Vasconcelos (1882–1959), and Henríquez Ureña. Amidst a swarm of intellectual activity and growing political fear and insecurity, Henríquez Ureña published another book, *Horas de estudio* (1910). This book, a record of his own intellectual evolution up to this point, was published in Paris and received praise from many intellectuals. For example, the reigning man of Hispanic letters, Spanish literary historian Menéndez Pelayo, commented how the book reflected "an exquisite intellectual education begun during early childhood and reinforced by exposure to the best books."[21] Literary success and all, Henríquez Ureña tried to abstain from getting directly involved in political matters, but his relationships with members of different political factions and the strong ties to Alfonso Reyes forced him to proceed with extreme caution. The streets of Mexico City were teeming with fear and hostility. During these times, Henríquez Ureña endured personal economic hardships. He was also the object of personal attacks by some jealous local journalists: "They have attacked me by calling me 'Menox,' in order to create a less flattering contrast between my name and my brother's, 'Max.'"[22] In Spanish, the juxtaposition of "Max" and "Menox" create the phonetic homonyms *más* and *menos*, which literally translate to "more" and "less." He attributed these initial attacks to the insecurities of those who envied his prestigious position within the Ateneo:

> I have been informed that Núñez y Domínguez is particularly resentful because he was not invited to join the *Ateneo* and blames me for the omission. While commenting on the foundation of the society in the newspaper *El Heraldo*, he insulted me publicly, by referring to me as *Menox* and as a *Haitian* author.[23]

Henríquez Ureña's racial profile was the object of attacks first in Mexico and later in Argentina.[24] It must be noted that many Dominicans consider being called "Haitian" one of the worst possible insults. Using the term "Haitian," his attackers questioned Henríquez Ureña's national origin and targeted his mulatto profile. As the revolutionary situation in Mexico grew more violent, the risk of physical danger for individuals like Henríquez Ureña became more acute. In 1913, Alfonso Reyes's father, General Bernardo Reyes, was assassinated. In 1914, Henríquez Ureña left Mexico and, after another brief stay in Cuba, returned to the United States, where he worked as a journalist, among other things.

After traveling and working in the United States, Spain, and Mexico again (1921–1924), Henríquez Ureña settled down in Argentina. In 1924, he arrived in Buenos Aires with his Mexican wife, Isabel, and his first-born daughter, Natacha. That same year, he joined the faculty of the Colegio Nacional de la Universidad de la Plata and began to work on a series of academic projects and new intellectual endeavors. It is during this period of his life that Henríquez Ureña began to amass his linguistic and philological oeuvre. In 1931, he briefly fulfilled his wish of returning to Dominican soil, assuming the role of national superintendent of education in Santo Domingo during the Trujillo regime. However, frustrated with the limitations of his position, as well as disillusioned with and in fear of the Dominican political landscape, he returned to Buenos Aires and continued teaching, investigating, writing, and publishing for the next 13 years. Along with Amado Alonso, he helped develop the institutional base for the discipline of Hispanic linguistics in Latin America. In 1946, at the age of 62, while he was grading and correcting students' work, Henríquez Ureña died suddenly aboard the train on his daily commute from Buenos Aires to La Plata.

Considering his roles in developing knowledge of classical humanism and Spanish-American literary tradition and in forging a critical consciousness in Latin America, Alfonso Reyes declared that our intellectual debt to Henríquez Ureña was immeasurable: "Educator by nature, he stirs up the spirit of his interlocutors, by teaching them how to listen, see, and think. He fittingly rewards all his followers by instilling in them a deep appreciation of culture and a serious desire to work."[25] Samuel Ramos (1946), another Mexican disciple, added: "Henríquez Ureña was an example of how Latin Americans must modestly assimilate European culture. A humanist by training, he cultivated Spanish letters, but he merged his interests in these areas with his interest in the study of Latin America's literary production and linguistic realities."[26] The flood of panegyrics following Henríquez Ureña's death is vast. It culminates in the year of his centenary with a significant homage, the two-volume *El libro jubilar de Pedro Henríquez Ureña*, edited by Julio Jaime Julia (1984). These texts reveal the high degree of reverence many Latin American intellectuals and scholars had for Henríquez Ureña because of his vast contributions to the collective knowledge and understanding of Latin America's cultural, linguistic, and literary history.

Henríquez Ureña, and his work, has been the object of numerous studies, most of them, naturally, laudatory. For over half a century, a host of researchers, who can be described as former friends, former colleagues, admirers, and students, have produced an extensive body of literature on Henríquez Ureña, which, while informative, mostly celebrates his charismatic personality and serious commitment to teaching. Enrique Zuleta Álvarez[27] (1998) has discussed how many of the critics who knew or dealt with Henríquez Ureña based their judgments of his intellectual production solely on his personal appeal and his leading role in key episodes of twentieth-century Latin American political and cultural history. Generally, Henríquez Ureña scholars can be divided into the following five groups: Latin American literary critics and intellectual historians; Dominican historiographers; Hispanic linguists, most of whom highlight Henríquez Ureña's role in the debate over the Andalusian nature of American Spanish (*andalucismo*) and in developing dialectology as a field of inquiry in Latin America; Dominican linguists who utilize and revise some of his data on Dominican Spanish; and a small but diverse group of scholars who, in varying degrees, problematize Henríquez Ureña's work. Despite this specialization on different facets of his work, Henríquez Ureña's oeuvre has not been appropriately contextualized (Pérez Guerra 2004, Sarlo 1998) and such lack of contextualization is most evident in the studies that approach his linguistic production.

Often classified by their country of origin, Henríquez Ureña specialists are far from homogeneous. However, their different theoretical concerns and ideological attitudes at times intersect. We can attribute to them the following five basic characterizations of Henríquez Ureña: (i) Henríquez Ureña as the primary advocate of a school of thought known as *americanismo* (Latinamericanism), (ii) Henríquez Ureña as an exemplar of patriotism and Dominicanness, (iii) Henríquez Ureña as an exiled intellectual, (iv) Henríquez Ureña as a linguist whose unique approach to Spanish in the Americas resulted in a wealth of dialectal observations, and (v) Henríquez Ureña as an intellectual whose rich and complex oeuvre demands critical attention.

The Advocate of *Americanismo*

The view of Henríquez Ureña as the primary advocate of *americanismo* is mostly advanced by Latin American literary critics (Álvarez 1981, Carilla

1988, Durán 1994, Febres 1989, Gutiérrez Girardot 1978, Zuleta Álvarez 1999). To them, Henríquez Ureña represents one of the greatest Latin American intellectuals of the twentieth century, comparable to nineteenth-century intellectuals such as Andrés Bello, Domingo Faustino Sarmiento, José Martí, and Eugenio María de Hostos, all of whom had a profound vision of the originality and value of Latin American culture. The significance of Henríquez Ureña's work, according to these specific scholars, resides in his search for the essence of Hispanic-American culture and its Hispanic roots. Enrique Zuleta Álvarez notes that, for some critics, "the sense of unity in Henríquez Ureña's writings emanates from his search for the manifestation of the spirit of Spanish American culture whose Hispanic roots were vitally important."[28] Scholars such as Rafael Gutiérrez Girardot, another unabashed admirer of Henríquez Ureña, affirm that Henríquez Ureña's oeuvre constitutes "an enlargement of the historical, spiritual, and cultural horizon which would clarify and facilitate the process of finding and expressing Our America."[29] Above all, Americanists find in Henríquez Ureña's oeuvre the best effort to combine knowledge of literature, history, and society in order to design, from the Hispanic base, the instruments and the proper continental vision that will lead to unity, solidarity, progress, and prosperity in Latin America.

The studies that emphasize Henríquez Ureña's *americanismo* are best illustrated by the words of the Dominican essayist Soledad Álvarez (1981):

> We hope to approximate Pedro Henríquez Ureña's Americanist thought. The "Great Motherland," as [Henríquez Ureña] called our America, constituted the Dominican intellectual's main concern. It came into full view in his work. Yet, sudden death interrupted the progression of these Americanist ideas, which were inching closer to our current interpretation of our reality.[30]

Soledad Álvarez explains Henríquez Ureña's *americanismo* as a continuum between conceptualizations of Latin America's history and culture expressed by progressives such as Simon Bolivar and José Martí and Marxist thinkers such as José Carlos Mariátegui.[31] Gutiérrez Girardot expressed similar ideas by characterizing Henríquez Ureña's political and scientific agenda as a Bolivarian and Martian vision that is radical and utopian but, nonetheless, historically founded.[32] These scholars situate Henríquez Ureña (the man and his work) within the paradigm of revolutionary thinking that was aimed at liberating and empowering Latin America. Sergio Pitol (2002) best summarizes how scholars regularly identify Henríquez Ureña's character and work with a series of Latin American ideals:

We identify Henríquez Ureña with specifically Spanish American ideals. What we call our "American Utopia" was the core of his intellectual life. To this passionate cause he attracted the likes of Alfonso Reyes, Ernesto Sábato, Ezequiel Martínez Estrada, Enrique Anderson Imbert, as well as a host of other friends and disciples.[33]

In general, Henríquez Ureña scholars regard his oeuvre as one of the pillars of contemporary Latin American thought. Their primary concerns, evident from their writings, have been to ensure his international recognition as an intellectual authority and to highlight his extraordinary effort in the description and interpretation of Latin American realities.

The Icon of the Dominican Intelligentsia

The second perspective belongs to Dominican intellectuals who believe that Henríquez Ureña's life and oeuvre were primarily dedicated to the glorification of his nation. For example, Emilio Rodríguez Demorizi (2001) and Juan Jacobo de Lara (1975 and 1982) suggest that Henríquez Ureña's Dominicanism trumps his Americanism. Consequently, no greater homage can be paid to the "premier man of letters of the Dominican Republic" than the proper appraisal of his *dominicanidad* (Dominicanness).[34] According to Rodríguez Demorizi, more than his wisdom and intellectual virtuosity, we ought to praise Henríquez Ureña's fervent Dominicanness. That is the best homage we can pay to "that spirit that resides in the lofty mansion of the just," because, quite simply, he loved his fatherland above all else.[35] Lara (1982) echoed this sentiment when he wrote: "Henríquez Ureña was a great patriot and a great americanist. His Americanism, however, never overshadowed his Dominicanism. He was a good Dominican who never changed his nationality and died a Dominican."[36] Lara (1975) also noted that "his Americanism does not represent the foundation of his unique talents."[37] With a few exceptions (Jimenes Grullón 1969, Piña-Contreras 2001, Soledad Álvarez 1998), Dominican scholars tend to see Henríquez Ureña as a messianic figure who, through his work as a teacher and his personality, instilled in others a passionate love for local cultures in Latin America, which he particularly exemplified through his Dominican oeuvre (especially his classic texts, *El español en Santo Domingo* and *La cultura y las letras coloniales en Santo Domingo*). Even though he spent most of his life abroad, Henríquez Ureña's exile is considered to be nothing more than a journey toward the fulfillment of his Dominican destiny. Carlos Federico Pérez y Pérez (1984) claims that Henríquez Ureña's love of Dominican culture and nationalism dominates his entire intellectual production.[38] According to the view adopted by most Dominican analysts, Henríquez Ureña's entire oeuvre has to be understood in relation to his departure from and his longing to return to his birthplace, Santo Domingo. There is a belief that his entire oeuvre constitutes an attempt to recreate what he left behind: the glories, ideals, symbols, and values of a nation built by generations steeped in Hispanic tradition.

Soledad Álvarez and Piña-Contreras are two Dominican scholars who slightly diverge from this line of thinking. Soledad Álvarez (1998), on the one hand, begins by noting that Henríquez Ureña's Dominicanness was reaffirmed while abroad and that, perhaps, his errant life can only be properly understood by Dominicans and by those Latin Americans who have been forced to emigrate and to develop culture in foreign soil.[39] Here, she echoes Rodríguez Demorizi (2001). However, she does not stop there. She does not make Henríquez Ureña's life and work a simple function of his national and biological kinship to one of the most enlightened and patriotic Dominican families. She further examines the specific sociohistorical factors that allowed Henríquez Ureña to achieve distinction and popularity among the historians of Latin American and Dominican cultures. Similarly, Piña-Contreras (2001), concentrating on details about his childhood and adolescence, explores in more detail the familial conditions and relationships that shaped Henríquez Ureña's character and perception as a Dominican citizen and as a budding intellectual. Therefore, these two authors only slightly depart from the traditional view that Henríquez Ureña's entire oeuvre can be explained in terms of his nationality and patriotism. Generally, Dominican scholars' analyses of his works, with the state's blessing, have contributed to making Henríquez Ureña a sacred and ubiquitous cultural icon[40] in the Dominican Republic.

An Outsider in Exile and Politics

With Henríquez Ureña in mind, Alfonso Reyes sketched a portrait of the modern intellectual: "Living in perpetual crisis, being a critic means being a guest in every city and a citizen of none. This condition constitutes a grave offense to the political meaning of life."[41] Studies that take into account Henríquez Ureña's status as an outsider, forced into exile in Mexico, the United States, Spain, and Argentina, comprise the third perspective on him. This is a view that troubles many who maintain the centrality of Henríquez Ureña's contributions to Hispanic studies. Nevertheless, his marginal condition in some contexts is increasingly attracting the attention of some Henríquez Ureña scholars[42] and leading to what Arcadio Díaz Quiñones (1994) calls "the renewal of Henríquez Ureña."[43] This trend originated with the Mexican historian Enrique Krauze (1985). In his analysis of Henríquez Ureña's intellectual development and vision, Krauze paid careful attention to the relation between Henríquez Ureña's personal circumstances abroad and the persistent image appearing throughout Henríquez Ureña's work of a paradise lost incarnated by the "privileged" history of his native country. Krauze wrote: "The image of a paradise lost always pervaded Henríquez Ureña's mind. The Caribbean island where he was born had been the novelty of the New World, the 'most beautiful place'... 'green and most fertile,' in the words of Christopher Columbus, who baptized it as *La Española*."[44] Krauze found an intricate connection between Henríquez Ureña's utopian vision, elaborated in his multiple texts, and his condition as an exiled intellectual from the Dominican Republic. According to Krauze, his utopias are a product of an exile's skepticism and melancholy for his origins.[45] Furthermore, contrary to critics who insisted on Henríquez Ureña's apolitical nature, Krauze believed that it is precisely this condition of exile that shaped his political attitudes and motivated his political writings, which appeared in several Latin American newspapers. While Néstor Rodríguez (2007) recently commented on Henríquez Ureña's political profile, the Latin American historian Tulio Halperín Donghi (1999) brought attention to some of his lesser-known political affiliations: "It is relevant to mention that during his whole life this discreet and measured humanist felt a quiet, unlike José Ingenieros, yet firm solidarity with the Soviet experience."[46]

Previously, there was a tendency among some scholars to focus on the question of whether Henríquez Ureña could be classified as a philosopher. For instance, the Argentinean critic Eugenio Pucciarelli[47] (1984) claimed that Henríquez Ureña belonged among Platonist philosophers by birthright and because of his love of beauty and passion for justice. These scholars were inclined to believe that the best way to fully appreciate Henríquez Ureña's significance as an intellectual was by deriving his thought from philosophical issues and Platonic ideas regarding the importance of reason in human affairs. This frequent association of Henríquez Ureña with philosophical currents neglects his intervention in political matters. Defining the position against this philosophical tendency, Liliana Weinberg (2002) stated that such considerations can only lead to an impasse and to endless, sterile polemics.[48] Weinberg centered on the relationship between exile and what others (Anderson Imbert 2001, Pérez de la Cruz 2003, Pucciarelli 1984) have labeled "philosophical thought" in Henríquez Ureña's oeuvre. She found that Henríquez Ureña was torn between the centripetal force emanating from the intellectual elite to which he belonged and the centrifugal force of alienating exile. As a result of this tension, he sought to root his life, personality, studies, and vision in the world of high culture.[49]

The image of Henríquez Ureña as member of an exiled diaspora is also the point of departure for Díaz Quiñones's studies (1994 and 2006). He proposes a reading of Henríquez Ureña's Hispanic-American oeuvre that takes into account exile as a persistent condition, the elaboration of culture as a type of order, and the redefinition of the colonial experience as a response to separatist nationalisms. Díaz Quiñones raises the following important questions with respect to the relationship between modernity, diaspora, and the construction of identities: How was Henríquez Ureña affected by his condition as a marginal, displaced figure, ultimately considered an outsider, in the countries where he lived and worked? What effect did the racial prejudice he encountered in Mexico and the United States have on his intellectual development? Was Henríquez Ureña's exclusion of Afro-Caribbean cultures a product of his effort to fully belong to a specific group and find a place for people of his intellectual pedigree in universal (i.e., European) culture? While exploring these and other similar questions, Díaz Quiñones finds in Henríquez Ureña an intellectual who experienced the tension of being an "outsider" and who proceeded to build traditions between what he perceived as the opposing forces of order and anarchy. According to Díaz Quiñones, "Henríquez Ureña was a marginal player seeking to play a central role."[50] Furthermore, with respect to the Dominican author's cultural representations, Díaz Quiñones notes:

> It was a project that allowed multiple traditions, provided that they could be integrated into the literate culture, which was not the case of that uncomfortable Afro-Caribbean world, a ghost that complicates their texts. Painfully and restlessly, national identity emerges with this exclusion, and perhaps, with deep and bitter overtones, so does the problem of these intellectuals' own identities.[51]

There is, in Díaz Quiñones's studies, an attempt to identify the various contexts or different perspectives surrounding Henríquez Ureña's intellectual enterprises. Díaz Quiñones examines the Dominican author's major cultural texts as well as a few of his linguistic texts in relation to the construction of a Dominican national tradition, the condition of the exiled intellectual in the modern world, and the practice of modernity defined in terms of order as an alternative to anarchy.

Linguist or Philologist?

Henríquez Ureña's visions of Latin America, his patriotic feelings toward his homeland, and the personal circumstances surrounding his elaboration of the texts in which he expressed his corresponding thoughts and feelings have been abundantly studied. In stark contrast, his linguistic production has received much less attention. Still, there are a handful of scholars who have examined Henríquez Ureña's linguistic texts (such as Ghiano (1976) in the prologue to the Argentinean edition of Henríquez Ureña's *Observaciones sobre el español en América*), examining their relationship to the body of his cultural and historiographical production and often taking positions either supporting or criticizing the Dominican's views on American Spanish.

Along with the Colombian Rufino José Cuervo, Henríquez Ureña is considered to be, especially by Latin American dialectologists (Álvarez Martínez 1998, Vaquero 1997), the founder of the linguistic discipline in Latin America. For instance, Juan Lope Blanch (1989) highlights Henríquez Ureña's pioneering role in determining the regional and dialectal origins of the New World colonizers.[52] In addition to explaining his theories on American Spanish, Hispanic linguists have been concerned with vindicating Henríquez Ureña's reputation as a linguist. There has never been a consensus among scholars as to whether to label him a linguist or a philologist. Scholars such as Lope Blanch (1989) are sometimes ambivalent:

> Concerning the Dominican philologist's extraordinary accomplishments as the initiator of modern Latin American dialectology at that time, I have already expressed my opinions on many occasions. But I should really highlight his role in Hispanic philology, giving the term "philology" its broad and generous original meaning of science that studies the spirit of a people through their linguistic manifestations—in both popular and folk-literary terms—and within the historical context which explains and conditions such manifestations. Like Menéndez Pidal, Henríquez Ureña was a true philologist, directing his scientific effort to the three domains of true philology: the linguistic, literary, and historical.[53]

Contrary to Lope Blanch, other Hispanic linguists disagree that Henríquez Ureña's language studies are fundamentally philological in nature. The Dominican linguist Carlisle González Tapia (1998), for example, dedicated an entire book to proving that Henríquez Ureña was, first and foremost, a linguist.

Until now, González Tapia's book *El pensamiento lingüístico de Pedro Henríquez Ureña* (1998) was the only full-length study that focuses solely on Henríquez Ureña's linguistic production. In the first chapter, González Tapia presents his main thesis: "Contrary to the view that Pedro Henríquez Ureña was a great philologist or that his language studies were philological in nature, we maintain that Don Pedro was primarily a linguist and therefore his language studies are essentially linguistic."[54] According to González Tapia, the majority of scholars who discuss Henríquez Ureña's language studies tend to situate them within the practice of philology.[55] He attributes this tendency to the nineteenth-century tradition of believing that philology was capable of encapsulating everything that had to do with language through the analysis of written texts. This notion, in varying degrees, persists today. González Tapia, however, insists that the object of Henríquez Ureña's language studies proper was oral speech, as exemplified in *El español en Santo Domingo*.[56] Furthermore, González Tapia insists that Henríquez Ureña can be perfectly situated in the field of structural dialectology because he approached the study of dialects from a structuralist point of view.[57]

González Tapia classifies Henríquez Ureña's entire linguistic production into the following four categories: dialectological-sociolinguistic, lexico-semantic, linguistic theory, and applied linguistics. The author provides a chronological commentary and brief analyses of Henríquez Ureña's contributions to each field. Cataloguing each text, González Tapia broadly reviews Henríquez Ureña's data, highlighting his major arguments or claims and, in some cases, raising questions as to their validity. In a similarly swift manner, González Tapia sums up Henríquez Ureña's striking position on the possibility, or lack thereof, of African linguistic influences on Dominican Spanish and gives his own evaluation. With respect to this and other major assertions of Henríquez Ureña on Dominican Spanish, González Tapia contends that the author's wide generalizations were a result of the impressionistic and subjective methodology that was the prevalent practice at the time. This practice consisted of generalizing a particular fact without sufficient empirical or statistical evidence. According to González Tapia, "a couple of words uttered by a single speaker were sufficient for the linguist to make definitive statements about a specific dialectal feature or to account for a particular speech phenomenon."[58] He characterizes this methodology as "linguistic impressionism." Nonetheless, González Tapia continues, "Don Pedro's excellent study [*El idioma español y la historia política en Santo Domingo* (1937)] presents a more accurate portrayal of 1930s Dominican Spanish, more real than fictitious, more objective than subjective."[59] González Tapia concludes by pointing out that Henríquez Ureña's notion of linguistic purism and his thoughts on the role of Spanish in the emergence of the Dominican state were somewhat misguided and influenced by traditional, and possibly racist, views.[60] This is a pertinent but brief observation. Yet, González Tapia does not provide a full discussion of some of the contradictions that Henríquez Ureña incurred while exploring the link between language and race. In this book,

I fully flesh out the racial implications of Henríquez Ureña's thoughts on language.

In short, González Tapia's study constitutes a brief chronological commentary of Henríquez Ureña's linguistic texts. He provides a general synthesis of Henríquez Ureña's major linguistic descriptions and assertions in order to reject the classification of Henríquez Ureña as a philologist. González Tapia insists that his work must be classified within a particular strand of modern linguistics: structural dialectology. This debate is typical in the scholarship on Henríquez Ureña, a tireless effort to enshrine him in the pantheon of this or that discipline. But more important is our understanding of his work in and relationship to each of those disciplines. The fact is that, within the context of his times, Henríquez Ureña was both a linguist and a philologist. Of particular interest is his work in philology, a discipline that, as Edward Said commented in *Orientalism*,[61] gave its practitioners an aura of power. As we will see in Chapter 3, philology was particularly vital for its practitioners because it made possible for them, among other things, the establishment and deployment of a text's schematic authority.

Zones of American Spanish

Within the field of Latin American dialectology, María Vaquero (1997) and María Ángeles Álvarez Martínez (1998) are two other researchers who have attempted to cement Henríquez Ureña's reputation as a pioneer dialectologist and theoretician of American Spanish. For example, Álvarez Martínez[62] (1998) highlights *Observaciones sobre el español de América* as groundbreaking work in Hispanic dialectology. Vaquero (1997) is even more emphatic when underscoring Henríquez Ureña's contributions to Spanish linguistics. According to Vaquero, for the first time in 1921, Pedro Henríquez Ureña formulated the problems of American Spanish.[63] He raised questions that we still continue to discuss: Is American Spanish the result of uniformity or variation? Is American Spanish an Andalusian offshoot? Are the features it shares with the Andalusian dialect the result of parallel development? Were its distinctive features shaped by external causes or internal evolution? Similarly, Lope Blanch (1989) acknowledged Henríquez Ureña's pioneering work: "The important thing is that Henríquez Ureña opened the door for this type of research, while raising serious questions about simplistic notions of the unity of Spanish."[64] However, Lope Blanch also recognized that there was some criticism of Henríquez Ureña's efforts to divide American Spanish into five zones based on geographical, historical, and cultural factors. Charles Kany

(1951), for example, identified Henríquez Ureña's tendency to outweigh indigenous linguistic influences in American Spanish and to make broad generalizations based on insufficient facts.[65]

Lope Blanch's acknowledgment of the limitations of Henríquez Ureña's dialectal division notwithstanding, Hispanic linguists locate Henríquez Ureña's linguistic ideas within the school of thought that postulates a diverse yet unified speech community grounded in the Spanish language. In this regard, they resemble the group of scholars who focus on Henríquez Ureña's account of America as a cultural unit. Álvarez Martínez and Vaquero situate Henríquez Ureña's linguistic work within the collaborative effort to scientifically prove Spanish America as a cultural and linguistic unit derived from a Hispanic base. In general, these Hispanic linguists concentrate on Henríquez Ureña's dialectal observations and dialectological arguments that allow them to establish, advance, or question the concept of "American Spanish."

Spanish and Linguists in Santo Domingo

Orlando Alba (1990), Max Jiménez Sabater (1975), Carlisle González Tapia (1998), and Irene Pérez Guerra (1992, 2003, and 2004) represent the group of Dominican researchers who have attempted to characterize Henríquez Ureña's work on Dominican Spanish. Pérez Guerra (2004) laments the scarcity of studies dedicated to Henríquez Ureña's linguistic production, especially in comparison with his literary and cultural work. Like other analysts, Dominican scholars (Lara 1975 and 1982, Rosario Candelier 1990) who focus on Henríquez Ureña's linguistic production generally hesitate to go beyond the exaltation of his contributions. Max Jiménez Sabater (1975) made a similar observation in reference to the prevalent attitude among Dominican analysts: "It is time for us to shake off that fetishistic attitude, typical of some Dominican language specialists and intellectuals, towards the scholars that represented the best of our national talent."[66] In more recent decades, however, some have attempted to overcome that attitude and further explore Henríquez Ureña's perspective on Dominican Spanish. One of the first Dominican linguists who scrutinized Henríquez Ureña's data on this topic was Jiménez Sabater (1975 and 1981). This linguist found some of Henríquez Ureña's characterizations of the Dominican speech community to be problematic, in that they suggested that Henríquez Ureña erroneously presumed that the Dominican Republic had remained the most isolated country in the Hispanic world:

> If we just look at Henríquez Ureña's lexical data, we would be forced to conclude that Dominican Republic has experienced much more isolation from

the rest of the world than any other country in Latin America, as if time had stopped for us alone and kept us at a remote distance for five hundred years.[67]

For their part, Alba (1990) and Pérez Guerra (2003 and 2004) have approached Henríquez Ureña's classic *El español de Santo Domingo* by explaining the value of the work as the first systematic coherent study of Spanish in the Dominican Republic. These researchers also highlight how the author's central idea, the linguistic archaism of Dominican Spanish, dictates the overall structure of the text, each individual chapter, as well as the collection and selection of data. They have, however, differing opinions with respect to the currency in Dominican Spanish of the archaic lexemes collected by Henríquez Ureña. Alba believes that archaic lexemes do not constitute a distinctive feature of this dialect. Alba explains that, while these archaisms could have been prevalent in the 1930s Dominican Republic, now a substantial number of them are not even part of Dominicans' passive vocabulary.[68] Moreover, Alba points out that the preservation of archaic forms is not exclusive of the Dominican Republic and can be found in other areas of Spanish-speaking Caribbean and in parts of Spain.[69] Alba provides a brief overview of the historical period in which Henríquez Ureña's *El español en Santo Domingo* emerged and ascribes its inaccuracies with respect to the features that Henríquez Ureña exclusively attributed to this dialect to the infancy of dialectology as a field of research. Alba also reiterates Hispanic linguists' and philologists' views regarding the immense value of the Dominican's pioneering work in the field of dialectology and its limitations. In addition, Alba cites Henríquez Ureña's prolonged absence from the Dominican Republic as a reason for the shortcomings of his research on Spanish in the Dominican Republic. Considering such circumstances, Alba argues, we can identify a possible explanation for the discrepancies between Henríquez Ureña's linguistic description and our current understanding of Dominican linguistic realities.[70] According to Alba, however, the empirical value and theoretical contribution of the work overshadow any problems inherent in the text.

Pérez Guerra (2004) also examined Henríquez Ureña's other linguistic texts and highlighted their special significance within his intellectual production. Her study, focuses primarily on the works that comprise Henríquez Ureña's Latin American dialectology, his take on *la expresión Americana* (unique American expressions), and the defense of the autonomy of Spanish in the Americas.[71] Pérez Guerra believes that the subject of Latin American linguistic unity is one of the keys to understanding his linguistic production. In contrast to Alba's assessment of lexical archaisms in the Dominican Republic, Pérez Guerra (1992) accepts Henríquez Ureña's characterization of Dominican Spanish, in spite of what she calls his "methodological apriorism." She argues that Henríquez Ureña's fundamental position with respect to the nature of Dominican Spanish is basically correct. His characterization of Dominican archaic vocabulary is still valid despite the social changes that have occurred since 1961, especially in the Dominican Republic.[72] Going beyond the lexico-semantic level, Pérez Guerra (1992) finds evidence in Dominican Spanish of archaic forms at the morpho-syntactic level. Among the evidence she highlights are double negation (*nadie no vino* (no one did not come)) and the use of the indefinite article plus possessive plus noun (*un mi amigo* (one my friend)).[73] While comparing Henríquez Ureña's linguistic claims with similar cultural claims he made in his *La Antigua sociedad patriarcal de las Antillas: modalidades arcaicas de la vida en Santo Domingo durante el siglo XIX* (1932), Pérez Guerra affirms that Henríquez Ureña's conclusions are also substantiated by some of the facts of nineteenth-century Dominican history.

The debate continues, mostly along the lines of whether Henríquez Ureña was correct regarding the linguistic archaism of Spanish in the Dominican context and whether his conclusions are valid today. Pérez Guerra diverges from Alba and insists that the relative density and frequency with which the phenomenon occurs in different Dominican regions is presently high enough to resemble previous stages of the dialect and to resist comparisons with other Caribbean dialects of Spanish, such as the one spoken in Puerto Rico.[74]

Bent on solely establishing the facts, these linguists shy away from exploring the sociological issues embedded in Henríquez Ureña's linguistic texts. This debate must evolve, and much more work is necessary in order to provide a fuller explanation of his linguistic ideas and conclusions with respect to Spanish in the Dominican Republic. The inquiry needs to go beyond questioning the validity of his claims or the currency of linguistic archaism in this dialect and move toward questions concerning the circumstances and ideological issues surrounding his characterization of the Dominican speech community. In fact, some scholars have suggested the need for problematizing the work of Henríquez Ureña. These are the ones who take the view that his work, while rich in many ways, demands critical attention.

Critically Reading Pedro Henríquez Ureña

Juan Isidro Jimenes Grullón (1903–1983), a historian and important Dominican political figure, was the first scholar to formally formulate the need for a more critical approach to Henríquez Ureña's work. Jimenes

Grullón was the first Dominican analyst to go beyond rendering homage and to seriously take issue with several of Henríquez Ureña's arguments: "Both in Spain and in Latin America Pedro Henríquez Ureña's intellectual prominence is widely recognized. But in what has been written about him, we often only find emotionally and ideologically charged judgments rather than balanced and in-depth assessments."[75] According to Jimenes Grullón, Henríquez Ureña was an excellent writer who skillfully cultivated the field of literary criticism and also excelled as a linguist and a philologist. Jimenes Grullón examined Henríquez Ureña's oeuvre in order to assess his characterization of colonial history, the construction of Latin American identities, the role of the intellectual in Latin American history, and the sociocultural configuration of the Dominican Republic. Recognizing the intrinsic value of Henríquez Ureña's scholarship, Jimenes Grullón was not deterred from detecting the ideological underpinnings of some of Henríquez Ureña's representations: "It cannot go unnoticed...his exalted concept of Hispanism on which he founded his Americanism."[76] In addition, Jimenes Grullón noted that, while in many of his writings Henríquez Ureña advocated for universal justice, he alienated certain groups of people who did not fit into his description of Dominican realities, namely, those of African descent and those from low economic classes. Jimenes Grullón found examples of this type of alienation in several of Henríquez Ureña's discussions on early colonial cultural processes:

> [Henríquez Ureña] claimed that this [music] was not indigenous...even though the new soil soon modified it, giving it an unmistakable aroma, for him, it was still European music. We can accept that European music arrived in our American continent, but should we assume from this fact that indigenous or African people renounced their music? We would think not. But Henríquez Ureña's Hispanist alienation tacitly but definitively led him to embrace the opposite conclusion.[77]

According to Jimenes Grullón, this considerable process of alienation can be attributed not only to his Hispanism but also to Henríquez Ureña's particular concept of history: "There is a tendency in Henríquez Ureña to view history as a process led by the privileged social class and its most notable figures, not as the work of a whole community driven, from beginning to end, by the class struggle."[78] It is not surprising that Jimenes Grullón made the most forceful statement in relation to the ideological dimension of Henríquez Ureña's oeuvre. This Marxist intellectual, founder of the Dominican socialist party (1961), sought to analyze many myths in his quest to dismantle, what he considered to be, within a classical Marxist framework, "the false consciousness" of Dominican society. Accordingly, he concluded, "Henríquez Ureña, driven by Hispanic fervor, lost his sense of reality."[79] From statements such as these, we get the sense that Jimenes Grullón adhered to a strict traditional Marxist perspective on ideologies. As we will discuss in the next chapter, standard Marxist theory uncritically associates ideology with false consciousness elaborated by power structures working to mask their existence.

The linguists Guillermo Guitarte (1958a) and Elvira N. de Arnoux (2001) have also paid attention to the ideological dimension of a portion of Henríquez Ureña's linguistic work. Arnoux (2001) analyzed the secondary role he played in the polemic surrounding the appearance of his *Gramática castellana* (1938), coauthored with Amado Alonso, in Argentina and the Spaniard's negative characterization of *Porteño* speech as *plebeyismo* (plebeian in nature). Arnoux's study is relevant because it highlights important and particularly political linguistic debates that were taking place during the period in which Henríquez Ureña was living, teaching, and writing in Buenos Aires. Arnoux characterized Henríquez Ureña and Amado Alonso's collaborative effort to promote a Latin American identity that would be built over the Hispanic linguistic base. She referred to this endeavor in the following terms: "This perspective amounts to a political culture that supports the spiritual unity of the Hispanic world as a way to defend a specific identity."[80] Arnoux highlighted the discursive strategies used in their grammar and other linguistic texts to impose a specific order on students' linguistic practices as well on the ways in which ordinary people should approach and think about the use of language. Arnoux's study introduces us to some of the specific language ideological issues that engaged Henríquez Ureña while he worked in the Buenos Aires of the 1930s.

Guillermo Guitarte (1958a) was the first scholar to coherently argue that Henríquez Ureña's important contributions to the emerging field of Spanish linguistics and his role in the *andalucismo* debate had to be problematized and understood in the precise context of their emergence. Guitarte emphasized the need to revise Henríquez Ureña's theoretical contributions using the critical tools of analysis that we have available today:

> Let us be clear. I am not saying that Alonso's and Henríquez Ureña's work is outdated simply because we have new techniques available or because new findings have forced us to modify their knowledge base. Clearly, this has occurred, but simply stating it is not sufficient ... What we need is not to solve the problems they raised and according to their terms, but, taking into account our new situation and, from it, reformulate these problems in our own terms.[81]

Not only did Guitarte articulate the need to reconceptualize the work of philologists and linguists such as Henríquez Ureña, but he also insisted on the need to focus less on the particular solutions that they intrepidly advanced with respect to certain linguistic and cultural problems and pay more attention to the principles that guided their work.

Apart from this line of inquiry by Jimenes Grullón, Arnoux, and Guitarte, most attempts to criticize Henríquez Ureña's work have been relatively genteel. The criticism is generally limited to pointing out that there are contradictions in Henríquez Ureña's analyses and interpretation of Latin American cultural and linguistic realities. Traditional authors do not actually analyze these contradictions in depth or the specific circumstances surrounding them. For the most part, analysts neglect the task of critically reading Henríquez Ureña's texts. Beatriz Sarlo (1998) catalogued the implications and tasks that are involved in a critical analysis:

> Reading Henríquez Ureña today involves a temporal displacement through which we counter the inevitable rhetoric imprinted on his texts by his times. Reading against time does not imply a charitable interpretation, always ready to justify differences as the result of cultural and historical distance. Rather, I would like to mean, in this case, bracketing the hallmarks of his writings in order to articulate certain aspects of his discourse which speak to our current concerns.[82]

Almost three decades ago, Soledad Álvarez (1981) remarked how critics had failed to scrutinize the depths of Henríquez Ureña's work. She pointed out several reasons why we needed critical approaches to the work of Henríquez Ureña:

> The question of his Americanism has been raised very often, but, paradoxically, we cannot find an insightful analysis of his ideas regarding Latin America. With regard to his anti-imperialism, the literature is non-existent. The broad range of issues present in the Dominican scholar's writings exposes the limitations of our narrow approach.[83]

Clearly, there is still a serious need for critical studies on Henríquez Ureña, especially with respect to his linguistic production. As noted even by devoted admirers such as Soledad Álvarez, rarely do we find analyses or reflections of the problems and contradictions that are present in Henríquez Ureña's cultural texts or, most relevant to this book, his linguistic production.

Knowledge and Ideology

The dominant tradition in Pedro Henríquez Ureña scholarship focuses on the reconstruction of his vision of Spanish America, which is known as Americanism. Within this tradition, scholars mostly expound on the

Dominican's intellectual brilliance, wealth of knowledge, and effort to develop and defend high culture in Latin America. Among Dominican analysts, the tendency is to extol Henríquez Ureña's Dominicanness or his symbolic value within the country's intellectual tradition and nationalism. With some exceptions, these trends are, in varying degrees, reproduced by those few analysts who focus on his linguistic work. Critically inclined analysts lament the limitations of highly evocative perspectives and the absence of detailed studies on Henríquez Ureña. Most studies attend to aspects of his personality and pedagogical practice and ignore the complexity of his ideas. A survey of studies on Pedro Henríquez Ureña, such as the one developed in the present chapter, reveals a dearth of critical approaches to his work. To focus solely on Henríquez Ureña's Americanism or his role in the *andalucismo* debate profoundly limits our appreciation and understanding of his work.

The most apparent limitation of the scholarship on Henríquez Ureña is the lack of studies that take into full consideration the significant impact of political and cultural ideology and context on his work. The few available critical approaches barely skim the surface of the ideological dimension of Henríquez Ureña's writings. For the most part, Henríquez Ureña scholars believe that he was able to reject ideological forces and concentrate on a "spiritual-like" search for knowledge. There is even a tendency to reduce the impact of ideological forces on Henríquez Ureña only to a mere preoccupation with philosophical problems of the "purely" epistemological kind. According to this perspective, ideology could not play a role in the intellectual activity of a man many consider incorruptible and impervious to politics of any kind. Nevertheless, as Jimenes Grullón and Guitarte argued, it is necessary to study Henríquez Ureña's oeuvre without forgetting that even brilliant thinkers such as Henríquez Ureña must adapt and respond to external pressures that ultimately manifest themselves in their work. Yet, despite some insightful studies on Henríquez Ureña's array of ideas on Spanish America, the majority of studies on his Americanism tend to focus on the aesthetic dimension of his oeuvre, and ignore its ideological dimension.

A primary apprehension among Henríquez Ureña specialists is that criticism can lead to a denial and radical rejection of the scholar's achievements. Additionally, there is the belief that the generational gap between Henríquez Ureña and us is now far too great for us to grasp the significance and implications of his work. Jean Franco (1998) suggested that the gulf that separates our generation from Henríquez Ureña's stems from a rupture with the past or a radical rejection of the idea that a powerful current, a human thread, runs through all great works.[84] However, Franco insists that we can accept the task of demystifying our humanist predecessors without necessarily trying to invalidate them. As Franco suggests, there is a need to develop a critical distance with respect to the works of the previous generation of "men of letters." This critical distance implies, first, acknowledging that it is insufficient to simply measure the quantity of knowledge that Henríquez Ureña accumulated and, second, understanding the conditions that allowed the acquisition and production of that knowledge in the first place.

Filling the Gap: A Language Ideological Approach

Some analysts attribute Henríquez Ureña's problematic assumptions, with respect to language and identity, to dialectology's relatively undeveloped methodology ("linguistic impressionism") in the early twentieth century, while others contend that some of his questionable claims are simply "insignificant" when compared with his achievements. Krauze, Díaz Quiñones, Jimenes Grullón, with their respective approaches, and Guitarte and Arnoux, with their metalinguistic approaches, represent a major departure from this tradition. Their analyses emphasize the need to adopt a more critical attitude toward Henríquez Ureña's ideas and even survey some specific problems that are present in his texts. Despite these calls for more in-depth analyses, the ideological implications and specific problems in his writings have not been fully considered. By and large, studies that have dealt with Henríquez Ureña's description of Spanish America as a cultural and linguistic unit say very little with respect to the specific strategies used by him in order to link language and identity in his construction of "Spanish America." This is a crucial limitation because it overlooks Henríquez Ureña's Dominicanness and Hispanoamericanism as two key ideological sites that articulate his work's discursive and textual realization. In this book, I take a specific language ideological approach that overcomes this limitation. Like Jimenes Grullón and Guitarte, I maintain that ideology was a powerful force in Henríquez Ureña's work and thought. Going a step further, I do not seek to simply identify which aspects of Latin American and Dominican cultural realities were distorted by Henríquez Ureña. Instead, I approach the problems of representation that surface in his work by examining specific semiotic and ideological processes as well as the degree to which these were triggered by specific conditions of production.

For this analysis, I critically examine the entire corpus of Henríquez Ureña's available linguistic texts.[85] In order to fully understand his linguistic production, I argue that it is necessary to read it in several contexts. First, Henríquez Ureña must be read in the context of the development of language studies in the Hispanic tradition, a tradition in which he grounded his own professional and intellectual development. Second, we must explore the context of the dialogue that Henríquez Ureña established between his linguistic production and the Dominican cultural and political field. Third, we must read his linguistic work in the context of the complex and contested construction of Dominican and Latin American identities. Confronting these contexts allows us a better glimpse into the issues and challenges that Henríquez Ureña attempted to resolve. On the one hand, by affirming the autonomy of American Spanish, he attempted to demonstrate the cultural unity and independence of Latin America. On the other hand, adopting a radically different perspective, he classified Dominican Spanish within the northern Iberian dialect continuum in order to settle the question of Dominican national identity. To some extent, it is perfectly clear that these linguistic representations respond to the sociopolitical circumstances that they attempt to articulate. However, we must understand the degree to which these linguistic representations, developed around the facts, naturalized these same sociopolitical circumstances under the cloak of science, thus constituting linguistic ideologies.

2

Linguistic Ideologies and the History of Linguistic Ideas

The concept of ideology and its epistemological status is a complex topic whose discussion involves many disciplines and theories. Terry Eagleton[1] (1991) provides 16 definitions of ideology, which reflect the different epistemological attitudes and theoretical commitments of the concept's proponents. Most of these definitions fall within two broad intellectual traditions. On the one hand, the philosophical tradition deals with the falsity and truthfulness of ideas and relates them to matters of cognition, reality, illusion, distortion, and mythmaking. On the other, there is a sociological tradition that deals with the functions of ideas in social life. The anthropologist Kathryn Woolard[2] (1998) explains that those that come from the philosophical tradition tend to highlight the representational-conceptual character of ideology (idea-ology), while those that come from the sociological tradition highlight issues of power and public and private conflict between social groups (id-ology). In this chapter, I review the history of ideology, examine the major approaches to the concept, and highlight the main characteristics of ideological phenomena in order to produce the most appropriate conceptualization for the study of the ideological dimension of Pedro Henríquez Ureña's linguistic texts.

The concept of ideology has some antecedents in the work of Francis Bacon (1561–1626). Regarded as the originator of the phrase "knowledge is power," Bacon advocated against what he called "idols," or bad habits of the mind that distort human thinking and prevent people from acquiring accurate knowledge of natural phenomena.[3] According to Bacon, debunking these idols was an important step in eliminating inadequate knowledge that was tied to special interest groups (e.g., the clergy). His main concern was how certain modes of interpretations (i.e., superstitions) impeded free thought while benefiting members of the church.[4] Bacon's critique constituted an attempt to comprehend ecclesiastical views of nature and relate them to the social conditions in which they emerged and the specific interest groups that, because of their social positions, were able to impose their views and modes of thinking on the rest of society.

French Enlightenment philosophers (Holbach, Condillac, Helvetius, and de Tracy, among others) adopted Bacon's ideas, which were generally about developing better methods for the study of nature, and applied them to knowledge of society, its structure, inequalities, and injustices. The goal of these philosophers was to develop methods of rational thinking and organization that could limit the arbitrary expansion and abuse of power and lead to a more rational organization of society. The scientist's task consisted of exposing social prejudice under the light of reason in order to reveal the nature of social institutions. It is in this context that the concept of ideology initially emerged. Toward the end of the eighteenth century, Destutt de Tracy (1754–1836) coined the term "ideology" while attempting to establish a "science" for the systematic and empirical study of ideas. According to de Tracy, ideas had to be broken down into their original elements in order for "one to ascertain everything that occurs when one thinks, speaks, and argues."[5] De Tracy considered the analysis of ideas the best method for achieving this task and progressively improving society and human life. The proponents of this theory were called "ideologues" and their objectives were not only theoretical but also political. Eventually, the antiauthoritarian position of the ideologues clashed with Napoleon Bonaparte, who had given up revolutionary idealism for absolutist pretensions. This political confrontation caused a rift between the ideologues and Napoleon, who had by then turned to conservative and religious groups for political support. Napoleon publicly attacked the ideologues, accusing them of being deluded theoreticians who were ignorant of the real issues and problems of the world of politics: "You ideologues destroy all illusions, and the age of illusions is for individuals as for peoples the age of happiness."[6] Consequently, Napoleon successfully diverted attention away from the original meaning of the word "ideologue" and infused it with negative connotations. Nevertheless, the concept of ideology emerged as a theoretical instrument that articulates political conflict and class warfare in a social arena. We can see in the ideologues' early formulations the basic lines of our current conceptualization of ideology as a discourse that naturalizes a context.

The point of departure for Karl Marx and Frederick Engels (1845) was a reformulation of Napoleon's condemnation of ideology, initially directed as an attack on their German contemporaries. Ideology became a polemical label for the kind of thinking that did not take into account material, social, and historical processes, including human consciousness.

In broad terms, Marxism developed three accounts of the concept: first, a system of beliefs characteristic of a particular class or group; second, a system of illusory beliefs—false ideas or false consciousness—that can be contrasted with true or scientific knowledge; and third, the general process of the production of meanings and ideas.[7] Contrary to common belief, it was Engels, and not Marx, who characterized ideological thinking as "false consciousness." Marx's approach to the concept of ideology was more complex and embedded in his general theory of alienation and consciousness.[8] Nonetheless, according to the authors of *The German Ideology* (1845), the production and reproduction of false consciousness took place in the struggle for class domination. For Marx and Engels, ideology stood against "science." The association of ideology with false consciousness and its opposition to the notion of "objective truth" became central to classic Marxism. In the process, this position produced some polemic reactions. The classic Marxist view of ideology has been challenged over the years on a number of grounds by non-Marxists and Marxists alike. Raymond Williams (1977), for example, a Marxist himself, took issue with the view that what is not ideology is pure positive science and that pure positive knowledge is free of ideology.[9] According to Williams, this position is excessively reductionist and overlooks the fact that thinking and imagining are, from the beginning, social processes.[10]

Presently, the term has acquired more acceptance and legitimacy due, in part, to interest in cognitive science. Teun A. Van Dijk (1995) defined the concept as a basic system of social cognition that facilitates the organization, monitoring, and control of specific group attitudes.[11] According to this cognitive perspective, we produce ideologies in our minds during our communication with members of our social group, starting with our family members and other close interlocutors. Essentially, cognitivists view ideologies as mental representations organized in the form of schemas. Their main function is to provide the common ground that sustains daily group interaction and discourse. Ideologies share many similarities with what cognitivists generally regard as "knowledge." Both are typically constructed and shaped by discourse and are bound by the limits of human cognition. For Van Dijk (2002), the difference between the two is that knowledge must not only be widely shared but must also pass tests that determine "the state of affairs" before it is accepted by a broader epistemic community.[12] Ideology, on the other hand, does not have to be accepted beyond the level of the group. Thus, according to this perspective, the difference between ideology and knowledge is only a matter of the size of the community that shares the set of beliefs. From a cognitive perspective it is possible to study the diverse ideologies of various groups, including feminists, racists, antiracists, fascists, environmentalists, and even sport fans, in order to learn significant facts about mental phenomena. The cognitivist approach to the study of ideologies is generally limited to questions of the mind, perception, and subjective experience. For a broader approach, more appropriate to the analysis intended in this book, we must return to the debates and problems social scientists faced in trying to cope with and overcome its association with the notion of false consciousness.

Critical Approaches to Ideology

The notion of ideology has been productively used to explore a vast array of complex sociohistorical phenomena. First of all, Antonio Gramsci exposed a serious flaw in the traditional Marxist understanding of ideology: the inability to see how ideology acted in a diffuse way. He advanced the notion of *hegemony*, the state's ability to govern, without force, through consent and ideology with the help of civil institutions that mediate between organizational and ideational processes.[13] Hegemony, a broader category that, in Gramsci's work, subsumes the concept of ideology, brings attention to the complex relationship between the leaders of a society and those that are led. For Gramsci, a social group must already exercise some form of intellectual or cultural "leadership before any power is firmly established."[14] An exuberant example of how hegemony unfolds can be seen in Henríquez Ureña's initial description of the role of intellectual politics in the Mexican Revolution:

> Soon enough we were addressing the public through conferences, articles, (a few) books, and art exhibitions. Our youthful revolution triumphed beyond our hopes. After a long and peaceful reign, our elders had forgotten how to fight. We were all young and like-minded. In 1909, before Diaz's government fell, Antonio Caso was asked to join the faculty of, what we now call, *Universidad Nacional*. His arrival there signified the beginning of the end [for the previous intellectual regime]. In 1911, when Madero arrived in power, the chief representatives of the old official ideology, most of whom were political figures in the old regime, retired from the University and their influence vanished.[15]

Ideological phenomena inevitably emerge in everyday life through the exercise of power and the signifying practices of social beings. To Gramsci, cultural hegemony is what guarantees the ruling classes' power over less powerful classes. It is achieved through control of a wide range of institutions, including the education system, religious organizations, and mass media that mediate between the economy and the state. In these institutional networks, we find agents who function as workers within the local economic system, but through these positions they also represent the state (or its enemies) and gather support within a specific zone of "civil society" for the state's monopoly (or its demise).[16] With control of these cultural institutions that are interwoven with habitual daily practices, the dominant classes educate the subordinated groups into accepting their rulers' supremacy and the ruling conditions as something natural and beneficial.

For Gramsci, ideology refers to the way groups articulate these power struggles at the level of signification. Accordingly, ideologies are psychologically and historically necessary in that "they 'organize' human masses and create the terrain on which men move, acquire consciousness of their position, struggle, etc."[17] Gramsci reminds us that Marx emphasized the historical nature of ideologies, always grounded in specific situations that require the organization of knowledge, popular beliefs, and action.[18] Therefore, the concept of ideology suits the analysis of belief systems that underlie certain social structures and articulate individual and collective behavior and consciousness.

The analyses of power relations show that ideology is a theoretically valid and useful concept that sheds light on recurring patterns of (political) thinking, for which there is concrete evidence in the real world. Ideologies involve thought practices intermeshed with and that inform material and observable practices and acts; they have both social and psychological manifestations that can be found in our actions and utterances. In Henríquez Ureña's writings, we find a variety of ways in which hegemonic ideas or pretensions are tied to language: "We have not given up writing in Spanish, and our problem of expression begins here."[19] Gramsci was fully aware of this link between hegemony and language:

> Every time the question of language surfaces, in one way or another, it means that a series of other problems are coming to the fore: the formation and enlargement of the governing class, the need to establish more intimate and secure relationships between the governing groups and the national-popular mass, in other words to recognize the cultural hegemony.[20]

To Gramsci, language and discussion about language constitute instruments of hegemony. Thus, he considered and reflected upon language in his analysis of the Italian cultural climate and the debates over his country's national destiny.[21] In these debates, Gramsci found evidence of power relations operating through linguistic practice. As we will find in Henríquez Ureña's linguistic texts, issues of differences among struggling social groups were reflected in speech and discourse on language. Analysts must pay serious attention to language as a central constituent element of hegemony: "Since this is the way things happen, great importance is assumed by the general question of language, that is, the question of collectively attaining a single cultural climate."[22]

Discourse: Where Language and Power Meet

The French philosopher and sociologist Michel Foucault also reacted against the traditional Marxist model of ideology as a simplistic and negative process whereby individuals were deceived into using ideas that were not in their best interest. However, Foucault's concept of "discourse" has been defined in dialogue with and in reaction to the classic Marxist definition of ideology.[23] Three issues stand out in this dialogue: the opposition of ideology to "truth," the role of "the subject," and the role of the economy in the determination of ideology. Foucault thought it was impossible to speak from a position of "truth," since one could only speak within the limits of what could be said at a particular time and place. Foucault referred to this combination of social, institutional, and sociolinguistic limits as "discursive frameworks," which are articulated by the effects of and struggle for power.

Foucault insisted that, in order to adequately understand historical processes, it was necessary to abandon the notion of "the individual subject" who is capable of resisting ideological pressures and controlling his or her actions. Instead, he proposed the study of the "micro-physics of power."[24] While Foucault paid considerable attention to state control and power relationships based on economic imbalance, he did not see economic relations as a primary feature of ideological phenomena (in the traditional Marxist sense). Foucault's discussion of power highlights the complexity of the relationship between socioeconomic positions and discourses: "In short, this power is exercised rather than possessed; it is not the 'privilege' acquired or preserved, of the dominant class, but the overall effort of its strategic positions—an effect that is manifested and sometimes extended by the position of those who are dominated."[25] He perceived the relationship between economics, social structures, and discourses as a complex interaction in which none of the constituent elements of the relationship were necessarily dominant.[26] He rejected the assumption that in a relationship of dominance there is only a powerful participant and a powerless one, who is duped into that position. In a sense, Foucault is essentially recasting the concept of ideology and moving away from the traditional Marxist view: "Perhaps, too, we should abandon a whole tradition that allows us to imagine that knowledge can exist only where the power relations are suspended and that knowledge can develop only outside its injunctions, its demands, and its interests."[27] Foucault's proposal has serious analytical implications: "We must cease once and for all to describe the effects of power in negative terms: it 'excludes,' it 'represses,' it 'censors,' it 'abstracts,' it 'masks,' it 'conceals.' In fact, power produces; it produces a reality; it produces domains of objects and rituals of truth."[28]

Foucault's preference for employing the term "discourse" was also tied to his desire to incorporate language into the analysis of the operations of power: "Historians have constantly impressed upon us that speech is no mere verbalization of conflicts and systems of domination, but that it is the object of man's conflicts."[29] Discourse, as an analytical category, focuses attention on the fact that language is a crucial site in the articulation of society and relations of power:

> Knowledge... is like language whose every word has been examined and every relation verified. To know is to speak correctly, and as the steady progress of the mind dictates; so to speak is to know as far as one is able, and in accordance with the model imposed by those whose birth one shares. The sciences are well-made languages, just as languages are sciences lying fallow. All languages must therefore be renewed; in other words, explained and judged according to that analytic order which none of them now follow exactly; and readjusted if necessary so that the chain of knowledge may be made visible in all its clarity, without any shadows or lacunae.[30]

Like Gramsci, Foucault overcame the hurdle of seeing ideology as a product and not as process and of focusing too much on the particular notion of false consciousness. They both contributed to an improved understanding of the complexity of ideological phenomena. They argued that ideology involves complex social phenomena and not just a kind of collective subjectivity, therefore alerting us to the fact that a dominant ideology reflects not just the rulers' worldview but the specific relations between the dominant and the dominated classes in society as a whole, in which the resulting dominant ideology will contain hybrid elements from the experiences of both classes.

Like Gramsci and Foucault, the French sociologist Pierre Bourdieu expanded our understanding of ideology with his notion of "habitus." This concept refers to the predispositions, attitudes, and modes of thinking based on past experience and associated with specific social conditions and relations of power. These predispositions constitute strategies in the mastery of social practice and make possible the achievement of diverse tasks. This approach to ideological phenomena allows us to explore how power legitimates itself in a field of competitive social relations by tacit rather than explicit agreement. These authors constantly remind us of the importance of considering the ideological functions of language in social life and historical processes in general. Bourdieu further claimed:

> Utterances are not only (save in exceptional circumstances) signs to be understood and deciphered; they are also signs of wealth, intended to be evaluated and appreciated, and *signs of authority*, intended to be believed and obeyed. Quite apart from the literary (and especially poetic) uses of language, it is rare in everyday life for language to function as a pure instrument of communication.[31]

Words and utterances are ideological because they are exchanged in an environment characterized by conflicts related to issues of difference, distinctiveness, material or symbolic resources, obedience, and defiance (i.e., relations of power).

The Russian literary critic Mikhail Bakhtin also discussed the complex socioideological dimension of language by going beyond traditional strictly formal linguistic concerns. For Bakhtin, the analysis of language in isolation was a problem. Language constitutes not a closed system but a complex system of polyphony and heteroglossia, synchronically and diachronically laden with all kinds of socioideological tensions. In other words, language is not simply an abstract mental structure. Its very nature and forms reflect the diversity and complexity of human activity and all the changes taking place in social life. Therefore, to investigate language is to explore social and ideological phenomena that involve tensions between the present and the past, different epochs, different social groups, theoretical currents, etcetera.

Bakhtin was particularly interested in the social character of linguistic activity because it spoke to issues particular to the science of language and to problems embodied in the traditional Marxist approach to the study of ideology. In *Marxism and the Philosophy of Language*, Bakhtin, under the pen name of V. N. Volosinov (1986), approached the linguistic sign as a fundamental and sensitive medium of social intercourse:

> Every ideological sign is not only a reflection, a shadow, of reality, but is also a material segment of that reality. Every phenomenon functioning as an ideological sign has some kind of material embodiment, whether in sound, physical mass, color, movements of the body, or the like. In this sense the reality of the sign is fully objective and lends itself to a unitary, monistic, objective method of study. A sign is a phenomenon of the external world. Both the sign itself and all the effects it produces (all those actions, reactions, and new signs it elicits in the surrounding social milieu) occur in outer experience.[32]

According to Bakhtin, "all its properties make the word the fundamental object of the study of ideologies."[33] The semiotic nature of ideology makes it possible to study these phenomena in relation to language, and, more specifically, in relation to concrete issues and problems engendered by the politics of language.

In sum, Bakhtin, along with Bourdieu, Foucault, and Gramsci, enriched our understanding of the interplay of language, society, politics, and history and laid the groundwork for the use of ideology as a crucial tool in the analysis of this interplay. Gramsci extended and enriched the notion of ideology with his introduction of the concept of hegemony. These authors problematized the classic understanding of ideology as false consciousness and of language as an instrument with which people are forced to believe ideas that are not true or in their best interest. Instead, as a result of their critical approach, we may view ideology as a form of discourse that produces and reproduces a hierarchy of truths, ideas, beliefs, images, and symbols, in order to naturalize, justify, legitimize, maintain, or challenge relations of power. In this new theoretical context, language is seen as inscribed in political and social reality and as an ideological site where political and social struggles are worked out. Above all, these authors have argued that knowledge and consciousness are mediated by the social position and the social processes in which we are involved, and that language is central to social practice and processes and therefore to the development of knowledge and consciousness.

The Concept of "Language Ideologies" in Linguistic Anthropology

Woolard (1998) identified four major interconnected strands of inquiry within the scholarly field known as *language ideologies*: investigations of the socioculturally motivated beliefs people utilize to rationalize and justify language structure and language (Bauman and Briggs 1990, Silverstein 1979); analyses of the underlying philosophies of language that bind particular speech communities together and shape their linguistic practices (Gumperz and Hymes 1972, Urciuoli 1991 and 1996); research into the actual mechanisms through which ideas about language are produced, valorized, circulated, and exchanged (Irvine 1989); and studies that focus on the status or values ascribed to particular linguistic systems, language varieties, the social identities associated with their users, and the interplay among different language groups (Gal 1987). Susan Gal and Kathryn Woolard (2001) defined language ideologies as "cultural conceptions of the nature, form and purpose of language, and communicative behavior as an enactment of a collective order."[34] Within Hispanic sociolinguistics, José

Del Valle (2007), following this line of thought, has provided the following definition:

> Language ideologies are systems of ideas that articulate general notions of language, languages, speech, and communication with politically or socially specific cultural formations. Although they belong to the realm of ideas, they can be viewed as cognitive frames that consistently link language to an extra-linguistic order; hence naturalizing and normalizing linguistic phenomena... It must be noted that language ideologies are produced and reproduced in the material world of linguistic and metalinguistic practices, among which we pay particular attention to the ones that are highly institutionalized.[35]

Linguistic ideology is therefore a concept around which anthropologists (Schieffelin, Woolard, and Kroskrity 1998), sociologists of language (Del Valle and Gabriel-Stheeman 2002 and 2004), and linguistic historians (Joseph and Taylor 1990) have converged.

Linguistic anthropologists embraced the concept of "linguistic ideology" as a result of their participation in debates over the need to incorporate a community's own theory of speech as part of any serious ethnography. According to Woolard, they reacted to Franz Boaz's (1858–1942) proposal that language is a cultural system whose primary structure has little to do with secondary rationalizations.[36] In contrast to this point of view, anthropologists advanced the view that "a grasp of language ideology is essential to understanding the evolution of linguistic structure."[37] Woolard explains that ethnographers of speaking (Bauman 1983, Gumperz and Hymes 1972, Ochs and Schieffelin 1981) delved into metalinguistics and folk theories of language in order to determine connections between language beliefs, linguistic practices, and key cultural ideas about identity.[38] These and other similar endeavors led them to focus more explicitly on the concept of linguistic ideology. This type of analysis is made possible by a conceptualization of language that triggers approaches that, as in the case of the authors discussed in the previous section, go beyond its formal material dimension. Combining knowledge of linguistic phenomena with social theories, linguistic anthropologists utilize their traditional skills in examining cultural conceptualizations of language and talk shared by members of a speech community and in relating them to their sociopolitical and economic positions and interests.[39]

Analysts have identified various aspects of language ideologies. First of all, according to Paul Kroskrity, language ideologies represent the perception of language and discourse that is constructed in the interest of a specific social group.[40] One must be aware of the fact that language users do not always behave disinterestedly. As Judith Irvine (1989) put it, "talk isn't cheap." Signs, words, verbal activity, speech can and do function as commodities and valuable resources in several ways.[41] For example, in her study of Nahuatl language ideologies, Jane Hill[42] (1998) found that talk and expressions about "respect" and "honor" in this speech community are implicitly and explicitly tied to native traditions and legitimate the political interests and social practices of distinct groups—the richer older men, the young men who hold jobs outside the community, and women. The main idea promoted by the group of male elders who defend the nostalgia-respect discourse is that the Nahuatl language, *mexicano puro* (Nahuatl without Spanish loanwords), and its most typical monolingual expressions are the most appropriate linguistic forms for certain types of social interaction in their community. At the same time, the group of women, which benefited from social and sociolinguistic change in the community, supports the new linguistic and social forms of interaction. Thus, in this particular sociolinguistic scenario, we find an example of a linguistic ideology that is grounded in social structure and relations and is connected to issues of power and inequality in a local system of production. This facet of language ideologies allows linguistic anthropologists to relate linguistic practice in a given culture with the exercise of power and questions of social inequities.

Second, language ideologies are profitably conceived as multiple because of the large number of meaningful social divisions (class, gender, elites, generations, and so on) within sociocultural groups that have the potential to produce divergent perspectives expressed as indices of group membership.[43] Thus, a characteristic of language ideologies within speech communities is "multisitedness" (Phillips 1998, Silverstein 1998). "Sites may be institutionalized, interactional rituals that are culturally familiar loci for the expression and/or explication of ideologies that indexically ground them in identities and relationships."[44] Therefore, it is helpful when analyzing language ideologies to explore institutional settings as well as actual contexts where speech and talk about speech take place. For example, Del Valle (2005 and 2006) has closely examined the pronouncements and discourses that come out of the various agencies in charge of Spain's language policy: the various autonomous governments, multinational corporations, the Spanish Royal Academy, the Cervantes Institute, and the newspaper *El PAÍS*, among others. These diverse institutions have produced a body of ideas about Spanish and endowed the image of the language with certain new properties. According to their views, Spanish is or has become a harmonious place of encounter, a global language, and an economic resource.[45] Del Valle explores precisely where these ideas originate, who expresses them, and under which conditions. In his analysis of the language ideologies surrounding the discussion of

"Spanglish" and the linguistic practices of Latinos in the United States, multisitedness becomes evident. Language ideologies range from what he characterizes as modernist (i.e., traditionalist, nationalist) to high modern (i.e., diasporic, globalist).[46] Examining the narratives of Latinos themselves, the testimonials of Latino intellectuals, the analyses of Latino and non-Latino academics, the statements of politicians and advocates of language legislations, and the proposals of Spain's language policy agents, Del Valle found opposing ideas that reflect the diverse interests of these distinct groups.[47] In this assortment of linguistic ideologies, one finds views of Spanglish as a type of linguistic practice that is at odds with the image of the United States as a monolingual nation and the image of Spanglish as the artificial creation of disloyal intellectuals. When we approach language ideologies with the understanding that they are multiple, we are in a better position to identify the different sources and sites of contention in a society and among individuals.

Third, members may display varying degrees of awareness of local language ideologies.[48] People develop different degrees of awareness of ideologically grounded discourse depending on the role that they play in a given community and the linguistic level under scrutiny. The following statement by a Dominican woman interviewed by Jacqueline Toribio (2000b) in the United States reflects one degree of awareness: "The Spanish language is a major part of Dominican culture. I would say that speaking [Spanish] is important, even essential, to being Dominican. A Dominican that does not speak [our dialect] might still feel proud, but he or she is missing something."[49] In this case, the speaker, to some degree, is explicitly aware of the extent to which the Dominican vernacular is a strong indicator of Dominican national identity in the context of the immigrant community. However, as Kroskrity indicates, there are cases in which the ideology must be read from actual usage.[50] For example, Robert Vann's (1999) study of linguistic ideologies in Barcelona showed that the ideological preference for Catalan varied according to the degree of exposure to Spanish in school. The more Spanish the individual had been taught in school, the less she identified with Catalan identity. Yet, a host of other factors may influence in the ideological awareness of speakers in a given community.[51] Ideological awareness is also determined by the language form or discursive phenomena that speakers are most likely to identify. According to Kroskrity, "nouns, our words for things, display an unavoidable referentiality that makes them more available for folk awareness and possible folk theorizing than, say a rule for marking the 'same subject' as part of verb morphology."[52] The challenge for the researcher lies in determining the degree to which ideologies are explicitly or implicitly expressed by speakers or members of a community. While the language ideologies of the state may be very explicit, the ideological arguments that underlie the analyses of linguistic scholars, for example, may be implicit. Therefore, we can expect to find evidence of language ideologies in a wide variety of sources and contexts.

Finally, members' language ideologies mediate between social structures and forms of talk.[53] Language users articulate their sociocultural experience and linguistic resources by indexically linking their linguistic and discursive forms to features of their sociocultural experience. We now turn to semiotic theories of communication for a more detailed explanation of this complex but fundamental aspect of language ideologies that we will encounter in Henríquez Ureña's linguistic texts.

The Iconicity of Language

Although from quite different perspectives, both literary and linguistic studies identify *iconicity* as a fundamental principle in the organization of language and text (Johansson 1999, Simone 1995, De Cuypere and Willems 2008). Literary scholars (Muller and Fischer 2003) explore iconicity and its manifestations through the analysis of metaphorical, iconographic, and mimetic devices in the production of texts and a great deal of their emphasis is on icons as aesthetic devices. Within linguistics, most discussions of iconicity center on the relationships between the linguistic sign and its referent. In its most basic formulation, iconicity refers to an isomorphic relationship between linguistic form (a word, phrase, sentence, or grammatical distinction such as singular vs. plural) and the semantic structure of a concept. For example, in the English sentence "Today I saw John," we might claim that there is a formal correspondence between the linear order of the elements and their semantic pattern. Thus, a direct object being closer to the verb (rather than the adverbial "today"), iconically reflects or diagrams a particular experience of the world. According to John Haiman (1985), "the most evident and often-noted iconicity of language structure is the linearity of the linguistic sign, which iconically reflects the linearity of time and causation."[54]

Cognitive scientists explore iconic phenomena using different conceptual models and terminology. For example, Bruce Hawkins (1997) defines an iconographic reference as "one that constructs an image of the referent which is intended to evoke a strong emotional response to that referent."[55] Hawkins focuses on the use of emotionally charged words and imagery typically found in the speech of demagogues. As an example, he offers Hitler's characterization of the Jews as "blood poisoning," which must be "removed from the national body."[56] Hawkins explains that "the effect of iconographic reference is to establish a powerful conceptual link between the referent and a particular value judgment."[57]

The concept of iconicity has a long tradition strongly associated with the model of semiotic communication developed by American philosopher Charles Sanders Peirce (1839–1914). In Peirce's view, the icon is a particular sign that exhibits its object by virtue of similarity or physical resemblance:

> An *icon* is a sign which stands for its object because as a thing perceived it excites an idea naturally allied to the idea that object would excite. Most icons, if not all, are *likenesses* of their objects. A photograph is an icon, usually conveying a flood of information. A piece of mimicry may be an auditory icon. A diagram is a kind of icon particularly useful, because it suppresses a quantity of details, and so allows the mind more easily to think of their important features... Many diagrams resemble their objects not at all in looks; it is only in respect to the relations of their parts that their likeness consists.[58]

In Peirce's theory of signs, icons are related to two other kinds of signs: indexes and symbols. Indexes (such as "this," "that," "mine," "yours," "here," "there," "now," and "then") encode relations between objects and contexts. Peirce explained that an index stands for its object by virtue of a real connection that forces the mind to pay attention to that object. For example, a possessive pronoun acts as an index in two different ways: "First it indicates the possessor, and second, it has a modification which syntactically carries the attention to the word denoting the thing possessed."[59] In other words, a possessive pronoun points to an object and also highlights one element (a noun) in a syntactic relationship. The indexical sign and its referent are copresent in the context of the utterance, which is conditioned linguistically by the cognitive existence of a semantico-referential grammar and socioculturally by the local standards of relevance and meaning.[60] Finally, a symbol is a sign that denotes an object solely by convention. It depends on abstract, semantico-referential values and, unlike icons and indexicals, does not convey meaning by virtue of physical similarities or of spatial and temporal contiguity.[61] Yet, to some degree, even sign-symbols incorporate iconicity.[62] These three signs are related to one another and to the general class of signs and are, therefore, crucial for the study of modes of signifying in general.[63]

These semiotic concepts are also crucial for researchers who study the social life of language. Within the field of linguistic anthropology, some researchers have further elaborated concepts such as index and icon in order to advance their study of language ideological phenomena (Bucholtz 2001). Michael Silverstein (1976 and 1985) was one of the first scholars to adopt Peirce's explanation of meaning derived by indexical contiguity in order to investigate how language users tend to associate particular linguistic forms with specific kinds of speakers. He observed, for example, that in the native American Muskogean language there was a phonologically variable suffix –s that tended to be preserved only with the inflected verb forms of direct (not quoted) utterances spoken by female individuals.[64] Thus, although the referential value of the verb forms that take this suffix is not changed, the use of this index provides relevant information regarding the social category of the speaker. Woolard (2007b) explains that "first-order indexicality involves the semiotic act of noticing" and "second-order indexicality brings ideology to bear on the relationship noticed."[65] First-order indexicality, for example, is at work when everyday language users associate particular linguistic features with specific kinds of speakers and contexts. In these cases, language users pay attention to linguistic patterns in order to determine the meaning or the appropriateness of utterances. Ideology is not necessarily at work in these cases. However, ideology comes into play when language users specifically attribute values to these linguistic indexes in order to determine the speakers' membership status in a given speech community. At the second level, therefore, speakers rationalize, explain, naturalize, and ideologize the sociolinguistic associations (indexical relations) that they noticed at the first order. Linguistic forms and codes can become indexes that point to social identities and the typical activities of language users. While this is not news to sociolinguists, less is known about the specific processes by which speakers often register, rationalize, and justify such linguistic indexes and the linguistic ideologies that claim to explain the source and meaning of the linguistic differences.[66] Woolard affirms that the operation of indexicality is very similar to the semiotic and politically loaded process that we call *iconization*.[67] While analysts do not necessarily abandon the difference between the concepts of index and icon, they prefer to focus on their potential for explaining in concrete terms how cultural conceptions of language, linguistic forms, and communication interact with language structure and language use. In this regard, terminology is secondary. However, the difference in terms such as iconicity and iconization reflects a difference in focus: the former emphasizes a product, while the latter emphasizes a process of mapping out social meaning and its conditions of production.

Linguistic Differentiation and Language Representations

Judith Irvine and Susan Gal (2000) propose three semiotic and ideological processes in the discursive construction of the social meaning of language and language forms: *iconicity, fractal recursivity,* and *erasure.* First, they appropriate iconicity in order to account for processes by which some aspect of or feature in the linguistic repertoire of a given community is perceived as an iconic representation of its members:

> Iconization involves a transformation of the sign relationship between linguistic features (or varieties) and the social images with which they are linked. Linguistic features that index social groups or activities appear to be iconic representations of them, as if a linguistic feature depicted or displayed a social group's inherent nature or essence. The process entails the attribution of cause and immediate necessity to a connection (between linguistic features and social groups) that may be only historical, contingent, or conventional.[68]

The authors offer as an example the iconization of click consonants among speakers of Nguni languages in southern Africa. Clicks were not originally part of the Nguni languages, but were acquired from Khoi languages via a process of lexical borrowing. They were borrowed in order to avoid, in the presence of particular interlocutors, native expressions that were deemed to be disrespectful. Thus, usage of Khoi loanwords became iconically associated with respect and deference to people and their social positions. The result was a click-laden respect vocabulary that came out of the semiotic process of iconization.[69]

Iconization works in tandem with processes of fractal recursivity and erasure. Fractal recursivity is defined as "the projection of an opposition, salient at some level of relationship, onto some other level."[70] For example, by means of the conspicuous click consonants viewed as icons of foreignness, speakers mobilized the contrast between Nguni and Khoi consonant repertoires to express social distance and difference within Nguni.[71] Erasure is defined as an ideological process that renders some people, practices, or sociolinguistic phenomena invisible. According to Irvine and Gal, in simplifying the sociolinguistic field,

> Facts that are inconsistent with the ideological scheme either go unnoticed or get explained away. So, for example, a social group or language may be imagined as homogeneous, its internal variation disregarded. Because a linguistic ideology is a totalizing vision, elements that do not fit its interpretive structure—that cannot be seen to fit—must be either ignored or transformed.[72]

Irvine and Gal found ample evidence of erasure, iconization, and recursivity in the representations of Senegalese languages by nineteenth-century European linguists and ethnographers whose work was heavily influenced by national and racial ideologies.[73] These scholars encountered a complex, regional linguistic situation in which linguistic repertoires were inscribed in equally complex religious and political relationships. Assuming that a language ought to correspond to one territory, one nation, and one race, scholars studied which languages were spoken where in order to "disentangle the supposed history of conquests and represent legitimate territorial claims."[74] Irvine and Gal explain how this language mapping project involved the three semiotic processes: (i) the language map depicted the relationship ideologically that was supposed to obtain between language, population, and territory (iconization); (ii) the map could only be drawn by tidying up the linguistic complexity, that is, by removing multilingualism and variation from the picture (erasure); and (iii) relationships between Europeans and Africans were the implicit model for a history of relationships within Africa itself (recursivity).[75]

Irvine and Gal's analysis offers a model for studying the relationship between linguistic ideology and linguistic forms and has implications for a number of fields of inquiry such as the historical fields of contact among peoples, the interplay of ethnicity and linguistic practices, and conceptions of language itself.[76] Their analysis has also shed light on the degree to which ideas that were forged in earlier historical periods remain embedded in our analytical frameworks and emphasize the importance of closely examining scholars' conceptions of language as they relate to categories of identity.[77] Consider the Dominican linguist Manuel Núñez's (2004a) claims that the first line of defense in harnessing the Dominican Republic's identity is language. It is not only speakers' theories about the nonarbitrariness of the sign that make a difference in the production, interpretation, and reporting of linguistic differentiation, but also the equally ideological descriptions of linguists.[78]

By paying attention to semiotic and ideological processes such as iconization and erasure, linguistic anthropologists examine the links between linguistic practices and social experience. We also learn how and to what degree ideational matters are inscribed in the lived relations of everyday life and that social life and its materiality are constituted through signifying practices such as linguistic communication. Accordingly, analysts (Gal 1998, Irvine 1989) utilize knowledge of these semiotic processes to advance the study of the material, cultural, economic, political, and social foundations and implications of language and discourses on language.

Language and Nationalism

The concept of language ideology has been very influential in studies on language and nationalism (Anderson 1983, Barbour 2000, Blommaert and

Verchueren 1998, Del Valle and Gabriel-Stheeman 2004b, Gal 2001, Joseph 2004). For instance, some researchers have focused on the idea, implicit in the majority of nationalist texts, that social differences are not desirable because they undo "natural" groupings and the national homogeneity that is necessary for democracies to exist. These undesirable "social differences" include linguistic differences. Jan Blommaert and Jef Verchueren (1998) characterized this language ideology as "the dogma of homogeneism," or the view that differences constitute dangerous centrifugal forces in society that would function better without intergroup differences:

> In other words, the ideal model of society is monolingual, monoethnic, monoreligious, monoideological. Nationalism, interpreted as the struggle to keep a group as "pure" and homogeneous as possible, is considered to be a positive attitude within the dogma of homogeneism.[79]

Thus, one primary area for language ideological research is the role that language plays in nation-building. Del Valle (2005) highlighted the basic conceptual structure of the ideology of linguistic nationalism in the following terms: a shared group or cultural (ethnic or political) identity, made possible by a common language, within a circumscribed territory.[80]

Joseph Errington (2000) explored linguistic nationalism in his study of the modernization of Indonesian culture and its process of linguistic standardization. "The New Order" regime in Indonesia selected a standardized dialect (Javanese) as the national language and as the main vehicle of their modernization project in a multilingual and multiethnic territory. Errington followed the ideological links between The New Order's nationalist program and the specific institutional proposals regarding the features and use of language and speech genres in the public domain *(exemplarism)*. Despite the fact that the standardized dialect lacked many native speakers, it was utilized as a propagator of national ideology and a symbol of "Indonesianness." These processes within the Indonesian nationalist movement naturalized a system of ideas, including the idea that "language indicates nationality."[81] According to Errington, in this context, schools became the primary institutional means of disseminating the standard language, the nationalist ideology, and the patterns of behavior that the state expected of its citizens.[82] Thus, the diffusion and naturalization of linguistic ideas, in the context of national development, also aimed at producing certain effects on the linguistic behavior and other social practices of men and women in this community.

In many Latin American contexts, the nation has also been conceived as a culturally and linguistically homogeneous "organism" and as the most suitable vehicle for the diffusion of knowledge necessary to develop industry, commerce, and prosperity in a society (Arnoux and Luis 2003, Ashley 2002, Centeno Añeses 1999, Colom González 2005, González Tirado 1987, Morris 1996, Toribio 2000b). The process of nation-building occurred unevenly throughout Latin America. It is characterized by a series of events that responded to the specific problems facing each country and followed different time frames. However, as Elvira N. de Arnoux and Carlos R. Luis (2003) point out, in each case, the state proceeded to consolidate its language, forging consent among its subjects and displacing, where necessary, the power of other institutions, in particular, the church.[83]

Especially since the nineteenth century, state functionaries, scholars, the cultural elite, and other social agents who participate in national projects, more often than not propose monolingualism and the Nation-State model as the only solution to most social problems. Although globalization and other transnational processes erode linguistic nationalism, we can still find tendencies to conceptualize language as a distinctive feature of "natural" groups and as the cause of divisions between groups. For example, the U.S. English Foundation insists on the image of the United States as a monolingual nation and the need for "preserving the unifying role of the English language."[84] This organization is committed to "keeping this nation unified through a common language."[85] Its efforts include spreading the idea that only English can provide the best cultural framework for national unity, economic prosperity, and democracy. In the case of the Dominican Republic, Toribio (2000a) has documented the degree to which an idealized form of the Spanish language still stands as the representation of national identity, even among the Dominican diaspora. According to Toribio, "in this predilection for the northern Iberian variety and emphatic repudiations of the influences of Haitian Creole, Dominicans ignore a central axiom of linguistics—language variation is normal—and affirm their *hispanidad,* a historical obsession."[86] In several statements, Toribio's Dominican informants confirm the existence of a (dominant) national linguistic ideology. In other words, while there are a number of identity markers for Dominicans, language is given priority, especially in the construction of national identity.

The Politics of Language and Hispanic Sociolinguistics

Within Hispanic sociolinguistics, specialists have approached language ideological phenomena, on the one hand, from a critical discourse analysis perspective, and on the other, from a historical and sociopolitical perspective *(glotopolítica*[87] *del lenguaje).* Scholars such as Arnoux (2003, 2006) and Del Valle (2002, 2004, 2005, 2007) have produced a body of research exploring the relationship between language and politics, the use of politicized language, and the history of politics and ideas about language in Spain and Latin America. Their line of research departs from the shared viewpoint that the relationship between language ideologies and language policies is a dialectical one (Arnoux and Del Valle 2010). But while Del Valle is mostly interested in historicizing language ideologies and thus exploring the institutional sites (especially those connected to the state) where they originate and the conditions that produced them, Arnoux primarily approaches them from the perspective of (textualist) discourse analysis. Arnoux (2007) searches for language ideological phenomena in an array of sources such as grammars, dictionaries, style and rhetoric manuals, school textbooks, fiction, radio programs, newspaper articles, interviews, political speeches, and pedagogical discourse.[88] In Arnoux's exploration of archival materials and in Del Valle's analyses of recent language policies in Spain, they have found and examined *ideologems*, or ideas, slogans, and metaphors, that articulate more complex ideological systems (e.g., "total Spanish," "polycentric language," "language of our homeland," "language of encounter," "*mestizo* language").[89] These labels are the product of ideological practices that assign various roles, functions, and values to the Spanish language and the pan-Hispanic speech community. In various contexts, the specific authors of these ideologems produce and reproduce messages that introduce, repeat, and exaggerate certain key phrases *(e.g., concordia* (harmony), *encuentro* (encounter), *cohesión* (cohesion)*)*.[90] Both Del Valle and Arnoux are primarily concerned with the role that discourse on Spanish has played and continues to play in the construction of cultural, political, and social hierarchies in Spain and Latin America in different historical moments.

In addition, these analysts have paid particular attention to ideological representations of language in the Hispanic world. Del Valle, Luis Gabriel-Stheeman, and their collaborators (2002 and 2004) examined metalinguistic discourses as sites where the postcolonial relationship between Spain and Latin America was being debated. They centered on discourses on language by Hispanic intellectuals of the nineteenth and twentieth centuries that reveal a willingness and determination to intervene in linguistic matters. More specifically, in concrete statements about Spanish, its domains, speakers, status, and future, these analysts uncovered efforts on the part of leading Spanish and Latin American intellectuals to rationalize, protect, promote, and, especially, control the institutional and symbolic power of Spanish. Such efforts, when analyzed in their proper contexts—that is, in light of the institutional settings from which they emerge and the contexts in which they operate—reveal intricate connections with political phenomena.

For example, Del Valle and Gabriel-Stheeman (2004a) and Del Valle (2007) show that, during the last few decades, some Spanish cultural agents, business executives, and political figures, working within specific institutional settings (Real Academia Española, Instituto Cervantes, Congreso Internacional de la Lengua Española, Asociación para el Progreso del Español como Recurso Económico) actively engaged in the construction and promotion of a new image of the Spanish language as a sign of pan-Hispanic identity and cultural patrimony as well as the exploitation of its economic profitability. In Del Valle and Gabriel-Stheeman (2004c), the authors highlight the words of one of Spain's language agents—the head of Asociación para el Progreso del Español como Recurso Económico (Association for the Advancement of Spanish as an Economic Resource)— that illustrate the articulation of a specific language ideology with concrete actions designed to impact in this case a specific speech community, Latinos in the United States: "If Spain manages to become a model or provider of identity for the Spanish-speaking community in the United States, it will easily secure and improve its positions in this country."[91] From the agent's point of view, Spain's socioeconomic position can improve, with the proper intervention, by transforming Spain into a source of identity for U.S. Hispanics.

The analysis of the politics of language centers on the nature and operation of language and discourse in a context defined in predominantly sociopolitical terms. Analyzing the politics of language implies fully fleshing out the social dimensions of language, by interrogating the details of each speech situation, the institution from which discourse emerges, and its conditions of production, in other words, by analyzing language in context. Similar to the anthropological approaches of Woolard, Gal, and Kroskrity, Arnoux and Del Valle investigate the linguistic ideologies surrounding Spanish and its political dimension, in relation to three central categories: (i) an ideology's contextuality, or the discourse's relation to a series of specific individual, cultural, social and political contexts; (ii) its naturalizing function, or the normalizing effect on the extralinguistic order (i.e., the Nation, the pan-Hispanic community); and (iii) its institutionality, or its production and reproduction in institutional settings (i.e., language academies, party platforms, radio stations, classrooms, research institutions, etc.) endowed with power and authority.

Arnoux (2000 and 2007), working within the Discourse Analysis perspective,[92] believes that language ideologies derive from wider ideological systems, but are readily accessible whenever people or institutions present language as an object of desire or an object to be acted upon.[93] Arnoux refers to this political field as *glotopolítica*. She borrows this category from Louis Guespin and Jean Baptiste Marcellesi (1986). These two

French analysts declared: "*Glottopolitical* refers to the different ways (conscious or not) in which a society attempts to impact language... The political analysis of language is necessary to establish all the facts surrounding political actions intended to impact linguistic behavior in a given a society."[94] Considered a branch of applied linguistics that focuses on issues of "language planning," glottopolitical studies analyze language ideologies in relation to language policies as well as the specific interventions of agents aimed at impacting the public domains of language. These phenomena are then correlated with social positions in an inquiry into their roles in the production, reproduction, and transformation of power structures in local, regional, national, or global contexts. Because of the connection between language ideologies and other aspects of ideological systems, Arnoux and Luis (2003) analyze a diverse corpus of materials, including linguistic texts. In addition, they analyze texts and discourses whose main subject is not necessarily language but that provide important clues as to the role of language in sociohistorical formations (e.g., historical texts that narrate the emergence of national states). Thus, from a glottopolitical perspective, analysts such as Arnoux apply the concept of language ideology in order to investigate the politically significant means by which social representations (particularly linguistic ones) are constructed and imposed in different institutional settings. A typical procedure includes examining archive materials from a specific country during a specific historical moment.

Within Hispanic sociolinguistics, this political analysis of language seeks to fully understand the prevalence of some ideas on the Spanish language, reflections on the origin of language, and the role of the intellectual in the production of discourse as products of theoretical and ideological options and strategies that were determined by historical circumstances. Arnoux and Luis (2003), in particular, examined the pervasive influence of Enlightenment thought (Gaspar Melchor de Jovellanos, Vincente Salvá, and Andrés Bello, among others)—with its emphasis on rationality, order, and progress—on the construction of the nation. The Spanish thinker and politician Gaspar Melchor de Jovellanos (1744–1811), for example, was a key figure in the adaptation of new historical currents and valued national traditions in Spain. He viewed language as an important site in the construction of the Spanish state, which, in his view, needed economic development, cultural homogenization, language standardization, the expansion of the education system, and greater communication with other European nations. This last particular feat required that citizens spoke foreign languages. As a result of this view, Jovellanos launched several education initiatives designed to increase knowledge of the national language, as well as French and English. He also produced grammatical texts that articulated theoretical positions within the Royal

Spanish Academy with Enlightenment thought as found in the work of the French philosopher Étienne Condillac (1715–1780).[95] Arnoux examined Jovellanos's reformulation of Condillac and, particularly, the series of displacements, substitutions, omissions, and reordering of Condillac's arguments. Jovellanos had to reformulate Condillac's discourse because he was addressing it to a different audience, but also because of major theoretical and ideological differences between the two authors. According to Arnoux, Jovellanos sought educational and linguistic solutions to matters of state. Some of these solutions were modeled on Condillac, but others were adjusted and transformed in order to conform to monarchic rule and the ecclesiastical apparatus that were trying to protect their interests in a changing world. Through Arnoux's ideological-discursive analysis, in this particular case, we are able to appreciate how Jovellanos intervenes in sociolinguistic problems of his time from a powerful yet vulnerable political position.

Thus, by closely examining these authors' discourses on language in relation to the sociopolitical circumstances that motivated and conditioned them, Arnoux and Luis (2003) were able to demonstrate the degree to which specific ideas about language were deployed for political purposes. While not necessarily identifying themselves as language ideological researchers, these authors illustrate how the concept of language ideology can be applied in order to situate representations of language within specific political contexts and thus gain a better understanding of their historical significance.

Critical Linguistic Historiography

The analysis that I develop in this book is situated between language ideological research and linguistic historiography. According to Konrad Koerner (1995), the three basic objectives of linguistic historiography are the establishment of the "climate of opinion" in which the given linguistic theories of a period were advanced (to which he refers as the principle of contextualization), the development of a historical and critical understanding of the linguistic texts in question (principle of immanence), and a final approximation with current conceptual frameworks and technical vocabulary (principle of adequation).[96] First, building on historian Carl Becker's (1932) original conceptualization, Koerner adopts the notion of "the climate of opinion" in order to analyze the intellectual environment in which certain linguistic ideas develop:

> Linguistic ideas have never developed quite independently of other intellectual currents of the time; the *Zeitgeist* has always left its imprint on linguistic

thinking. At times, the influence of the socio-economic and even political situation must be taken into account as well. For instance, the historiographer of linguistics should be aware that the "natural order" discussion in 18th-century France, intended to demonstrate French superiority, and not only linguistic superiority, took place in a political climate of autocratic rule and supremacy aspirations of France.[97]

Second, Koerner insists that the researcher must fully understand the ideas in question within the general theoretical framework in which they were originally embedded. Moreover, the specific terminology used in the texts must be analyzed internally. Finally, and only after the first two principles have been satisfied, can we attempt to approach the ideas and the texts in terms of the issues and problems that are relevant to us today. In other words, the present must find the most adequate means of entering into dialogue with the original historical context.

Throughout this endeavor, Koerner emphasizes the need to develop an appropriate framework, methodology, and epistemology:

> It is important to realize ... that because of the particular nature of the subject of investigation, namely, theories of language (as well as theories of linguistics) and their application as well as their evolution through time, historians of linguistics must find their own framework, their methodology and epistemology, and cannot expect to be able to apply methods and insights from other fields directly to their own subject of investigation.[98]

Although highly focused on practical and methodological considerations in establishing a historiography of linguistics, Koerner believes that the application of these principles can help researchers in achieving an adequate understanding of the history of linguistic ideas and the establishment of linguistic myths within the field of language studies.[99]

Paul Laurendeau (1990) also elaborates on the notion of climate of opinion, which he prefers to call a "theory of emergence." Like Koerner, he wants to establish a methodology that can be applied to the study of linguistic ideas in their historical context.[100] He contends that historians of linguistics typically describe the origin and developments of ideas as the result of the institutional clout of certain strong personalities. He finds one example of this approach in the linguists J. C. Chevalier and P. Encrevé's (1984) description of interpretations of Ferdinand de Saussure's formalism and the influential role attributed to Antoine Meillet's role in securing Saussure's fame: "Meillet dominated linguistics in French universities until his death in 1936. Guillaume's fate is an example of that domination. Nobody would have thought of appointing another linguist without

Meillet's approval. Once Meillet had spoken, everyone followed."[101] In contrast to this traditional approach to the history of linguistics, Laurendeau proposes a historicization of linguistics:

> This *historicization* of linguistics, a subdivision of the *science of history,* is limited to the knowledge of the relations between the ideological and/or scientific reality of linguistics and the objective reality of *history*. This includes many things. Because knowledge is something more sophisticated than a simple tool.[102]

Laurendeau argues that linguistics emerges and exists as the result of the tense interaction between practical knowledge about an empirical reality and the ideological conditions surrounding it:

> This implies certain theoretical positions about history. Historical materialism provides the general framework for the *theory of emergence*. This theory sees in every school of linguistics an indirect and relatively autonomous product of concrete socio-historical contexts, and tries to describe the *emergence* of a linguistic school, proceeding backwards from its established results towards the complex mix of its theoretical and material sources.[103]

In the study of the emergence of schools of linguistics, the researcher's tasks include identifying the sources of tension between science and ideology and recognizing how the tension manifests itself in texts that are products of sociohistorical conditions. Laurendeau refers to these processes as *critique* and *hermeneutics,* respectively:

> We mean by *critique* a "first-degree" reading that postulates the tension between science and ideology in every intellectual product, and that looks less for what-is-true-and-what-is-false than for the manifestations of the *struggle* between positions. Conversely, we mean by *hermeneutic* a "second-degree" reading that does not look for *data* or *symbols*... but for clues of a socio-historical reality in the text. *The passage from a (dialectical) critique to a (materialistic) hermeneutic is the global method proposed by the theory of emergence.*[104]

Laurendeau explains that a critique centers on the contents of the linguistic texts as a source of information, while a hermeneutical approach considers the texts as "a system of more or less intentional codings" to be analyzed with reference to specific cultural representations.[105] In short, this linguistic historiographic approach seeks to understand linguistic ideas in relation to a specific intellectual context and the sociohistorical ground in which they emerge.

The History of Linguistic Ideas

Since its inception as a legitimate scholarly field, linguists have sought to identify their practice as a science that explains language according to exclusively empirical criteria (scientific evidence, purely objective quantifiable facts, etc.). The epistemological and ideological foundation of modern linguistics rests on the following statement by Saussure: "The true and unique object of linguistics is language studied in and for itself."[106] Accordingly, language is defined as an autonomous system of signs that expresses ideas and should be studied separately from speaking as well as social and political phenomena.[107] As Roy Harris (2001) pointed out, although this synchronic definition of language and linguistics liberated linguists from unnecessary theoretical, pedagogical, and normative commitments, it also meant that "students could become fully qualified academic linguists without bothering at all about the history of the language they were studying, even where historical materials were available."[108] It also meant the displacement from the academic space of those who were not adhering to the synchronic study of language, which was regarded by some interpreters of Saussure as the most legitimate, "even though it was actually directly contrary to the holistic letter and spirit of Saussurean synchrony."[109] As a result of the rejection of language's social dimension, certain topics such as the relationship between language and nationality; language as a key historical site; language use as an instrument of exclusion; and language as a class, race, and gender-related phenomenon were relegated to the margins. In order to study the interrelated phenomena of language ideologies that we find in the writings of Pedro Henríquez Ureña, we must abandon the traditional definitions ascribed to Saussure.

Thus, whether he intended it or not, our intellectual debt to Saussure includes his delimitation of *langue* and his apparent rejection of history— in the sense of the products of human affairs and material labor—as an obstacle to the scientific study of language. Tony Crowley (1996), examining the arguments for and against approaches to language in history (i.e., the theories of Saussure and Bakhtin), argues against this view. He explains that, contrary to common belief, Saussure did not entirely fail to address historical questions but simply relegated "important matters" of language and race, nation and political history to the realm of "external linguistics," while prioritizing the system of language as the focus of "General Linguistics."[110] According to Crowley (1996), "there is no absolute rejection of history then, but a new positioning of the historical viewpoint in the field of linguistic study. There is evidence that it is a viewpoint which Saussure might have favored once the arduous task of clearing the ground for the science of language had been completed."[111] This evidence includes the following statement by Saussure in a letter to Meillet: "In the last analysis, only the picturesque side of language still holds my interest, what makes it different from all others, insofar as it belongs to a particular origin, the almost ethnographic side of language."[112]

Nevertheless, the underlying assumption for most modern linguists was that their research—as well as the linguistic phenomena they study—was immune to the sociopolitical world and cultural facts. Koerner (2001) concurs: "At least since the establishment of the so-called 'Boppian paradigm' of comparative-historical linguistics, historians of the field have succeeded in presenting us with the image of the field as objective, value-free, in one word 'scientific.'"[113] In the pursuit of their task, linguists often forget, ignore, or even deny the degree to which their own cultural precepts, professional demands, and personal prejudices leak into their scientific investigations (Joseph and Taylor 1990, Newmeyer 1986). Therefore, within the field of language ideologies, a series of studies surfaced focusing on two major concerns: the circumstances in which historical matters are ignored in linguistic description, and the ideological pressures that permeate the study and descriptions of language at different periods; in other words, we aim to analyze the production and reproduction of language ideologies in specific institutional domains such as the well-established disciplines of linguistics and philology.

Focusing on the scientific ideologies of professional linguists, the studies included in John Joseph and Talbot Taylor's *Ideologies of Language* (1990) offer excellent examples of the analysis of the history of linguistic ideas. Taking note of ideas coming from history, politics, and race, they demonstrate the degree to which many different belief systems penetrate linguists' judgments about what constitutes a language, language change, grammar, language contact, language mixing, codeswitching, creolization, and language decay. For example, Paul Roberge (1990) explored Afrikaans linguistic scholarship in light of the subjects of race, racism, and politics in South Africa. He examined the intellectual roots of the prevailing purist and albocentric ideology in Afrikaans historical linguistics and found connections to the comparative paradigm that dominated Europe during the nineteenth and the early twentieth centuries. More concretely, he identified the ideological underpinnings of the fundamental descriptions of white Afrikaans-speaking linguists concerning the history of their language. A body of evidence shows that Afrikaans comprises a semicreolized variety of Dutch that emerged from contact between Europeans, the aboriginal Khoikhoi, and slaves of African and Asian origins. Nevertheless, some white South African linguists have nullified such evidence. Roberge identified the historical determinants and the mechanisms by which Afrikaans language historians have proposed certain features of the language as symbols of racial purity. Afrikaans linguistics emerged in the struggle of white Afrikaaners to maintain racial separation from black South Africans as well as linguistic separation from English. Furthermore, the National (political) party gave further impetus to the crystallization of these purist linguistic ideas by incorporating them as symbols and goals in its quest for political dominance.[114] Thus, the author explains that Afrikaans scholars wrote the history of the language and perpetuated their scholarship as value-neutral at a time when miscegenation, Creoles, and mixed languages were taboo subjects in South Africa.[115] In addition, Roberge demonstrated how the history of the Afrikaans language was written and rewritten to align with South African racial and nationalistic ideologies.

Another example of language ideological phenomena from the perspective of the history of linguistic ideas can be found in Del Valle's *Menéndez Pidal, National Regeneration, and Linguistic Utopia* (2002b). In this case, the author argues that Ramón Menéndez Pidal's philological and linguistic production can be read as a response to Spain's intellectual and cultural crisis, which reached its peak in 1898 when Cuba and Puerto Rico, the last of the Spanish colonies in Latin America, were lost. Ramón Menéndez Pidal believed that once a modern Hispanic community had been built, Spain would regain its position of leadership. Del Valle observes that Menéndez Pidal's classic text *Manual elemental de gramática histórica española* (1904) was consistent with neogrammarian doctrine in organization, methodology, and its conception of language change, a fact that attests to the scientific rigor of Menéndez Pidal's research activity. Yet, in his linguistic theorization, language was equated with culture and nation and Castile's elite played the key role. Menéndez Pidal (1926) noted that "the Castilian dialect displays in all its characteristics a unique character in comparison to the other dialects of Spain, as a rebellious and dissenting force that emerges in Cantabria and adjacent regions."[116] The military metaphor *fuerza rebelde* (rebellious force) is interesting because, as Koerner (2004) remarks, military analogies are a common characteristic of ideologies.[117] Del Valle (2002b) concludes that, for Menéndez Pidal, "the inherently superior qualities of the Castilian dialect explained its projection not only in time but also in space."[118] According to Del Valle, Menéndez Pidal was indeed committed to an accurate description of the Spanish language and its history, but he did so in the broader context of his commitment to the construction of Spanish as "a spectacular icon: glorious symbol for the nation's past and a sophisticated vehicle for its race towards a brilliant future."[119] Del Valle reaches this conclusion after a thorough and close reading of Menéndez Pidal's popular texts and his historical-linguistic texts in the context of Spain's political and intellectual crisis at the turn of the century. Once properly contextualized, these texts reveal the degree to which political ideas seep into the philologist's conception of the past, present, and future of Spanish and the collective identities of Spanish-speakers. Thus, Del Valle was able to show the degree to which Menéndez Pidal's linguistic descriptions were not value free and how they emerged under specific cultural and political circumstances.

The relevance of these studies for our present purpose is that they constitute a scholarly tradition in which, through historical contextualization of particular linguistic ideas, we can identify the underlying ideologies of linguistics. Identifying their ideological roots does not necessarily challenge their scientific status. While a particular description may comply with the scientific protocols dominant at a given time and produce an accurate representation of a segment of reality, it may have origins and implications beyond the realm of what is strictly scientific. In the process of analyzing language ideologies, we end up raising fundamental questions of power and authority in which language plays a central role and are able to explore a range of phenomena, including how certain linguistic ideas emerge in service of the linguistic self-image of certain groups of speakers.

Linguistic research grounded in the notion of language ideologies raises a number of questions relevant to our study of Pedro Henríquez Ureña's writings: What does the political dimension of language consist of? What roles does language play in politics and nation-building? How do languages and speakers of specific languages derive their symbolic power? How is language deployed in historical processes in general? Which variety best represents the language? Why? Who gets to decide? How do linguists approach historical and social variation? Under what circumstances would historical and social variation not be taken into account in linguistic description?

In addition, language ideologies research represents a theoretical and methodological position appropriate for the analysis at hand. First, it permits us to relate the linguistic practices of members of a speech community, their beliefs about language, and the descriptions of such practices and beliefs by experts to various social positions and interests. Second, it invites an integrated study[120] of linguistic and social phenomena usually taken up by different disciplines. Finally, it gives us a gamut of theoretical-methodological resources (from sociolinguistics and linguistic historiography) that in this present project will enhance the analysis of Henríquez Ureña's linguistic work and his representations of Dominican national identity.

While some might only understand language ideologies as conscious fabrications and distortions of a given linguistic reality by interested parties, most uses of this theoretical category have assumed a broader definition. The critical approaches to culture on which language ideological researchers have based their work (Bakhtin, Bourdieu, Foucault, and Gramsci) do not simply confront ideologies with objective reality. They locate ideologies in practices (discursive, institutional, social, and ritualistic) that tend to normalize and naturalize many aspects of social life, including linguistic behavior.

Building on these methodological principles established by Koerner and Laurendeau as well as the theoretical landscape described, I propose a language ideological analysis and historiography of Henríquez Ureña's linguistic work. In order to understand his linguistic ideas and claims, we have to explore the events, struggles, debates surrounding the language and culture he sought to represent. In trying to contextualize Henríquez Ureña's linguistic work, it is necessary to examine the interrelation of language and race, nation, political history, institutions, and literature in the Dominican Republic as well as in the broader Latin American context. In his work, we expect to find, among other things, the emergence of what Gramsci calls "the historical personality," or an active relationship between the intellectual and the sociocultural environment he or she is purporting to describe and modify.[121] Hence it is necessary to study these intellectuals as speaking subjects themselves, whose professional practice includes articulating the political functioning of their respective societies with certain forms of empirical knowledge and the construction of identities and collective consciousness in which language plays a crucial role.

3

Nationalism and Hispanoamericanism in the Dominican Republic and Latin America

Specific cultural and political circumstances contributed to Pedro Henríquez Ureña's writings on Dominican and Latin American identities. Therefore, Henríquez Ureña's linguistic texts, especially those in which he affirmed the independent development of American Spanish, cannot be fully understood without reference to the questions of Latin American identity that have preoccupied intellectuals from this continent. Furthermore, Henríquez Ureña's insistence in embedding the Dominican variety of Spanish within the northern Peninsular dialect continuum acquires its fullest meaning if read against the backdrop of Dominican nation-building. In line with the theoretical framework laid out in the previous chapter, this historical contextualization is crucial to properly understand the cultural and historical specificity of Henríquez Ureña's representations of language.

Although Spain's imperial adventures continued until well into the twentieth century in Africa, with disastrous consequences, the onset of the nineteenth century marked the beginning of the end of Spanish colonialism and the emergence of independent Latin American states. The independence movements were hardly homogeneous, but they did share certain characteristics, including calls for administrative reform, dissatisfaction with the distribution of wealth and power, and caste wars. These and other sociopolitical conditions led to numerous rebellions, the rejection of the principle of monarchy (both royal and Catholic), the official adoption of various forms of liberal republicanism, and the emergence of independent states.¹ The second half of the nineteenth century saw the formation of modern Latin American export economies. The prolonged phase of neocolonialism encompasses the "national period" and postindependence Latin America. No longer controlled by the Spaniards and Portuguese, the ensemble of productive resources was geared for external markets. Historians such as Tulio Halperín Donghi (1998) refer to this phase as "neocolonial" because the ownership and control of the basic resources for exports were in the hands of British and German business interests.² Nevertheless, this economic trend was responsible for the industrialization and modernization of Latin America and the changing appearances of its major cities (Buenos Aires, Rio de Janeiro, Säo Paulo, Lima, Mexico City, and Caracas) where the educated classes were advancing new political ideas and absorbing secular and materialistic culture.³ Thus, this neocolonial phase is one initial framework from which to approach certain aspects of the intellectual production and consciousness and debates on identity in Latin America.⁴ In the 1880s, while the rest of Latin America was undergoing the agitated phase of economic growth and crisis that consolidated the neocolonial order, the Dominican Republic remained economically stagnant, desperately clutching onto its colonial past. Meanwhile, in Cuba, still a Spanish colony, slavery had not been abolished but the struggle for independence had begun (just as it had in Puerto Rico). In the newly formed Dominican state, the ruling class was struggling to institutionalize and maintain political independence.

Intellectuals and the State in Latin America

According to Julio Ramos (2001), in Latin America, the institutionalization of rational discourse through literature, art, and education was at odds with the practices of subaltern ethnic groups and traditional cultures. In some cases, the state sought to vanquish these groups from the national landscape as they did not seem fit for modern society.⁵ Of course, there was resistance to this form of organization and development, as Ramos observed, in the work of José Martí.⁶ Some analysts (Castro-Klaren and Chasteen 2003, Martínez-Vergne 2005) suggest that the construction of the nation took place at many levels. Nonetheless, there is, in the foundation of Latin American republics, a discourse comprised of texts that aimed to construct modern subjectivity or create the legality of the state and authority over its citizens. One of the most appealing features of this modernization project, says Beatriz González Stephan (1995), "was the effectiveness of its rationality, which involved a uniformed strategy of homogenization at every level for the sake of the greater good of nation-state."[7] Intellectuals of the Enlightenment, or *letrados*, such as Andrés Bello[8] (1781–1865) and Eugenio María de Hostos (1839–1903), played key roles in the realization of these state-formation and nation-building projects by disseminating Positivist ideas and rationalizing and reordering the public sphere and public life (i.e., government, legislature, school system, and other public institutions).[9]

According to Michiel Baud (2005), the leading social and educated classes in Latin America attempted to build nations in the name of "progress." This particular concept of progress was synonymous with the desire for rapid modernization and an obsession with Western modernity.[10] Because the growth of the state, the economy, and the nation depended on it, education was immediately relevant to the operations of the state. Thus, intellectuals began to reflect on the role of the state in the modernization of society and their particular roles in contributing to this process. While they had hoped to function independently of politics, intellectuals were cognizant of the fact that they could not have any influence outside the realm of the state.[11] According to Rafael Gutiérrez Girardot (2001b), if not for their didactic functions, Hispanic intellectuals had no social basis.[12] And the basis of their work was the political interpretation of history and subsequent pedagogical intervention on the national scene. Therefore, intellectuals wavered between the need to preserve their intellectual and political independence and the need to be part of the state apparatus. In the nation-building project, they assumed various tasks, including the creation of a reading public, preparing a citizen body, and the formation of a national identity and national discourse:

> The thinker has a duty to present evidence in order to substantiate his claims. So, if he is right in affirming that this evolving society whose material foundations are not yet grounded is worthy of history, we will owe it to the rational domain of facts and not to blind emotion or naïve illusion.[13]

Consequently, intellectuals perceived themselves as essential to the development of the basic functioning of the state as well as the organization of social life within the nation.

The discursive practice of writing[14] was crucial to shaping, organizing, and expressing the collective aspirations and organization of society. As Domingo Faustino Sarmiento (1811–1888) ironically noted, solving the state problem of organizing a society was only feasible through historical, sociological, geographical, philosophical, and juridical studies, the kind of work that was beyond the comprehension of dictators like Juan Miguel de Rosas (1837–1852).[15] During the foundational period, writing was adopted as the adequate medium for bringing under control the disruptive ("barbarous") elements of society and creating dispositions that were much more suitable for life in the newly independent states. There was already a precedent for these types of juridical, administrative, and discursive practices: the class of educated men *(letrados)* that for three hundred years had documented legal decisions, drafted government edicts, maintained Church records, and authored literature throughout Latin America.[16] In the nineteenth century, the *letrados* and agents of the state produced laws, norms, books, manuals, catechisms, and similar discursive devices that would achieve the ultimate sociopolitical objectives by acting as a force of cohesion on the citizen body.[17] In Henríquez Ureña's own words: "Our legislation was often at odds with the social facts in our anarchic societies, but in defiance of all skeptical opinions, it played a prophetic role and gradually shaped the unwieldy mass of reality."[18] Consolidating the power of the state required the proliferation of institutions (i.e., workshops, schools, correction centers, orphanages, prisons, insane asylums) and discursive practices (i.e., constitutions, registers, censuses, maps, grammars, dictionaries, etiquette manuals). One of the main functions of constitutions and grammars, in particular, was the creation of the citizen body and the national identity, in the sense of a field of culturally and linguistically homogeneous groups of people best suited for a viable government. In its most basic formulation, governability was equated with homogeneity. For example, Hostos wrote:

> The group comprised by [the three great islands] is especially homogeneous. Obeying Nature and the principles of political organization is all that is required to become in history what they represent in geography: a clear and naturally constituted Nation.[19]

Therefore, during the foundational period, Latin American intellectuals articulated their functions and relationship to the state through specific discursive practices designed to sustain and justify their own existence. Although they could not easily eliminate the tension created by their vulnerable positions in society and in relation to the market, these writers accepted their place and function (as the voice of reason) in the emerging states.[20] Henríquez Ureña observed:

> In the already independent countries, literature in all its forms kept all the public functions it had assumed with the movement of liberation. In the midst of anarchy, men of letters were all in favor of social justice or at least in favor of political organization against the forces of disorder.[21]

Postindependence Dominican intellectuals, as Teresita Martínez-Vergne (2005) points out, "continued to rely on government appointments and do so even today, not only because their livelihood was 'precarious' but also because the state was, after all, the medium through which some of their ideas could become a reality."[22] Moreover, Martínez-Vergne declares:

> Intuitively, maybe, Dominican intellectuals perceived the state as a political actor with whom they shared goals, and they promptly surmised the inchoate bourgeoisie had little to offer by way of ideas or economic support. They might have been correct in their assessment but ignored the dangers of becoming the co-opted supporters or ritual opponents of a strong state. Thus, the notion of an independent thinker, an impartial social critic by virtue of his isolation—Gramsci's "traditional" intellectual—was a fiction. As if having no social base were not bad enough, Dominican intellectuals could easily become "the accomplices of the ruling group in the battle of hegemony."[23]

In the Dominican Republic, as well as in Latin America, we find a number of thinkers, educators, and writers who provided not only intellectual leadership but also developed the ideology that was necessary for the expansion of the state and the construction of the citizen body. In most cases, the ideology functioned as a discourse that attempted to naturalize specific types of social formations. The explanation of sociocultural phenomena is full of references to nature, as we observe from Hostos's statement. In all, these writers did not see their practice so much as an intellectual occupation or even a form of livelihood as much as a "career in nation-building."[24]

Hostos, Positivism, and the Discourse of "Progress" in Santo Domingo

Eugenio María de Hostos was extremely influential in the intellectual landscape and cultural scene of the Dominican Republic and he exerted an enormous influence over three generations of the Henríquez Ureña family (1875, 1879–1888, 1899–1903). Although preoccupied with all the major problems that were affecting the Hispanic world, the most difficult and intense phase of Hostos's intellectual work was carried out in the Dominican Republic. He first arrived there in 1875. That same year, Hostos founded several magazines *(Las Dos Antillas, Las Tres Antillas,* and *Los Antillanos)*, where he proclaimed and discussed his ideas on Antillean independence and confederation, and analyzed Dominican socioeconomic and political events. He was well received by General Gregorio Luperón (1839–1937), one of the main leaders of the restoration movement and the head of the The National Liberal Party. El Partido Azul (The Blue Party), as it was called to distinguish it from the Conservative Red Party, was founded around 1857. With the support of Luperón and his Partido Azul, Hostos established the Escuela Normal de Santo Domingo (1880), the birthplace of the so-called *normalistas,* a new class of Dominican intellectuals. This class was considered "new" because its members publicly sought to distinguish themselves from the previous generation, such as Pedro Francisco Bonó (1828–1906) and Francisco Gregorio Billini (1844–1898), who opposed Hostos or were indifferent to him.[25] This institute became Hostos's laboratory for educational reforms and a platform for his political causes. In La Normal, he trained a generation of Dominican men and women using the most modern pedagogical methods available. Francisco Henríquez y Carvajal and his brother Federico Henríquez y Carvajal assisted Hostos during his second stay in the Dominican Republic (1879–1888). The liberal political climate made it possible for Hostos to reform Dominican schools and spread Positivist ideas, but it also led to greater opposition from the conservative sectors of Dominican society that rejected Positivism and its ideology of *Progress.*

Positivism is the key to much of the social and political as well as intellectual history of Latin America in the second half of the nineteenth century. Positivism is the philosophical position that maintains that the only genuine knowledge is what can be obtained using the methods of science. It constitutes a broad segment of Latin American thought that is organically tied to the structures of power of the enlightened elites and, since the mid-nineteenth century, has become the theoretical base for the development and modernization of society.[26] Positivism, first elaborated by Auguste Comte (1798–1857) and later developed by John Stuart Mill (1806–1873) and Herbert Spencer (1820–1903), was hailed by Latin American intellectuals as the doctrine of progress that would overcome the deficiencies of Spanish imperialism and the tyranny of Catholic theology. As interpreted by Spanish *krausistas,*[27] Hostos's teachers, Positivism opposed evolution to creation, reason to revelation, experiment to dogma and rational discourse to traditional rhetoric.[28] Ever evolving, Positivism reflected an assortment of ideological manifestations throughout Latin America. However, it continued to be based on two basic principles: (i) that positive principles, which could be scientifically investigated, underlie social structures; and (ii) that human history was evolving toward a rational humanism, a process that, though inevitable, could be aided by education. Closer to Comte, Hostos's brand of Positivism can be summarized through six fundamental sociological principles—Sociability, Work, Liberty, Progress, Self-Preservation, and Civilization or The Law of the Ideal—that produce "the true social order."[29] Hostos understood society as a living organism made up of six organic parts: The Individual, The Family, The Community, Religion, The Nation, and Humanity. To Hostos, natural laws subjected humans to proper living, the improvement of individual existence, and the development of society.[30] Hostos promoted the view of science as a revolutionary and radical vehicle for organized action and for the improvement of society.[31]

As the only independent state in the Hispanic Caribbean, Hostos enthusiastically viewed the Dominican Republic as the ideal place for him to experiment with liberal ideas, which he hoped to later implement in Puerto Rico and Cuba while promoting his vision of a free and unified Caribbean. According to Henríquez Ureña, Hostos dedicated himself to the development of Caribbean citizens for a confederation and future nation only after establishing himself in Santo Domingo.[32] Hostos dreamed of turning the Dominican Republic into a model nation that would ignite nationalism all over the Caribbean.

Before Hostos's arrival in 1875, the country lacked anything akin to a humanistic tradition. While teaching and writing in Santo Domingo, Hostos produced a corpus of texts through which he introduced rational discourse to the country. With the support of Partido Azul liberals including Luperón, and members of La Sociedad de Amigos, such as Henríquez Ureña's parents, Hostos promoted rational thinking in the Dominican Republic as a school of thought and a form of social organization. In particular, Positivist ideas became the artillery used in the fight against the influence of the Dominican clergy in society. Hostos's Positivist project became indissolubly bound to the Partido Azul's democratic and nationalistic project. Led by members of the Henríquez Ureña family, the new class of Dominican intellectuals converged around both projects in La Sociedad, and sought to create a system of education[33] that would contribute, above all, to the development of reasoning among Dominicans and a rational Dominican society.

In 1880, Henríquez Ureña's father, Francisco Henríquez y Carvajal, became the Secretary of President Monsignor Fernando Arturo de Meriño (1880–1882)[34] of the ruling Partido Azul. While promoting the "new science," Henríquez y Carvajal became a leader in the Dominican cultural revolution and, amidst the enthusiasm for the acceptance and expansion of Positivist ideas, married Salomé Ureña, who also had a leading role in the ideological debates. Salomé ceased writing poetry and dedicated herself exclusively to disseminating Positivism and the education of women and her own children. This group of intellectuals collaborated with Hostos, working within the Enlightenment paradigm whose key element was the opposition of civilization and barbarism. Hostos maintained:

> The century is not going to let us follow in the same direction and end up barbaric, corrupt, dissolute, leprous, and lacerated. With all the

evidence, History tells us that we can no longer afford corruption or destruction... Those who cannot achieve a small amount of progress, if only to become their own masters in a small corner of the world, must become civilized. The present order is clear: civilization or death.[35]

In order to overcome or incorporate the barbarous elements of society, Hostos advocated for, among other things, an education with "rational order in the curriculum," and "a reasoned method in teaching."[36]

Two years after Henríquez Ureña was born, General Ulises Heureaux[37] returned to power with a more repressive form of government (1886–1889). With its mistrust of Positivist ideas about freedom and the like, Heureaux sought to repress and limit the work of the most active intellectuals. The dictator forced Hostos and Henríquez y Carvajal to leave the country.[38] Following Heaureaux's assassination in the summer of 1889, Francisco Henríquez y Carvajal returned to his country from exile, as did his mentor Hostos, who wanted to resume his educational reforms before the onset of yet another dictatorship. Among those who contested Hostos's discourse in the Dominican Republic was Pedro Francisco Bonó (1828–1906), who had a different proposal for social progress. As Pedro L. San Miguel (2005) indicates, this author, who preferred to distance himself from the Enlightenment ideology embraced by the Dominican intelligentsia, emphasized the social substratum of political processes and institutional life.[39] He advanced the idea that the development of prosperity, democracy, and national identity depended more on the ability and creativity of the lower classes and not so much on the powerful socioeconomic institutions. In contrast, Hostos believed that "for the Republic to recover, it was essential to establish a rational order in education, a reasonable method of teaching, the influence of a harmonizing principle in teachers, and the ideal of a superior system aimed at developing public education."[40] It was Hostos who laid the groundwork for several generations of Dominican intellectuals, writers, and teachers. With the building of academic institutions and the promotion of rational discourse, Hostos exerted an enduring influence over the Dominican intellectual landscape for well over half a century.

Nation-Building in the Dominican Republic in the Nineteenth and Twentieth Centuries

Three important elements in the Dominican Republic's political history in the nineteenth century are nation-building post-Haitian rule (1809–1844), nation-building post-Spanish annexation (1859–1865), and the presence of Cuban and Puerto Rican patriots such as José Martí, Ramón Emeterio

Betances, and Hostos. Dominican history and nationalism are intricately connected to the affairs of its neighbor, Haiti.[41] Dominican nationalism emerged in the nineteenth century along with the project of a nation-state proposed by a group of young liberals led by Juan Pablo Duarte[42] (1813–1876). Dominicans had to separate from the political jurisdiction of Haiti, which, having gained its independence from France in 1804, retained control of Santo Domingo until 1844. Haitian military leaders pursued control over the eastern part of the island in order to unify Hispaniola under the banner of the Haitian state. Haitian leaders believed that they were legally entitled to the eastern territory. General Jean Pierre Boyer (1776–1850) extended Haitian sovereignty over the entire island, its troops, and inhabitants and declared "this [eastern] territory can no longer be considered Spanish."[43] Moreover, in the pursuit of unification, Haitian leaders claimed to have embodied the principles of Haiti's universal struggle for liberty of people of African origin against white oppressors of European origin (Price-Mars 2000, San Miguel 2005). Franklin Knight (1990) described how "in the process of creating the new State, Haiti destroyed its white elite and promoted its African heritage as the proud, homogenizing symbol of the new State, a beacon for all black Americans."[44] Therefore, in the ethnopolitical discourse of both states we find the opposing ideological symbols: black *Saint-Domingue* and white Santo Domingo. The drawn out process of independence from Haiti and the various military attempts of Haitian leaders between 1844 and 1855 to bring back the Dominican Republic under their rule gave rise to a nation-building ideology that produced a powerful element of self-identification in opposition to Haitians.

Subsequently, in the foundational and ancillary texts of the Dominican state, we find definitive statements about the Dominican nation and about what their authors consider to be two of its most basic and fundamental characteristics: race and language.[45] As early as 1822, for example, years before independence, José Núñez de Cáceres (1776–1846), a local political leader and the first hero of Dominican independence, declared, when handing the keys to the city of Santo Domingo over to Haitian General Boyer, that the Haitian plan for the political unification of the island was bound to fail based solely on linguistic grounds:

> Linguistic diversity, the rule of ancient law, and powerful customs rooted in childhood, have always played influential roles in politicians' state-formation and the transmutation of different peoples into one. Words are the instruments of communication among men. There is no communication without mutually comprehensible speech. Therefore, we see [in the Spanish language] a separation wall, as natural and insurmountable as were the Alps or the Pyrenees.[46]

According to Dominican historian Roberto Cassá (1998), Núnez de Cáceres uttered this statement aware that the colored Dominican majority favored annexation to Haiti.[47] However, even prior to Dominican independence (1844), in their struggle to maintain the political and cultural integrity of their territory, the Spanish authorities opposed Hispanic traditions to encroachment by other colonies. We can observe this, for example, in Antonio Sánchez Valverde's *La idea del valor de la isla Española* (1785). In validating many of his claims before the Spanish Crown, the author described the many splendors of the island's colonial past, highlighting, in particular, the growing number of Spaniards in the population. He considered this group the essential element in the community's *criollo* identity.[48] According to Haitian historian Jean Price-Mars (2000), due to the racial ideology prevalent in the eastern Hispaniola, its inhabitants found it unacceptable that they be incorporated into a nationality that they considered infinitely inferior to their conditions as whites.[49]

Cassá (1998) explains that the first phase of Dominican nationalism unfolded as some members of the miniscule and fragile bourgeoisie realized potential for growth and urgently sought the development of capitalism in Dominican territory.[50] The realization of this phase, however, would be considerably delayed due to the fact that the bourgeoisie[51] in the Dominican Republic, in the strict sense, did not stratify or consolidate for many years. However, after its independence from Haiti in 1844, the Dominican Republic was officially recognized as a state. For the next 40 years, political independence and some favorable economic conditions contributed to a renewed interest in literary and artistic activity and in the idea of a Dominican nation-state.[52] Only after a few years of political independence, Spain annexed the Dominican Republic in 1861, with the consent of the most powerful local groups and other European empires and its belief in its legal rights over the Spanish-speaking part of Hispaniola. Pedro Santana (1801–1864), the first constitutional President, justified the annexation to Spain in the following terms:

> We still conserve purity of religion, language, beliefs, and customs. Although there is no shortage of those who have attempted to dissolve such precious gifts. And the nation that has bequeathed so much to us is the same one that today opens it arms, like the loving mother who recovers her son from the shipwreck in which his brothers perished... Spain protects us with a shielding flag and weapons that will overcome foreign forces. Spain recognizes our liberty and together we will defend ourselves and form one people, one family, as we always were.[53]

The period of annexation (1859–1865) was characterized by a crackdown on religious liberties, masonry, and other forms of civil association, the practice of common-law unions, and a return to previous Spanish despotic practices. Although Spanish diplomats promised never to reestablish slavery and grant more autonomy to Dominican governments, Spanish authorities basically recreated the previous colonial order. The Spanish rulers replaced the *criollo* administrators with Iberians at every level and reinstituted the old racist caste system, which pegged Spaniards at the top of the social hierarchy, followed by white *criollos, mestizos,* and blacks, respectively. As Frank Moya Pons (1995) points out, this attitude of white superiority had its effects on Dominicans themselves: "The lighter skinned people began to avoid contact with darker skinned friends for fear of being associated with them or of being considered inferior by the new, Spanish, rulers."[54] The removal of Dominican civil and military leaders caused conflicts between Spaniards and Dominicans and created general discontent with the new administrative-political order. As a result, the idea of a nation-state became popular again. This time, it was fueled by overall discontent among the population and economic conflicts between the new administrative class and previously ruling local class who had lost a considerable share of its wealth and power.[55]

The problem of Spanish annexation and the question of a Dominican state brought the Henríquez family (unheard of until then) to the public arena. Representatives from the rural masses, the commercial bourgeoisie, the political petit bourgeoisie, and foreign interests largely supported the war of restoration (1861–1865). The Germans, for example, who had significant control of the tobacco industry, contributed financially to the armed struggles.[56] Following the war in 1866 and after regaining independence, there was a renewed sense of economic and political freedom and passionate pleas for national unity. From the Dominican Senate, Henríquez Ureña's grandfather Nicolás Ureña continued to articulate the cause of national sovereignty.

This same year (1866), El Instituto Profesional opened and replaced the Colegio Buenaventura as the leading school of professional education in Santo Domingo. Hostos collaborated in this institute as professor of public law and political economy. The Instituto also housed a school of medicine and was the birthplace of the group of professionals who began to institutionalize "Dominican" culture by creating other necessary institutions for national life in the late nineteenth-century Dominican Republic. Both Federico and Francisco Henríquez y Carvajal played important roles in this prominent professional institute and ideological site where Hostos lectured. Although not a completely homogeneous group, several of these *fin de siecle* Dominican intellectuals were inextricably linked to the upper classes and power. Both conservative and liberal intellectuals converged on the tasks deemed necessary for the construction and consolidation of the nation. Some helped to create, unify, and expand the institutions necessary for national life, while others helped produce the body of symbols necessary for national consciousness. From cultural institutions, publications, such *El Progreso* (1853), *Letras y Ciencias* (1892–1899), and literature, intellectuals took on a host of national issues including economic development, mass education, and the constant threat of annexation, the perceived Haitian threat, and the political violence among the *caudillos* who wanted power and control of the government.[57]

A few years later, the political situation became very unstable again and the economy was stagnant. In power from 1879 to 1886, El Partido Azul represented the interests of the tobacco cultivators and merchants of the wealthy Cibao region, while the Conservatives represented the great *latifundia* of the cattle ranchers and the woodcutting interests. The Azul party, a diverse group led by military figures, such as General Gregorio Luperón,[58] became strongly associated with Dominican nationalism and the idea of creating a citizen body apt to be governed. Luperón believed that the necessary conditions for an autonomous nation-state were missing and had to be produced.[59] Subsequently, a generation of Dominican intellectuals would begin the necessary work to overturn these conditions. The Henríquez and the Ureña families belonged to one sector of the Azul party, and were especially involved forging and promoting national and cultural institutions during the party's political hegemony in the last two decades of the nineteenth century.[60]

In 1868, a group of Cuban exiles, escaping the war of independence, arrived in the country. With the support of the liberal government and other prominent local groups, they began to revive and transform the sugar industry in the Dominican Republic. Some historians affirm that the Cuban immigration to the city of Puerto Plata alone represented an increase in capital of "two million *pesos* strong;" the Cuban émigrés were greatly responsible for injecting more dynamism into the economy.[61] Moreover, they founded political organizations such La Antillana and the Delegación Revolucionaria Cubana, dedicated to the cause of Cuban independence and open to all its sympathizers. Thousands of Cubans devoted themselves to work, in the city or in the neighboring rural areas. At the same time, their leaders were conspiring against Spain.[62] Meanwhile, the local Dominican political climate continued to change: the Buenaventura Baez government (1849–1853, 1856–1858, 1865–1866, 1868–1874, and 1876–1878) became a dictatorship and attempted to lease the Samaná Peninsula to the United States. After Henríquez Ureña's grandfather (Nicolás Ureña) was forced into exile for publicly challenging this plan, his uncle Federico Henríquez y Carvajal took up the cause in La Sociedad Cultural de Amigos del País.

President Buenaventura Baez was a target of the intellectual debates held amongst members of La Sociedad, a Paris-styled intellectual salon that had sprung throughout Latin America.[63] Baez was president five times (1849–1853, 1856–1858, 1865–1866, 1868–1874, and 1876–1878) and constantly tried to have the country annexed, first by France, then Spain, and finally the United States.[64] Through organizations such as La Sociedad and newspapers, pro-restoration intellectuals carried out an intense campaign against the Baez dictatorship and disseminated the latest liberal ideas brought to the Dominican Republic by the most recent wave of immigration. Intellectuals who supported and identified, to different degrees, with the Azul party's ideals of modernization, progress, rational government, and national sovereignty, such as Pedro Francisco Bonó, Francisco Gregorio Billini, Mariano Cestero (1838–1909), and José Gabriel García (1834–1910), among others, mounted a campaign against the inadequacy and tyranny of Baez's government. Most of these intellectuals voiced and promoted the idea that the *Azules* (Blue Party supporters) represented the only option for the institutional modernization of the state; as a result they helped to forge important political alliances between different social groups and economic interests. These and other similar sociopolitical ideas were taken up by La Sociedad, whose oppositional ideology can be summed up with Hostos's maxim "civilization or death."[65] The members of La Sociedad were willing to stake their livelihood and reputation on this credo. Accordingly, they labored intensely in order to create modern institutions and spread the rational and progressive ideas that were necessary for life in a "civilized" modern society. Enrique Deschamps recognized their contribution:

> Amigos del País has realized great cultural work. Among a thousand other things of national interest, it has elevated the concept of the Dominican intellectual with notable publications such as Antonio del Monte y Tejada's voluminous *Historia de Santo Domingo* and the poetry of Salomé Ureña and Manuel Rodríguez Objio.[66]

La Sociedad was a center for writers' meetings and readings but it was also a discursive institution and a platform for the diffusion of a progressive ideology and Dominican nationalism. It was the target of political opposition and military aggression.[67]

Occupation and U.S. Relations

A strong nationalist movement emerged again during the U.S. military occupation of the Dominican Republic (1916–1924). Almost immediately, the occupying forces took measures to prevent uprisings and to reorganize the socioeconomic and political life of the country.⁶⁸ These measures included the prohibition of arms among Dominican civilians, censorship of the press, the building of infrastructure, the creation of the Dominican National Guard for the suppression of future revolutionary movements, and the creation of a national primary public school system. During the course of the occupation, the Dominican economy grew to levels never seen before, but Dominicans did not reap the benefits because all of the country's commerce was tied to the United States. Resistance emerged in different sectors. In addition to producing the legal and moral arguments, nationalist intellectuals such as Américo Lugo (1870–1952), Fabio Fiallo (1866–1942), and Emiliano Tejera (1841–1923), among others, continuously agitated the people of Santo Domingo to rally behind their identity and language in opposition to U.S. occupation. In particular, some of these intellectuals urged Dominicans to defend against what they called the "Americanization" of Spanish.⁶⁹

The occupation began the same year that Henríquez Ureña accepted a position as a lecturer in the University of Minnesota, in the United States. In Minnesota, Henríquez Ureña taught a series of courses on language and literature, while pursuing and obtaining his doctorate. However, Henríquez Ureña's success in North American academia was marred by the U.S. occupation of the Dominican Republic and its continued intervention in Latin America. Since 1914, as a foreign correspondent for the Havana daily *Heraldo de Cuba*, he had been evaluating U.S. policy in Latin America. The following are some of the more significant remarks Henríquez Ureña made in regard to the ensuing North American interventionism, particularly in the Caribbean:

> It is generally known that since the treaty of 1907, the U.S. maintains vigilance and control as the administrator of Dominican customs. Roosevelt proudly acclaimed the role of his government in this context. Republican politicians referred to this situation as proof of the influential benefits of the United States in the Caribbean, pointing to the mystical and peaceful virtues of their own country. However, since 1912, we have had to attenuate the praise of these virtues.⁷⁰

A few years later, at a conference at the University of Minnesota, Henríquez Ureña evaluated the Monroe Doctrine: "The Caribbean Sea is the focal point of the Monroe Doctrine. The doctrine, as now conceived, is only applied up to the equator. It has very little application to the south."⁷¹ In addition, some dubious statements by journalists appeared in the American press regarding the Dominican Provisional President's son's alleged preference of the United States over the Dominican Republic. In order to clarify his situation and some of his positions, Henríquez Ureña granted a few interviews to *The Minneapolis Journal*. In one such interview:

> Mr. Henríquez Ureña declared he was not a hyphenate. "I admire the United States and the people. You are a great and happy people; we of Santo Domingo are small and poor people, but my allegiance is entirely with my own country, I have been accused of preferring this country. I do not."[72]

While still in Minneapolis, Henríquez Ureña authored a series of significant articles related to U.S foreign policy: *Mexico and Panamericanism*, and *The Dominican Republic—Another Test of Mr. Wilson's Sincerity*.[73] At one point, he joined a Dominican commission that was negotiating the terms of the occupation in Washington D.C. Among the leaders of the commission was his father, the former President, who had been traveling throughout Latin America denouncing the occupation. Francisco Henríquez y Carvajal had been a key figure in Dominican politics since the days of La Sociedad, where, along with Salomé Ureña and his brother Federico, he was directly involved in the development and diffusion of Hostos's Positivist doctrine in the Dominican Republic. The U.S. occupation was an emotional and very personal ordeal for Henríquez Ureña.

National Identity and Race in Latin America and the Dominican Republic

It is impossible to comprehend the political and intellectual history of Latin America during the last two centuries without reflecting upon the key debates on the roots of national identity. Latin Americans' pursuit of modernity was fraught with tensions and contradictions. While there was a modernist ideology geared to progress and socioeconomic change, a nostalgic rhetoric revealed a conservative tendency that manifested itself particularly in the construction of Latin American identities. Oddly, we find the *jíbaro* or *gaucho* (peasant) as a symbol of national identity in many Latin American countries such as Argentina, Colombia, and Venezuela as well as in Cuba, Puerto Rico, and the Dominican Republic. Thus, in the modernization of their societies, Latin American states focused their energies on the modernization and civilization of the rural masses. Many Latin American intellectuals had hoped that the benefits of modernization would resolve the question of race that linked white, Indian, and black, but they became disappointed when this did not occur. Therefore, issues of race played an important role in the discussions of national identity in Latin America and the Caribbean during the nineteenth and twentieth centuries.

According to Telesforo García (1901), in their proposals, many Latin American intellectuals primarily conceptualized race, not necessarily as a social group of common ethnic origin, but as a psychological identity shared by collectivities that consciously or subconsciously converge around common goals. For example, anticipating José Vasconcelos's *La raza cósmica* (1925), Hostos (1870) remarked:

> Beaten but not vanquished by their European conquerors, the *cholo* (Peruvian of mixed race) possesses the organic qualities of the Indian race. Colonialism could not completely overwhelm them. Once the *cholo* has developed the intellectual vigor bequeathed by Europeans, he will become an active, intelligent, and useful member of Peruvian society. Natural mediator of the elements of the two different races which he represents, the *cholo* will promote their dynamic merger... The result will be a mixed race of heroically stoic Indians and intellectually vigorous whites which will join the ranks of human progress, thus provisionally repairing the iniquities perpetrated by one of the parent races.[74]

The merging of racial differences was, according to Hostos, something natural and necessary for achieving social cohesion and progress. Yet, not everyone was of the same opinion when it came to the relevance of race in the construction of identities. In contrast, José Martí rejected racial distinction and deemed the issue pointless due to the fact that race was too imprecise and too abstract as a theoretical category: "There is no racial hatred because there are no races. Puny thinkers, thinkers in dim light, who string together and rehash fictitious races which the just traveler and friendly observer look for in vain in the justice of Nature."[75] According to Jean Muteba Rahier (2004), the challenges that racial diversity posed to the liberal nation-building model, led to narratives of white supremacy and the concomitant concept of *blanqueamiento* (whitening).[76] The notion of whitening was based on Positivist views of society as an organism that similar to biological organisms needed to evolve and rid itself of its "dysfunctional" and "inferior" organs (i.e., black and indigenous populations): "Many Latin American intellectuals of the late nineteenth and early twentieth centuries shared the idea that race mixing between 'superior' and 'inferior' races was unnatural."[77] The rejection of people of color as well as the rejection of popular culture was quite characteristic of the foundational period. Julio Ramos described it in the following terms:

> A period traversed by the circulation and prevalence of representations of Latin America as a sick body, contaminated by racial impurities and the survival of traditional cultures and ethnicities presumably destined to disappear in the unfolding of progress and modernity.[78]

Thus, for many Latin American intellectuals and members of the leading social classes, miscegenation had to be avoided in the discursive construction of the uniquely Latin American identities.

The situation was slightly different in the Dominican Republic, where "the problem of race" was projected outward in the direction of Haiti. In fact, we cannot understand nation-building or define Hispanism in the Dominican Republic without taking into account anti-Haitianism. "While a wave of anti-Hispanism swept the Americas, the Dominican elite, which based its position on land ownership and Spanish descent, returned to their links with the motherland."[79] Therefore, Dominican intellectuals such as Emiliano Tejera (1841–1923), scholar and minister of foreign affairs during the Ramón Cáceres administration (1905–1911), wrote profusely about the development of the Dominican character in relation to the undesired Haitians and the affirmation of Spanish ancestry.[80] Carlos Dobal (1984) reports that

> Many positions have been advanced for or against the influence of different races (white, black, Indian) on our particular idiosyncrasy and mixed make-up... The arguments have always been extremist: one is the notion that white European elements prevail; another is the simplistic but persistent idea that native genes determine our behavior... and if the discussion turns to the subject of whites, the emphasis is on Spaniards, whose contributions are highly valued by Dominicans, regardless of the skin color of the people or the region.[81]

Although with previous ideological antecedents, this dominant Dominican discourse on race originated in the context of the struggle for independence and nation-building described earlier. The discourse emerged in order to support, justify, and legitimate the military and political efforts of the country's ruling class and intellectual and moral leadership, which includes the Church. Undoubtedly, Dominicans are aware that their country is racially mixed with large enclaves of Afro-Dominican communities and their concept of race, as Silvio Torres-Saillant (2000) reminds us, has been quite elastic.[82] However, the Dominican Republic's historical process has been characterized by a anti-black and pro-white ideology that was instrumental in establishing the concept and symbolic value of *dominicanidad* (Dominicanness). This concept of Dominicanness is firmly embedded in Hispanic tradition, culture, and, above all, language.

Pedro Henríquez Ureña's Dominicanness

Like his predecessors before him, Henríquez Ureña saw his task as contributing to the full realization of the Dominican community by obtaining full access to two fundamental elements of (in this case, Spanish) civilization: language and identity. Throughout this process, he maintained a steadfast faith in the belief of his predecessors that the glories of progress are always achieved thanks to the will of a select few, the enlightened minority: "Intellectually gifted men and women are those that should guide the masses."[83]

After 1901, Henríquez Ureña returned to the Dominican Republic only on two occasions: a few days in 1911 and for 18 months from 1931 to 1933. However, he remained emotionally, politically, and intellectually connected to his native land. Although he often expressed a remarkable nostalgia for his homeland, as Jorge Luis Borges observed, Henríquez Ureña was able to circumvent it through his belief in being part of the greater and beloved Hispanic community, or what Borges called "the sense of *hispanoamericanidad*" (Americanness).[84] The idea of his eventual return to *La Patria* (the fatherland) continuously obsessed Henríquez Ureña, but the ever chaotic and repressive political climate with its perennial dictatorships prevented his return.

In 1926, in contemplating a possible return to Santo Domingo, Henríquez Ureña wrote to Américo Lugo, a prominent Dominican historian and architect of early twentieth-century nationalism: "If only I could find a position there for my intellectual activities and a safe and comfortable home for my family, I would immediately go."[85] That same year, he wrote to Alfonso Reyes from Argentina:

> Many people do not know that I live thinking about how I can return to Santo Domingo. And even Isabel, who finds Argentina not too interesting, so desires it... But what do you expect? The Yankees, the enemies, are eternally ruling and, quite stupidly, they would not allow me to serve my country.[86]

Finally, in 1931, thanks to his brother Max's intervention and an invitation from the Trujillo regime, the frustrated hope of returning to his native country was temporarily relieved. Henríquez Ureña arrived in Santo Domingo in order to assume the role of the national superintendent of education. It is probable that, at this point, he was not well aware of the despotic and ruthless nature of the Trujillo dictatorship. Trained by U.S. Marines to maintain order after the occupation (1916–1924) and quickly rising to high rank, Rafael L. Trujillo (1891–1961) overthrew President Horacio Vásquez in 1930. The association with the Henríquez Ureña family offered Trujillo the opportunity to seize two important attributes he most desired in relation to the public perception of his regime: intellectual pedigree and nationalistic pride.[87] Henríquez Ureña prudently fulfilled his duties despite many limitations that included the scarcity of resources and growing disillusionment with the local political atmosphere. He pursued a series of educational reforms, helped to establish the Humanities faculty at the Universidad de Santo Domingo, gave multiple lectures, and conducted archival research on Spanish in the Dominican Republic. After two-and-a-half years under a totalitarian regime and mounting disillusionment, Henríquez Ureña left for Europe under the pretext of visiting his family, whom he had sent to Paris months earlier. Soon after reuniting with them, they returned to Argentina where Henríquez Ureña continued to teach, investigate, write, and publish until his death in 1946.

For Henríquez Ureña, the nineteenth century represents a bridge to a presumed Dominican Golden Age: "I always tell my friends that I was born in the seventeenth century."[88] With this statement, Henríquez Ureña expressed his fascination with the Dominican patriarchal society that was the object of many of his philological investigations: *La catedral* (1908), *Cultura antigua de Santo Domingo (La española)* (1910), *La antigua sociedad patriarcal de las Antillas: modalidades arcaicas de la vida de Santo Domingo durante el Siglo XIX* (1932c), and *La cultura y las letras coloniales en Santo Domingo* (1936). In many ways, this patriarchal Dominican society emerged from the imagination of the *fin de siecle* Dominican Romantics (Félix María del Monte (1819–1899), Salomé Ureña, José Joaquín Pérez (1845–1900), Gastón Fernando Deligne (1861–1913), and Arturo Pellerano Castro (1853–1916), among others), to whom Henríquez Ureña attributes Golden Age Spanish as their linguistic and literary model.[89] But the Dominican Republic that Henríquez Ureña knew firsthand was his parents' fatherland, the *fin de siecle* country, where, in the face of poverty, political instability, fierce competition among the military and commercial elites, and conflictive relations with Haiti, the educated classes were desperately fighting to institutionalize the ideology of *Progress* (Positivism), consolidate the nation-state, legitimize the national identity founded on the Hispanic tradition. Henríquez Ureña's family became famous working and fighting to save this tradition. According to Diony Durán (1994):

> The link between Pedro Henríquez Ureña and his family is rich in suggestions that may shed light not only to his patriotism and unquestionable devotion to Americanism but also on the essential relationship between a modern writer like Henríquez Ureña and the nineteenth century. The ideas, concepts, and guidance he acquired at home were exceptionally influential in his subsequent training and development. Therefore, he received a unique education that enabled him to carry out his literary scholarship and life of integrity.[90]

Patriotism and enthusiasm for nation-building were vital elements in the intellectual climate in which Henríquez Ureña grew up. He devoted a huge portion of his work to the ideas and ideals championed by his family. This mixture of idealism and ideology included unconditional love for the foundations, traditions, and symbols of his homeland. These foundations included the formation of an exclusively Hispanic identity.

Núñez de Cáceres's statement regarding the perceived linguistic divide between Haiti and the Dominican Republic constitutes one of the first affirmations of the existence of national language, a language that was central to defining the Dominican Republic's national identity. Since the beginning of this phase of Dominican nationalism, Dominican intellectuals have semiotized language and made it one of the bases on which to build the nation, create a national consciousness, and enact a Dominican national identity. In 1912, language planners made explicit the language policy of the state. A committee of public officials, led by prominent Senator Ramón Lovatón, persuaded the Dominican Congress to officialize the Spanish language.[91] The words of Américo Lugo, who wrote profusely about Dominican nationalism, highlight the importance of language: "For all practical and theoretical purposes, Dominican culture, although politically weak at the moment, is essentially Spanish. This is evident in the language, forms of worship, customs, heritage, history, traditions, and collective memory."[92] Admittedly, some of the authors of Dominican nationalism did not always succumb to the dogma of homogeneism and the firm opposition to Haiti. For example, in 1908, Lugo declared: "With the term 'nation' I am not only referring to Santo Domingo. Haiti is also my nation. Our only uncontested claim to international status stems from our sharing and ruling together over one single island."[93] These statements were pronounced while arguing in favor of a Caribbean confederation that would oppose U.S. imperialism. Nonetheless, throughout the process of national development, the majority of Dominican intellectuals have maintained, to quote the conservative Dominican historian Manuel Arturo Peña Batlle, that "Dominicans fully developed a national consciousness as a result of the struggle to remain Spanish."[94]

Almost invariably, many Dominican intellectuals have tied the question of national sovereignty to racial issues and relations with Haiti in their discussions of Dominican nationalism and identity, especially since the nineteenth century. Although not necessarily part of the wealthy Dominican upper classes themselves, many *letrados* (poets, novelists, and historians) represented the educated group who most helped to establish the hegemony of the political elites and the concept of Dominican identity, especially in the 1870s and 80s (Matos Moquete 1986, Sommer 1991, Vellejo 1995). Deschamps (1906) lamented that before the arrival of this generation ("the Galváns, the Meriños, the Delignes"), the state of Dominican letters was quite deplorable.[95] Deschamps linked such a state of affairs and its impact on the language to the break in relations with Spain "due to the lack of interaction with the motherland, little contact with the classics, and the overall preference for French works, most of our writers are oblivious and produce an adulterated Spanish."[96] However, Salomé's generation, propelled by the work of Hostos, effectively changed all of that by reestablishing links with the classic tradition. Manuel Matos Moquete (1986), in his discussion of the relationship between periods, authors, and texts, shows that even in our era the very concept of "Dominican literature" is subsumed by the discourse of the state. According to Matos Moquete, the circulation and prevalence of specific literary images conflate the idea of having a body of literature with the idea of documenting purely Dominican phenomena. The existence of all things Dominican justifies the existence of a national literature: "The cover of any text on the 'History of Dominican Literature' or an 'Anthology of Dominican Literature' immediately announces a linear search for purely Dominican literature and purely Dominican characteristics."[97] Matos Moquete argues that the authors themselves are partially responsible for establishing this type of literary historiography and ideology:

> As everywhere else in Latin America, Dominican authors have been responsible for reducing literature to this state of affairs... Considering themselves to be invested with socially formative powers, they have truly believed in the revolutionary and transformative role of literature.[98]

Many *letrados*, aligning themselves with the dominant political forces, produced narratives and images of the nation's history and social composition that reveal the following objectives: the whitening of Dominican society, the promotion of cultural traits associated with the dominant classes, and the erasure of those associated with the popular classes. The subsequent generations of Dominican literary figures and literary historians would only intensify these particular discursive practices in service of the state and the ruling political forces. Matos Moquete asserts, "this brings us to a nationalization of the relationship between literature and politics. Thus, literature is transformed into an instrument of the state or history, and, in effect, becomes an instrument in the service of the search for an assumed national identity."[99]

Analogous with other Latin American and Caribbean contexts, many Dominican intellectuals have also proposed social theories that view blacks and Haitians as "inferior races" that are obstacles to modernization and progress. Any discussion contrary to this civilization-barbarism dichotomy is deemed treasonous and unpatriotic. The concept of race, in this Dominican context, is carefully crafted to fit a specific view of the nation and is evident in the advice Henríquez Ureña gives to his brother Max regarding the revision of his book, *Los Estados Unidos y la República Dominicana* (1919):

> Add a few pages about Santo Domingo, gently explaining the country's history with very few factual details, while being very clear on the fundamental aspects, such as the dynamic national character. In addition, modify the usual concept of "black people," without entering into contradictions, reminding readers of the existence of Indians and large groups of *mestizos*.[100]

It is easy to label these comments as racist, but they have to be carefully read in light of the surrounding circumstances. These editorial suggestions were partially motivated by another problem: the need to respond to the specific racism of the occupying North American soldiers. As noted by Gérard Pierre-Charles (1985), these soldiers treated Santo Domingo as a conquered land inhabited by a few whites but mostly mulattoes and blacks whom they considered racially inferior.[101] As we will see in Chapter 3, in several of his own texts, Henríquez Ureña strongly objected to the references of Dominicans as blacks that appeared in international publications.

Following the resurgence of Dominican nationalism during U.S. occupation, Henríquez Ureña declared his absolute rejection of North American imperialism in several journalistic articles. He refocused his attention on Latin America's situation in relation to growing U.S. interference. In a series of newspaper reports (most of them published in *El Heraldo de Cuba*, 1915–1917) Henríquez Ureña consistently criticized U.S. foreign policy and in a few of his essays began to delineate Hispanoamericanism as a utopian cultural ideal and reformulate Dominican nationalism as an alternative to North American imperialism.[102] In *La República Dominicana* (1917), Henríquez Ureña remarked: "Living precariously but properly for more than four centuries, Santo Domingo represents a fragment of the great Hispanic family. And it will strive to remain so as long as it can count one last descendant of the colonizers among its inhabitants."[103]

Undoubtedly, Henríquez Ureña's ethnolinguistic construction finds its source in and provides continuities for the Enlightenment and cultural discourses elaborated by members of his own family and some of the founders of Dominican historiography.[104] It is in relation to these discursive continuities that his understanding of Dominican nationalism emerges. According to Martínez-Vergne:

> Pedro Henríquez Ureña emphasized a longer intellectual process [of national development] that occurred throughout the nineteenth century among

literate groups and the bourgeoisie, who professed the island's sovereignty as they fought for independence from Haiti and rejected foreign rule and its proponents.[105]

Dominican nationalism emerges in the historical narratives, the foundational texts, and the analyses of Henríquez Ureña as a will to modernity, but also as an expression of faith in the idea of a Dominican nation-state, patriotism in the form of love for the Hispanic tradition, fear and loathing for Haitians, and indifference toward people of African descent. Consequently, adds Martínez-Vergne:

> Dominicans, as other Hispanic-descent peoples of Latin America, had internalized the value of whiteness and even cultivated it vis-à-vis their neighbor Haiti. To accentuate this tendency, scientific racism had introduced the notion that progress and modernity depended on the appropriate racial mix. Given these circumstances, it was incumbent upon the intelligentsia to claim nationhood on the basis of racial unity by subsuming blackness into the discourse and by erasing it through white immigration.[106]

Nineteenth-century nation-building discourse, anti-Haitian rhetoric, and the anti-North American sentiment all converged into the Dominican nationalism of the 1920s and 1930s. This particular brand of Dominican nationalism set forth a series of measures implemented by Dominican leaders during the Horacio Vasquez (1860–1936) presidency (1924–1930). The expression and promotion of xenophobic ideas became more vociferous and aggressive during the Trujillo regime (1930–1961). Trujillo controlled most of the country's sources of income and led one of the most repressive regimes in the world. At one point, Trujillo, his acolytes, and government officials were distressed by the number of Haitian immigrants in the country. They began projects to "Dominicanize" the border and force out as many Haitians as possible. In 1937, when some of these policies failed, Trujillo ordered the massacre of thousands of Haitians by the military.[107] In order to distinguish dark-skinned Dominicans from Haitians, a shibboleth test was applied, in which only those that could pronounce the flap (apicoalveolar) r instead of the uvular r (as in French) in the word *perejil* (parsley) would not perish.[108] This disastrous event drew heavy international criticism.[109] Jesús de Galíndez (1915–1956), a scholar from Spain who was tortured and ultimately killed per Trujillo's orders (1958), described the series of events:

> In 1936, it seemed that the causes of misunderstanding between the Dominican Republic and Haiti had forever vanished and that its two respective presidents had at least begun friendly official relations. This state of

affairs lasted a little over a year. In late 1937, a most horrible event occurred, suddenly creating the widest gulf in the relations between the two countries in more than a century. The killings took place several days between the second and third of October. But the first news regarding the killings did not circulate around the world until nearly three weeks later. In the Dominican Republic, news agencies remained totally silent for more than a month... Its first official reaction is a note from the Dominican Legion to the New York Times, dated October 23rd, which includes a joint statement from the Dominican Foreign Minister, Joaquín Balaguer and the Haitian Ambassador in Ciudad Trujillo [Santo Domingo], Everemont Carrié, declaring that the relations between Haiti and the Dominican Republic "have not been impaired." However, the scandal had taken on international proportions. Major news agencies had sent reporters to the country to find out what happened.[110]

This period saw the consolidation of politically conservative forces and the militarization of Dominican culture (Galíndez 1984, Peguero 2004). The worst elements in the military, the bourgeois bureaucracy, the Jesuit wing of the Catholic Church, and one of the most powerful dictatorships in Latin America's history converged in the exploitation and domination of the Dominican masses and in legitimating absolute despotic rule.[111] It was a very reactionary period in the life of the country. All over, it was a time of serious pessimism, which Henríquez Ureña, borrowing from Luis Arquistain (1928), described as "the Caribbean agony." The Caribbean agony included the dictatorships, the fall of the sugar industry in Cuba, the U.S. colonization of Puerto Rico, and the migration of Anglophone and Francophone West Indian workers to the Hispanic Caribbean. While Arquistain lamented the politically bleak future of Puerto Rico, Ramiro Guerra Sánchez (1927) described the general sociopolitical outlook of the Caribbean in the following fatalistic terms, concluding that Caribbean decline would inevitably become a reality: "Immigration will result in irreversible harm to all these Caribbean countries. Cuba will not realize its potential and destiny as a leading country. Unable to influence the fields of agriculture, industry, and science, Cuba will not achieve social progress."[112]

It is in this general political climate that the instrumentalist and hegemonic approach to language and history became the standard practice for Dominican historians and philologists. Their practice authorized images of the language as representative of *lo dominicano* (Dominicanness) and "cultivated speech" that had to be protected from anglicisms, gallicisms (or rather Haitian creolisms), barbarisms, and "deterioration" at the hands of the lower classes. Matos Moquete (1986) argues that instrumentalism and elitism have paved the way in the definition of language and history in the Dominican Republic. Historians and other scholars have advanced the privileged Dominican standard form of Spanish against the presumed barbarism and damaging effects of other lower varieties.[113] These sociolinguistic concerns intensified along with racial tension and the active policies of eradication of Haitians and increased European immigration pursued by the Trujillo government. In addition to *El español en Santo Domingo*, the year 1941 saw the publication of Emilio Jiménez's *Del lenguaje dominicano* and Patín Maceo's *Dominicanismos*. Further elaborating the ethnopolitical discourse of the state, Matos Moquete highlights the favorite and recurring themes of Dominican intellectuals, such as "language is our homeland," "language is our national soul," "language is our flag and shield," and "language is our treasure."[114] In the Dominican context, the discourse on language revolved around the issues of Dominican national identity and the demands of hegemonic forces, which were embedded in what Matos Moquete calls "the genealogical tree of Hispanism."[115]

Pedro Henríquez Ureña's Devotion to Hispanoamericanism

The history and use of the term *hispanismo* (sometimes opposed by *hispanoamericanismo, americanismo,* and *panhispanismo*) typically evoke ideological conflicts and extensive discussions of its sociopolitical origins. One of the most difficult questions to tackle in these discussions is whose *hispanismo* (Hispanism) are we referring to?[116] The discourse on Hispanism began to develop after the independence of Latin American states in the 1820s. In his classic study, Frederick Pike (1971) defined Hispanism as "[the] unassailable faith in the existence of a transatlantic Hispanic family, community or 'raza'... A *raza* shaped more by common culture, historical experiences, traditions, and language than by blood or ethnic factors."[117] Carlos Rama (1982) also discussed the meanings of the categories of *hispanismo* and *americanismo* by comparing and contrasting the different political aspects of liberal and conservative thought that articulated cultural relations between Spain and Latin America. Recently, Isidro Sepúlveda Muñoz (2005) defined *hispanoamericanismo* (Hispanoamericanism) as

> A movement whose goal was to build a transnational community over a cultural identity based on language, religion, history, and social customs or practices; an imagined community made up of Spain and [Spanish-speaking] Latin American states in which the former colonial metropolis held a position of seniority, if not dominance, captured by the widely used expression of Motherland.[118]

In the latter half of the nineteenth century and the first half of the twentieth century, Hispanoamericanism[119] exhibited two major branches that converged on various ideas and proposals that centered on the historical and cultural bonds between Spain and the Spanish-speaking countries in America. On one hand, the Spanish branch, composed of Spanish conservative and liberal politicians and intellectuals, defended the formation of a transatlantic Spanish community or identity that justifies Spain's cultural presence, commercial interests, and foreign policy in Latin America. They proposed a shared (idealized) identity of the Peninsular and American people, on the basis of a cultural community comprising historical, linguistic, philosophical, and religious elements that underlie the constitutions of the respective states and transcend the political divisions that followed the wars of independence. The American branch, on the other hand, was composed of various Latin American intellectuals who, preoccupied with resolving conflictive relations with Spain and the emergence of the United States as an imperial power, rejected or embraced cultural traditions and identities. It would be a mistake to define Hispanoamericanism in terms of this dichotomous relationship. The fact is, as Carlos Rama indicated, there were different proponents and versions of this political and cultural ideology in both Latin America and Spain, including liberal Spaniards who were pro-America, the government officials and public functionaries who refused to accept Spain's colonial losses, the rich and powerful *criollo* classes in Latin America who wanted a return to monarchic rule, and the Latin American progressives who desired a totally new political and sociocultural horizon, among others. Obviously, even within these groups, Hispanoamericanism engaged a wide array of individuals who, with different ideological attitudes, sought to define and construct Latin American identities in a variety of ways. José Del Valle and Luis Gabriel-Stheeman (2004d), following Pike and Rama, propose that Hispanism, in particular, generally consists of the following ideas: (i) the existence of a unique Spanish culture, lifestyle, characteristics, traditions and values, all of them embodied in its language; (ii) the idea that Spanish American culture is nothing but Spanish culture transplanted to the New World; and (iii) the notion that Hispanic culture has an internal hierarchy in which Spain occupies a hegemonic position.[120] Of particular interest to Del Valle and Gabriel-Stheeman, and to us, is the manifestation of linguistic Hispanism.

Between 1885 and 1936, as Del Valle and Gabriel-Stheeman and their collaborators have shown (2004a), philologists and intellectuals from both sides of the Atlantic were passionately debating ideas about the crucial role of the Spanish language in the construction of national identities, preserving the purity and the unity of the language, and the means for promoting the language and culture. They were particularly preoccupied with developing ideas, some opposing, some complementary, about a pan-Hispanic cultural community embodied by the Spanish language. In the vision of some intellectuals, Spanish became ideologized in such a way as to foster the spiritual (psychological) identity of all Spanish-speaking countries, naturally, with Spain as its focal point.

Hispanoamericanism initially appears in Henríquez Ureña's work as a theoretical preoccupation and powerful ideological current when he arrived in New York under the profound influence of the Uruguayan essayist José Enrique Rodó (1872–1917).[121] According to Henríquez Ureña: "My impressions jostled a bit, but I saw everything through the anti-North American prejudice that *Ariel* (1900) had reinforced on me thanks to its literary prestige."[122] The Spanish defeat of 1898 in Cuba and the manifestation of the power of the United States prompted the publication of Rodó's famous essay, *Ariel*. In it, the author calls for young Latin American intellectuals to reject the materialism of North America in favor of the Greco-Roman humanistic traditions of free thinking and self-improvement and to develop and concentrate on their own culture. Henríquez Ureña admired Rodó as the best stylist and one of the first Latin American modernists, to whom he attributed the aesthetic renewal of language.[123] Henríquez Ureña's reading of *Ariel* awakened in him, as it did in other young Latin American intellectuals in the 1910s and 1920s, a desire for cultural affirmation, a search for national "essences," and a preoccupation with defining Latin America's cultural landscape or Hispanoamericanism.

Another area of concern for Henríquez Ureña, after reading *Ariel*, is language: "In fact, the importance of our language is not even taken into account in France. In the Anglo-Saxon world, the idea that Castilian is a dying language is gaining ground."[124] Language, in Henríquez Ureña's reading of *Ariel*, is one of the main forces capable of unifying the dispersed elements of the Spanish race.[125] Early on, Henríquez Ureña absorbed one of Rodó's fundamental ideas: the transformation of our societies depended in the cultivation of knowledge and culture and not in the development of machinery and technology. In *Ariel*, Henríquez Ureña found a specific plan of action that called for showcasing the Spanish language ("our language") and fighting against the (French and Anglo-Saxon) idea that Spanish was a dying language. Furthermore, Rodó reformulated in modernist terms the old civilization—barbarism opposition. Henríquez Ureña wrote: "Today, Ariel crosses the Atlantic with his weightless wings and illuminates the head of young Próspero. He comes to help Próspero overcome Calibán who intends to take over the island devoid of civilization called America."[126] Henríquez Ureña accepted the image of *Ariel* as a symbol of the intellectual's commitment to the development of civilization and the erasure of barbarism in the former colonies. According to Louis-Jean

Calvet (2005), paraphrasing Roberto Fernández Retamar: "Basically, the intellectual history of colonized people is the history of making a choice between the path of Calibán and the path of Ariel, between collaboration and resistance."[127] Henríquez Ureña belonged to that generation of young intellectuals, inspired by Rodó, who wanted to portray the right image of Spanish in order to, first, help construct a cultural and linguistic whole and, then, secure and enjoy Latin America's membership in universal culture. For this important mission, Henríquez Ureña absorbed the lessons of generations of writers and scholars who exploited the political dimension of language and discourse:

> The flourishing of literature was not enough for modern languages to become established as proper instruments of thought and philosophy. They had to wage battle. At the point of highest linguistic development, it was necessary for writers themselves to assume the defense of these languages. Therefore, in Italy, we find Dante leading the charge with *On the eloquence of the vernacular*... In France, the Italian influence produced *La defense et illustration de la langue française* by the wise and sophisticated Joachim du Bellay. Before France, Spain had its own protectors of the Spanish vernacular. First of all, there was Pérez de Oliva,[128] who called for the preponderance of Romance throughout his work. Secondly, there was Juan de Valdés... who used Spanish as the model for writing and avoided Latin.[129]

While Henríquez Ureña did modify his use of some of these concepts throughout his productive career, this particularly ideological conceptualization of language would play a key role in his representations of Spanish. Henríquez Ureña's Hispanomericanism is an amalgam of the values and ideals inculcated by his family, experience gained from teaching and writing about Spanish literature and language in various settings, and his love for the intellectual history of Latin America and a "higher spiritual world." It first emerges out of a dialogue with Rodó and his opposition of Latin culture to Anglo-Saxon culture, Menéndez Pidal's vision of the Hispanic culture, and Vasconcelos's *La raza cósmica*. Essentially, Henríquez Ureña's Hispanoamericanism maintains that, despite the obvious influences from Spain and the rest of Europe, Latin Americans constitute linguistically and culturally diverse groups. In this sense, he is a very unique type of *hispanoamericanista*.

Henríquez Ureña belonged to the movement that Leopoldo Zea (1943) called *generación asuntiva*, or the intellectual group (Martí, Rodó, Vasconcelos, Manuel Ugarte[130]) that reacted against the search for identity carried out specifically by nineteenth-century intellectuals who favored European or North American models. For Latin American *hispanoamericanistas* such as Reyes and Henríquez Ureña, searching for the specificity of Latin America, involved the following tasks: (i) reincorporating Peninsular literature within a humanities framework that included other European literatures (namely, French, German, and English); (ii) applying the new methods of Hispanic philology as developed by Marcelino Menéndez Pelayo and Menéndez Pidal and his Madrid school to the study of language and culture; and (iii) providing the proper historical framework in which to reevaluate and reformulate the question of Latin American identity, or what Henríquez Ureña referred to as "the question of why nations are as they are."[131]

In their search for answers to such question, the Latin American *hispanoamericanistas* turned their attention to the concepts of race and language. At the beginning of the twentieth century, however, adherence to racial discourse, heavily influenced by French biologists, was the rule more than the exception.[132] One of the most celebrated elaborations of the racial category was Vasoconcelos's *La raza cósmica* (1925). In this essay, the author tried to oppose to growing U.S. hegemony and European racism his vision of Latin American *mestizaje*, or the construction, over the foundations of the Spanish legacy, of a new and improved cosmic race: "A race made from all the best of previous races, the ultimate race, the cosmic race."[133] Relying on Gregor Mendel's[134] (1822–1884) biological theories, Vasconcelos initially rejected the supremacy of one race over another. He believed that the "Latin race" was bound to triumph in the political and cultural struggle, because this group, in particular, was the most naturally inclined to mixing. Racial mixing was essential as the most certain means of bringing about the final and most improved "cosmic race." According to Vasconcelos, this could only take place in Latin America with a population (of indigenous and European mixture) already prepared for the task.

Vasconcelos exploited the emotional charge of this concept without hesitation in the elaboration of the emerging discourse on Latin American identities. As a result, his account of identity formation became extremely influential. Henríquez Ureña, on the other hand, was not so easily swayed by racial proposals in his own elaboration of Hispanoamericanism. Like Martí, Henríquez Ureña believed that the idea of a unified Latin America organized along racial lines was an erroneous oversimplification: "Certainly, these simplistic but emotionally-charged references to race are scientifically inaccurate."[135] According to Henríquez Ureña, from an anthropological perspective, the racial proposal was not acceptable:

> From the point of view of anthropological science, the multicolored groups of people who speak our language from the Andes to the Pyrenees and

from the Balearic and Canary islands to the Antilles and Philippines hardly constitutes a race ... but the word "race," despite its blatant inaccuracy has become commonplace for us.[136]

This cultural view clearly contrasts, as we will discuss, with the racialized one he adopted in his construction of Dominican national identity. Nonetheless, as far as his *hispanoamericanista* vision of the Latin American culture was concerned,

> What unites and unifies this race, in theory, is a culture primarily made up of a speech community. Each language encapsulates an everlasting repertoire of traditions, beliefs, and attitudes towards life that resist changes, revolutions, and disorders ... Describing our Latin American nations, Sarmiento used to say that we belong to the Roman Empire. We belong to the Roman family, or the Latin race, to use the often repeated phrase.[137]

Henríquez Ureña adds the caveat that this is an abstract illustration of race and not an empirical one. Certainly, Henríquez Ureña has Vasconcelos's racial discourse in mind in his explanation of the social realities of Latin America.

According to Henríquez Ureña, language was a more essential factor than race in the empirical foundation of a social reality (as well as the construction of what he called "The Great Concert of Nations," or Latin America's *Magna Patria*). There is, in Henríquez Ureña's discussion of language in his cultural texts, despite his acknowledgment of its heterogeneity, a basic belief in the unifying force of language. In his view, language reflects "historical unity, a unity of purpose in political and intellectual life that transforms Our America into an organic whole. Our Great Fatherland is an ensemble of nations that are destined to unite more each day."[138] Also in his preference of language over race as the basis of Latin American identity, we find him slipping into one of several contradictions. With his insistence on language as an essential component of a cultural unit, he sides with Menéndez Pidal and other Peninsular *hispanoamericanistas*. However, Henríquez Ureña maintains a critical distance from them by insisting on the specific American conditions of development of this essential (linguistic) component. He is reluctant to give up what he sees as *nuestra expresión*, Latin America's claim to "spiritual originality" and contribution to universal culture:

> We have not renounced to writing in Spanish. This fact is relevant to understanding our unique way of being. Each language is a crystallization of ways of thinking and feeling. Regardless of the subject, everything written in Spanish absorbs this language's particular properties.[139]

Hispanoamericanistas such Henríquez Ureña believed that it was possible and necessary to derive the idealized community from the common language, but disagreed with the priority assigned to Peninsular Spanish in the construction of Latin American identity. For that reason, he devoted a great deal of time and energy to a rigorous study of dialectal zones from Latin America and its specific linguistic features. In one of his classic linguistic works, *El supuesto andalucismo de América* (1925a), he strongly rejected traditional accounts of American Spanish, held by linguists and philologists,[140] as a derivative of the Andalusian dialect. In this instance, he sought to create a vision of American Spanish removed from its Peninsularist mold; a vision not so profoundly influenced by Peninsular tradition. This representation of American Spanish was a perfect fit for his brand of Hispanoamericanism, or the view of a politically unified Latin America, immersed in, yet emancipated from Spanish culture.

Ironically, the case is not the same in Henríquez Ureña's particular depiction of national identity and Spanish in the Dominican Republic. In order to understand this dilemma, it is important to go back and reexamine the different nature of Hispanoamericanism in the Dominican Republic. It is possible to use the categories of *españolismo* or "hispanophilia" to distinguish the Dominican brand, but our adopted terminology and a basic description of its characteristics will suffice. Dominican Hispanism is a political and cultural ideology based on the concept of the Dominican national identity as pure, white, and Spanish. The historian Carlos Rama noted: "The Dominican Republic is a very particular case. This country was surrendered to France by Spain during the Basel treaty of 1795. Between 1809–1822 and 1861–1865, it suffered through French and Haitian occupations and two restorations of Spanish power. The Spanish restorations were supported by the archdiocese and the Spanish clergy, all of whom were monarchists. The main objective was to turn Santo Domingo into a colony because apparently at this juncture Dominicans still considered themselves to be Spanish, white, and Catholic."[141] As mentioned, not all Dominicans accepted this self-image and neocolonial status. The most commonly noted exception is the equally complicated *mulataje* (the mulatto community) discourse that promotes the categorical view of Dominicans as fully mixed racially.[142] However, the ideology of Hispanism became, and is still, dominant. Thus, in Henríquez Ureña's linguistic work, we find the following seemingly divergent representations: American Spanish as the product of the independent will and collective effort of the American people versus Dominican Spanish as a Northern Castilian archaic dialect without the possibility of African influence. Why did Henríquez Ureña abandon his complex Hispanoamericanism for the traditional Hispanism of the Dominican ruling class and the intellectual elite? To answer that question we must initially look at the political and cultural circumstances surrounding his native country as well as the political and cultural conditions surrounding intellectual production in Latin America, while exploring the complex interplay of Dominican nationalism and Hispanoamericanism.

In the Dominican Republic as well as in the broader Latin American context, on the basis of the historical and ideological reasons that I have discussed, identity continuously emerges as a central question. In analyzing this question, intellectuals felt that it was crucial to link identity to language. In the process, they not only formulated an identity but they also produced a particular vision of the language, which, under varying circumstances, they felt compelled to defend and protect. In addition, however, we must situate Henríquez Ureña's linguistic production in the tradition of language studies in the Hispanic world. Of utmost importance for our purpose is the question of how exactly were these problems and issues dealt with by analysts in the tradition of language studies in Latin America and what dictated the terms of their approach.

4

Pedro Henríquez Ureña in Hispanic Linguistics

Similar to the elaboration of the ideology of Hispanoamericanism, the development of language studies in the Hispanic world involved the collaboration and opposition of many individuals, groups, and institutions. In order to fully understand the origins and implications of Pedro Henríquez Ureña's linguistic work, it is necessary to place it against the backdrop of the contributions made by the principal figures in language studies in the Hispanic world and to identify the distribution, circulation, and operation of fundamental ideas about language that informed his approach to linguistic matters. As indicated in Chapter 2, this particular analysis is grounded on the principles of critical linguistic historiography according to which the historical emergence of a particular form of linguistic description cannot be solely interpreted by virtue of its factual rigor, but must also be understood in relation to the general goals and objectives of the linguists who established them as well as in relation to the cultural, political, and social contexts in which they were formulated. Therefore, I situate Henríquez Ureña's linguistic studies in a particular intellectual context and climate of opinion and reveal the degree to which his work developed in dialogue with the specific sociolinguistic, political, and intellectual circumstances. This chapter explores the how, when, and why, since the seminal work of Andrés Bello, Hispanic philologists and linguists have tried to legitimate their occupation, help create independent nations and modern societies, and define the pan-Hispanic community.

In the nineteenth century, students of philology and historical grammar were laying the epistemological and methodological foundations for the "new" science of language that gravitated more and more toward the natural sciences such as botany, chemistry, biology, comparative anatomy, paleontology, and geology: "The science of language is to be regarded as a modern one, as much so as geology and chemistry; it belongs, like them, to the nineteenth century."[1] The nineteenth-century American linguist William Dwight Whitney (1827–1894) thought that developments in the study of language were similar to developments in the natural sciences but not identical.[2] Nonetheless, philologists such as the German August Schleicher (1821–1868), who wanted to prove that languages could be studied scientifically, argued that they functioned like natural organisms and began to develop a theory of language that emphasized its systematic character. By the late nineteenth century, philology had achieved three major accomplishments: the establishment of comparative grammar as a method, the reclassification of languages into families, and the elimination of the idea of sacred languages.

For European philologists, the interest in a language's systematic development was also directly linked with the Romantic preoccupation with determining the developmental process of national consciousness: "[The science of language] seeks to know what language is worth to the mind, and what has been its part in the development of our race. And less directly, it seeks to learn and set forth what it may of the history of human development, and of the history of the races, their movements and connections, so far as these are to be read in the facts of language."[3] The relationship between national consciousness and language became a fundamental problem for nineteenth-century philologists. As Edward Said reminds us, from their scientific perspective, philologists saw and seized an opportunity to drive out supernaturalism in order to see nature and reality more clearly.[4]

The neogrammarian[5] model dominated Europe until the appearance of Ferdinand de Saussure's *Course in General Linguistics* (1916). Saussure established that the essential tasks of linguistics should be to describe and trace the history of all observable languages, to determine the universal forces and principles around which all languages develop, and to delimit and define itself.[6] The first works in Spanish linguistics were historical grammars mostly by German philologists (Diez 1882, Meyer-Lübke 1890) that included descriptions of Spanish. Subsequently, Ramón Menéndez Pidal (1904, 1926), working within Schleicher's paradigm, concentrated his efforts in establishing the study of the history of the Spanish language as a separate discipline.[7] However, in the nineteenth century, other scholars in the Hispanic world had already expressed serious interest in the scientific study of Spanish.

Andrés Bello and National Grammars

At the time that Friedrich Diez (1794–1876) was developing the foundations of Romance philology in Germany, Andrés Bello (1781–1865) worked on his *Gramática de la lengua castellana destinada al uso de los americanos* (1847), considered the first scientific study of Spanish.[8] The Venezuelan-born Andrés Bello, an exemplary figure in Latin American cultural history, is often considered the precursor of language studies in Latin America.[9] Bello spent 20 years in London where, under difficult circumstances, he forged personal and intellectual ties with several important Latin American and Spanish exiles and European thinkers such as James Mill (1773–1836) and Alexander von Humboldt (1769–1859), through whom he learned about Alexander's brother Wilhelm von Humboldt's (1767–1835) work on language. Bello's major works were in the fields of philology, literature, law, philosophy, and education and were mostly carried out during his life in Chile after 1829, which was a critical juncture in the history of this emerging South American republic.

Bello conceived of his Grammar as an important tool for maintaining linguistic and cultural unity as well as civic order in and among the newly independent nations: "I deem important to preserve the language of our fathers in all its possible purity as a beneficial medium of communication and a fraternal bond between the various nations of Spanish origin scattered over the continent."[10] Bello wrote his Grammar in order to control and maintain language standards that would presumably curtail the danger of linguistic, cultural, and political fragmentation. The standardization process consisted of selecting and using the (pan-Hispanic) norm that most closely resembled the educated speech of Peninsular speakers instead of the "pernicious" regional forms.[11] The preference for a Peninsular norm is not explicitly stated, but it can be inferred from Bello's writings. Consider the use of the verb *transar* (to yield, to reach an agreement) in Chile, a practice of which Bello disapproved because he believed it had no precedent in Peninsular Spanish: "It does not exist in Spanish."[12] Bello referred to the linguistic norm as: "Castilian ... the language spoken in Castile and which Castilians brought to America along with their weapons and laws is today the common language of Spanish American states."[13] Bello selected and recommended the Castilian linguistic norm, naturally entrenched in the Castilian legal tradition and bolstered by power, as the national language for the new republics. Thus, in spite of putting the process of language standardization at the service of the new nations, Bello helped reproduce some colonial hierarchies.

During Bello's time, the fear of linguistic fragmentation was intense and widespread: "Like the Babylonian chaos of the middle ages, our America will soon produce a confusion of languages, dialects, and jargons. These nations will lose one of their most powerful fraternal bonds and one of its most precious means of communication and commerce."[14] Fearing the possibility that the Spanish language might fragment into multiple

American dialects (as had occurred with Latin following the end of the Roman Empire), Bello specified the preservation of linguistic unity as the principal motivation behind his Grammar.[15] Bello believed that the preservation of the unity of the Spanish language and national unity was directly related to an expansion of the linguistic code used by the leading class and educated people that could circumscribe the linguistic diversity and chaos of the newly independent states of Latin America:

> Intelligent readers who read my Grammar with close attention will confirm the care I have taken in demarcating the proper use of our language and its limits. In the midst of imprecise and changing speech habits, I have also identified the sources of corruptions that most affect us today, pointing out the existing differences between Castilian and foreign expressions. Despite a certain degree of resemblance, we should exercise better judgment and avoid using these foreign expressions.[16]

While insisting on the separation of Spanish and foreign modes of expressions, Bello was associating geographical and linguistic boundaries. This type of association played a large role in the work of those who were working on ideological formations (i.e., the nation) in the context of Latin America.

Bello's *Gramática castellana* became the model and the inspiration for the next generation of scholars who participated in the debates over Latin America's linguistic reality. Following the appearance of Bello's Grammar there was a surge in the publication of provincial vocabularies in many Latin American countries, including Juan de Arona's *Diccionario de peruanismos* (1882), Zorobabel Rodríguez's *Diccionario de chilenismos* (1875), Joaquim de Macedo Soares's *Diccionario brasileiro da lingua portuguesa* (1888), and Alberto Membreño's *Vocabulario de los pronvincialismos de Honduras* (1895). According to Guillermo Guitarte (1998), these dictionaries from the "pre-scientific" era are primarily the products of amateurs who shared the notion that American Spanish was corrupted in relation to the Spanish spoken by Spaniards.[17] These dictionaries reflect the practice of lexicographers, amateur or not, who were only too eager to assist in the ideological tasks of nation-building, such as the standardization of the national language. This was done specifically through the legitimization of provincialisms and the defense of an orthography based on the particular local pronunciation. Yet despite this separation from what was regarded as the Peninsular norm, these lexicographers, with varying degrees of success, tried to emulate Bello's reflections on language in the context of the modern Latin American states. Henríquez Ureña remarked:

In his *Grammar of the Spanish tongue* (1847) and in his *Principles of orthology and metrics* (1835), [Bello] established the study of language and of its verse on a basis of fact which had been obscured latterly by a blind adherence to Latin models, although the grammarians and prosodists of the fifteenth century, Nebrija and Encina, had originally taken the right road. Bello's Grammar is still, after nearly a hundred years, the most complete synchronic description of our tongue and one of the best of any modern language.[18]

Henríquez Ureña recognized Andrés Bello and Rufino José Cuervo, the two pioneers of language studies in Latin America, as the building blocks of the system of knowledge known as *el saber hispanoamericano* (Hispanoamericanism). This knowledge is a fundamental base on which Henríquez Ureña built his own representations of language and culture in the Latin American context and it is, therefore, no accident that Hispanoamericanism is the tradition with which he is most often associated.[19]

Lexicography, Rebellion, and Liberty

The appearance of the Cuban-Dominican Esteban Pichardo's *Diccionario casi razonado de voces y frases cubanas* (1836) signaled the emergence of lexicography in Latin America and the Caribbean. Even the author was amazed by the Dictionary's successful reception in Cuba: "the public lavished the most generous praise upon it. Literary celebrities, farmers, clerks, lexicographers, all adopted and commended the work."[20] The author was also pleased by the reception accorded to it by the Real Academia Española. To Carlos Rama (1982), its greatest achievement was the recording of new lexemes derived from local speech.[21] According to Fernando A. Martínez (1968), the concept of a genuine record of local speech inspires Pichardo's Diccionario *de Voces Cubanas*, "which opens nineteenth century lexicography, and which springs from living experiences with the language and with different neighboring countries (Cuba, Santo Domingo, and Puerto Rico). It offers a direct testimony of lexical varieties, of their sources (terms from other languages), and their most marked changes in meaning."[22] As exemplified by Pichardo, the lexicographer's practice consisted of providing a broad view of the American world through its lexicon. It included descriptions of a given region's flora, fauna, resources, and industries as well as the practices and customs of its inhabitants.[23] In addition, these lexical corpora contained linguistic expressions that were presumably unique to a province, state, or country (e.g., *argentinismos, chilenismos, hondureñismos*): "only in Puerto-Rico have I heard the word *embullamiento*; our *marañón* is *cajuil* in Santo Domingo."[24] Lexicographers such as Pichardo conceptualized regional dictionaries as more than simple compilations of provincialisms:

> Some people think that the *Diccionario cubano* only amounts to an indigenous lexicon... On the other hand, others would like to incorporate neologisms and rare words with a discussion of incorrect popular usage. To all of them, my answer is no. The *Diccionario* presents all the words peculiar to the island of Cuba.[25]

Regional lexicons became associated with distinct national territories and therefore a theoretical tool for explaining national cultures.

Among Henríquez Ureña's contemporaries, we also find the Puerto Rican lexicographer Augusto Malaret (1878–1967), who significantly contributed to the spread of this type of studies not only in the Caribbean, but also in Latin America. While his *Diccionario de americanismos* (1925) was considered, at one point, the most complete lexical count of American Spanish,[26] his *Diccionario de provincialismos de Puerto Rico* (first edition dates to 1917) was highly regarded as well. This work attempted to collect linguistic and folkloric material from remote corners of Puerto Rico. The result was a list of 3,209 lexical items used throughout the island.[27] The *Diccionario de americanismos* is organized around three central elements: the definition and status of lexical items within the academic establishment, information regarding certain grammatical contexts in which lexemes appear, and information regarding lexemes's sociolinguistic variation, if any. These lexicographers' attitude toward sociolinguistic variation was complex. While some acknowledged that many of the so-called provincialisms were widely used throughout Latin America or were in fact archaic Hispanisms, they tended to emphasize their local character. In some cases, they were not too receptive to their own local lexical variation. Regarding *afronegrismos* (words of possible African origin), for example, Malaret wrote (in his 1937 edition of *Vocabulario de Puerto Rico*):

> The contribution of Africans to the Spanish variety spoken in Puerto Rico is certainly negative. Falling outside the scope of this study, there is no need to mention their errors of pronunciation. While we find African lexicons published in Cuba and we may find in Santo Domingo the minor influence of Patois from neighboring Haiti, in Puerto Rico, we can count on our hand the number of Africanisms that have passed into conversational Spanish: *calalú, guigambó, macandá, malanga, mandinga, ñame... baquiné, calambé, marinada, o mariyandá*.[28]

Nonetheless, these lexicographers were devoted to compiling a proper inventory of Americanisms and provincialisms and ensuring their preservation. In the process, some of them could not avoid adopting neologisms derived from new economic, cultural, and ideological conditions generated by independence and nation-building.[29] Along with grammarians and philologists, lexicographers were shaping nationalism in Latin America.[30] The following remarks by the Peruvian Juan de Arona (1882), in his *Diccionario de peruanismos,* exemplify the degree to which lexicography was put at the service of the discursive construction of the nation:

> In the same spirit of independence, rebellion, and liberty that we always demonstrate, we have also shaken off the yoke of orthological and prosodic tyranny. This tyranny prescribes that we substitute the vowel *o* with the diphthong *ue* in some derived nouns which includes *buñuelo* from *buñuelero*... In the case of *pañuelón* instead of *pañolón,* we detect the presence of Peninsular writers among us. Would a nation that has forged ahead, overcoming the force of civil law and social customs, allow itself to be subjugated from abroad by the grammar of Castile?[31]

The basic idea shared by these Latin American lexicographers was that, in adding American regionalisms to or correcting the ones already included in *Diccionario de la Real Academia Española* (DRAE), they were presenting and solidifying the foundations of their respective national identities and their recently won freedoms.

Rufino José Cuervo and the Foundations of Latin American Philology

At the end of the nineteenth century, following very closely the latest development in European linguistic research, Colombian philologist Rufino José Cuervo (1844–1911) began his studies reacting against the amateur lexicographers and ended up as one of the most eminent figures in Hispanic philology. Henríquez Ureña admired Cuervo's erudition and knowledge of the science of language. To him, Cuervo represented the pinnacle of Hispanic philology: "In Europe or America, no one, not even Bello, was as well-versed in the history of our language or the history of every word and changes in meaning."[32] In addition, Cuervo took strong positions against Spanish neocolonial impulses, a fact that was of utmost relevance to the debate over the origins and evolution of American Spanish.[33] But more importantly, Cuervo opposed Spanish intellectuals' attempts to continue their dominance of the public discourse on language.

Cuervo explained that it was through satire and criticism that he initially tried to reach and then educate a local public that found literary and intellectual gossip more appealing than linguistic problems.[34] Nevertheless, despite these publicity tactics, the author saw his *Apuntaciones* as a serious endeavor and commitment to the development of his national culture, which, one way or another, needed the establishment of scientific disciplines and "scientific culture."[35] Cuervo's desire to scientifically study language was so strong that he taught himself German in order to read Franz Bopp, the founder of scientific philology of the Indo-European languages. Cuervo's philological work initially emerged as part of an effort to establish different categories of change in the meaning of words. Cuervo's *Diccionario de construcción y régimen* (1866) established him as the leading authority on Spanish philology. His *Apuntaciones críticas sobre el lenguaje bogotano* (1876) combined on a comparative basis a firsthand study of the local language with far-reaching considerations of linguistic principles. More specifically, Cuervo explained the use and history of a large number of lexical items in Bogotá speech while reflecting on important phonetic, morphological, and syntactic phenomena. With *Apuntaciones*, Cuervo sought to contribute to the development of scientific studies in the region, thus, putting linguistic research at the service of his society.

The possible fragmentation of Spanish into multiple dialects is another central theme in Cuervo's work. Like Bello, Cuervo was deeply concerned with the idea that, in order to prevent the split, it was necessary to reestablish a clear and prestigious linguistic authority. However, Cuervo was the first scholar to express coherent views on the subject. He saw the ever-increasing appearance of regionalisms in works of literature, combined with the decreasing cultural influence of Spain, as indication of the linguistic fragmentation of Spanish in Latin America. According to Cuervo, three important factors played a role in this situation: the natural evolution of languages assisted by different climates and the practices of social and ethnic groups, Spain's collapse as a unifying cultural and intellectual force, and the lack of contact among Latin American countries.[36] He made reference to the historically parallel case of Latin, which had to make way for other European languages with the break-up of the Roman Empire.[37] The Colombian's views regarding these linguistic issues led to a polemic with the *hispanomaericanista* Juan Valera (1824–1905). The Spanish writer reacted acrimoniously to Cuervo's ideas, especially the idea that "with the exception of four or five [Spanish] authors whose works we beneficially read with pleasure, our intellectual life is derived from other sources."[38] Valera replied that essentially the stability of the language and its future was secured and guaranteed by the pride and loyalty of Spanish speakers everywhere to Spain and its colonial history.[39]

Valera's position, infused with the political and cultural anxieties of his days, anticipated Menéndez Pidal's views on Spanish as well as the ideological spiraling of this subject in the Hispanoamericanism debates.[40] Although Menéndez Pidal (1944) had admitted that Cuervo was indeed a linguistic authority, he believed that the Colombian was incorrect and attributed his fragmentation theories to old age.[41] This was, of course, a rhetorical strategy he employed to indirectly discredit the Colombian philologist.[42] Menéndez Pidal proposed to the subsequent generation of scholars that the unity of Spanish was firmly established. Throughout the debate with Valera, however, Cuervo demonstrated the breadth of his knowledge of the linguistic history of America and a determination to establish empirically based facts concerning linguistic phenomena. Yet his belief that defending the unity of Spanish was an intellectual responsibility counterbalanced his so-called linguistic pessimism. As the debate over the unity of Spanish continued, scholars such as Henríquez Ureña seriously took into account many of Cuervo's ideas on the subject.

Characteristic of Cuervo's linguistic thought is the assimilation of the dominant ideas in linguistics at the end of the nineteenth century. Well versed in these prevalent linguistic ideas, Cuervo understood the evolving character of language as revealed by objective linguistic studies: "Every language represents perpetual evolution, changing, becoming richer or poorer, and each epoch represents one stage of a language's evolution."[43] He also acknowledged the fact that linguistic evolution responded to historical circumstances:

> Regional linguistic differences can be explained by the presence of the remains of a dialect that was succeeded by another, which achieved literary and political dominance. We can find examples of this phenomenon in the many peculiarities of the Castilian spoken in Aragón and Galicia. But some of these changes can also represent subsequent developments from the establishment of the national language, as it is the prevalent case in other parts of Spain and America. Therefore, when we study popular or literary language in each region of the Spanish-speaking world, we must consider all these circumstances. In light of political and literary history, we will apply the necessary criteria and be able to clearly determine every stage and every step in the evolution of language.[44]

While Cuervo had a broad conception of language change, he was also mindful of the academic tradition begun by scholars such as Bello who viewed defending the concept of unity of the Spanish language as their intellectual responsibility.[45] Cuervo wrote: "Linguistic development is induced by force everywhere, including Spain and America. If we truly want to maintain linguistic unity in literature, the only domain where that is possible, then both Spain and Latin America must do their part to achieve it."[46] Faced with the possible fragmentation of Spanish, Cuervo explored the possibilities of preserving linguistic unity. In *El castellano en América* (1901b), he examined the history of American Spanish, its status at the turn of the century, and its possible future, which he viewed with a certain degree of pessimism or, at least, skepticism.

Cuervo had enormous impact in the development of language studies in Latin America, professionally and ideologically. He is recognized as the founder of Latin American philology.[47] His writings, which considerably evolved throughout his career, reflect a unique effort to approach linguistic matters in a scientific manner. In the analysis of the local speech of his native Bogotá, he uncovered archaic lexical forms that had been incorrectly classified as American neologisms. Cuervo came to the defense of Latin American speakers who had been accused of corrupting the Spanish language, stating that historically Spaniards were responsible for bringing to America the linguistic practices that they then censored and ridiculed among Latin Americans. Over the years, as his professional and intellectual development expanded, Cuervo's view of American Spanish evolved. Nevertheless, some of his lessons and opinions strongly resonated with successors like Henríquez Ureña, especially the idea of combining scientific endeavors with patriotic duties. Another significant suggestion that resonated strongly in Henríquez Ureña's representation of Latin American cultural identity is Cuervo's idea that, except for four or five exceptions, Latin America no longer derived its intellectual inspiration from Spain.[48] Thus, in the origin and development of philology in Latin America, we see the consolidation of a scientific as well as political field.

The Internationalization of Hispanic Philology

The foundation of linguistic studies in Latin America owes a great deal to intellectuals like Cuervo and Bello, but also to their most immediate successors (of foreign extraction), the German linguists working in Chile, Friedrich Hanssen (1857–1919) and Rudolph (Rodolfo) Lenz (1863–1938). Hanssen contributed with studies on the systematic historical phonology of Spanish as well as on Old Spanish conjugation, syntax, dialectology, metrics, and textual criticism. Lenz advanced phonetic studies as well as research in historical phonology. Contributions such as Lenz's and Hanssen's benefited language studies in Latin America by developing more modern methods, but, more importantly, by increasing the exchange of scholarly information between European and Hispanic language scholars.[49]

Lenz, an honorary Chilean who immigrated from Germany in 1890, thought that Bello's and Cuervo's proposal of developing a scientific, psychological, synchronic grammar needed more work. According to Helmut Hatzfeld (1947), Lenz tried to advance in Latin America the idea that language study is not possible without a descriptive and experimental phonetics.[50] He insisted that training in phonetics was absolutely necessary in order to analyze, describe, locate, imitate, and correctly pronounce the sounds of present languages and dialects.[51] Lenz's *La oración y sus partes* (1920) is the culmination of efforts to modernize Bello and Cuervo. Other contributions by Lenz included *El español en Chile* (a collection of studies of Chilean Spanish published in Germany in 1891 and translated and edited by Amado Alonso in 1940) and *El diccionario etimológico de las voces chilenas derivadas de lenguas indígenas americanas* (1905–1910). Some of the issues considered by Lenz in *El español en Chile* would become fundamental in the next phase of language studies. Of particular interest are his observations on how the phonetic analysis of speech can be utilized in the characterization certain dialectal varieties and the nature of particular national groups. In *El español en Chile*, Lenz tried to demonstrate the scientific value of the study of popular speech. However, the main focus of this work was the influence of *araucano* in the pronunciation of Spanish in Chile and the following key question: "are today's Spanish-speaking Americans descendants of Spaniards, Indians, or other groups, or are they *mestizos* derived from distinct races?"[52]

While Cuervo (1876) elaborated the concept of the (linguistic) "base" of American Spanish, Lenz (1892–1893) was the one who formalized it.[53] For Lenz, the concept was enmeshed with other neogrammarian concepts such as ancient (pre-literary) speech, Vulgar Latin, original language, primary form, and nation, but he thought that this linguistic base was equivalent to the popular Spanish brought to America by Spanish colonizers. Cuervo's conceptualization was different. For the Colombian, the concept meant a particular dialect or the midpoint between educated speech and common everyday speech.[54] While a relatively simple concept in Cuervo, in Lenz's work it is more complex. Lenz equated the concept of "the linguistic base of Spanish" with the notion of "popular Spanish." *El habla del pueblo* (popular speech) is a type of speech that, unlike written classical Spanish, primarily represents the essence of a social group (i.e., the nation). Lenz's concept was laden with the Romantic meanings associated with folklore, nationalism, and the German tradition represented by Johann Herder:

> Clearly, the development of popular language in Spanish America can only be properly studied when we have collected all the words used by the people in every country... I do not lose hope that some of my old students from the Pedagogical Institute will take the initiative of collaborating in the elaboration of a popular Chilean Spanish Dictionary. It is a national patriotic task. And when has Chilean patriotism failed to achieve success in any task![55]

Lenz's linguistic nationalism had ethnolinguistic implications for his investigations. In his view, ethnological factors determined the aspiration of syllable final s in Chile and Argentina.[56] Lenz's (Romantic) views on the concept of the linguistic base, nonetheless, led to an important discussion on the conditions of development of American Spanish. Guitarte (1998) highlighted the importance of Lenz's role and the development of this concept and related issues in Hispanic philology. According to Guitarte, the problem was the reality of Spanish as a transplanted language. As such, it could not be explained simply as a geographical dialectal extension. Spanish developed in America through a handful of speakers that had minimal communication with their Peninsular counterparts. Therefore, the diverse historical circumstances and the process of acculturation prevented Spanish from following the same evolutionary patterns it did in Iberia. Instead, Spanish evolved from a new base, the new set of conditions it encountered in America.[57] Lenz's work contributed to the increased sophistication of language studies in Latin America. During the next phase of development in Hispanic philology, scholars (Alonso 1930, Henríquez Ureña 1921c and 1940) picked up his important theoretical concept of "base" in order to further elaborate it and use it for various purposes such as developing a polygenetic theory of American Spanish.

Ramón Menéndez Pidal and Linguistic Hispanism

Some intellectual figures become institutions onto themselves and in turn exert an enormous influence on others. Ramón Menéndez Pidal (1869–1968) was one such figure. The decline in German prestige after the First World War and the emergence of Menéndez Pidal's Madrid school of philology reflected a change in the intellectual climate surrounding research on Spanish. In an essay written in 1914, Henríquez Ureña described "Don" Ramón Menéndez Pidal as a model researcher.[58] The Spaniard Menéndez Pidal was a decisive figure whose philological and linguistic work was crucial in the development of Romance and Hispanic philology in the twentieth century. He took it upon himself to bridge the gap between the old tradition of Spanish philology and the (then) new science of Romance linguistics. His major contributions included *Manual elemental de gramática histórica española* (1904) and *Orígenes del español* (1926), which, as Henríquez Ureña (1922) asserted, were (and still are) the point of departure for every student of the history of the Spanish language.[59]

In *Manual*, using data from the *leonés* dialect, Menéndez Pidal anticipated what became more explicit in *Orígenes*, an integrated view of linguistic change that rendered the neogrammarian and dialectological perspectives compatible.⁶⁰ The general organization of the book, the proposed methodology, and the author's conception of language change were highly consistent with neogrammarian doctrine, or language science. In *Manual*'s chapters 2 and 3, Menéndez Pidal presents the linear phonetic changes that operated in the transformation of the standard Castilian form of Spanish from Latin. Despite dedicating one chapter (Chapter 4) to sporadic changes, the emphasis in the analysis and description is on the regularity of the phonetic changes. Accordingly, Menéndez Pidal focused on the most regular, most constant, and repeated aspects of phonetic evolution from Latin to Castilian.⁶¹ The prominence of regularity principles and the use of analogy to explain language change reflect a strict adherence to theoretical and methodological principles proposed by neogrammarians. Menéndez Pidal's *Manual* made the case—to Spanish readers—that Spanish could and should be studied scientifically. But, as José Del Valle (1997) argues, it also contributed to a vision of the language in which the heterogeneity of its past is absorbed by the consolidation of a homogeneous standard.⁶² According to Menéndez Pidal, "Castilian, having become the medium for the most important literary tradition in Spain and, most importantly, having absorbed the two most important Romance languages spoken in the Peninsula (*leonés* and *navarro-aragonés*), can be aptly called the Spanish language."⁶³ Later, the author adds: "This Hispano-Roman language, continuously and naturally evolved, is the same language that appears as a fully formed literary language in The Poem of the Cid, the same language that Alfonso the Wise perfected. It is essentially the same language in which Cervantes wrote."⁶⁴ In these statements we observe the emergence of a monumental image of Spanish grounded on a number of old linguistic documents as well as on the canon of Hispanism: El Cid, Alfonso X, and Cervantes.

Menéndez Pidal's *Orígenes* is a rigorous study of the political and linguistic history of Spain from the fall of the Visigothic monarchy in 711 to the end of the eleventh century. In *Orígenes*, Menéndez Pidal is no longer completely bound by the neogrammarian model. At this point, taking into account the contributions of modern geographical dialectology, he concluded that the focus should be not on sound laws but on word history. His extensive study of the evolution of words through many documents revealed that each word has its own history and the sum of the history of each of these words reveals to us the establishment of a sound law.⁶⁵ Menéndez Pidal further explained that, on the basis of the physiology and psychological reality of sounds, which are very similar for all humans, all sound changes may be characterized as spontaneous and natural. Yet, he insisted, every change in every country has its own particular history, which linguistics is bound to investigate.⁶⁶ History, as Menéndez Pidal saw it, corresponded with his concept of tradition, which constrains collective action and causes linguistic changes to yield one unique result. His investigations centered on those particular language forms that contributed to sustain or support his theory of tradition and *el estado latente* (cultural latency). As a result, certain dialects and geographical areas acquired greater relevance in his attempt to reconstruct the origin and development of Spanish since the Middle Ages.

José María López Sánchez (2006) suggests that the work of members of Mendendez Pidal's research team, particularly the elaboration of the Linguistic Atlas of the Iberian Peninsula and the writings of Amado Alonso on the linguistic classification of Catalan, aimed at legitimating a political unit and defining a historical tradition.[67] Although mindful of evolutionary conditions and language contact phenomena, Menéndez Pidal considered tradition as the spiritual nucleus that binds the history of the Spanish language and literature and allows for the uniform characterization of some of its most unique features. According to Menéndez Pidal, the Castilian temperament and its unique ("euphonic") features best represent this tradition and history of Spanish.[68] Del Valle (2004) argues that, for Menéndez Pidal, the old documents, philologically scrutinized in *Orígenes*, offered proof of Castile's destiny as the leading sociopolitical force in the history of Spain.[69] Menéndez Pidal wrote: "Some countries show a more natural and decidedly solid process of language stabilization. In this regard, Castile proved to be ahead of all related dialectal zones."[70] Proving this Castilian manifest destiny was important to Menéndez Pidal for a number of reasons, but primarily, as Del Valle points out: (i) to forge a positive image of Spain, the Spanish language, Spanish identity, and the civilization it had created over the centuries; and (ii) to neutralize the possible spread of fragmentation theory proposed by individuals like Cuervo and Bello.[71] Therefore, besides helping to stream into the Hispanic world some of the most intensely debated linguistic theories from Europe, *Manual* and *Orígenes* also articulated the interplay between theory and the ideological context. Del Valle (1997 and 2002b) shows how Menéndez Pidal's linguistic work (i.e., his description of the history of Spanish) is part of a project of constructing an image of the language, of the Spanish nation, and most relevant to Hispaonamericanism, of Spanish civilization, while establishing the canon of Hispanism.

Center for Historical Studies

Through his scholarly research, textual production, and various institutional roles Menéndez Pidal had tremendous impact on generations of scholars. He was the Professor of Romance Philology at the University of

Madrid (1899–1939) and also director of the Centro de Estudios Históricos (Center for Historical Studies) (1910–1936) in Madrid. Through this particular institution, he created a school of research, brought together a community of intellectuals and created a dialogue with his contemporaries. In this institution, he also designed programs, courses, research projects, methodology, and publications that contributed to the development of some of Spain's most renowned intellectuals in the twentieth century. The Center was the specific site where these scientific and patriotic efforts began to take shape (López Sánchez 2006). Created by the government agency La Junta para la Ampliación de Estudios, the Center's operations included the advancement of philological research, active participation in field research, the training of a select group of students in methodology, participation in scholarly conferences, the creation of a specialized library, and the establishment of relations with analogous institutions abroad.

From the school's inception, philological research received priority. For example, Menéndez Pidal encouraged Amado Alonso, who began translating into Spanish Wilhelm Meyer-Lübke's *Romance etymological dictionary* in the 1920s, to challenge the German scholar's classification of the Catalan language. The main issue of contention was whether certain Catalan phonetic features were wrongly attributed to substrate effects. According to Guitarte (1958a), this controversy agitated the philological community in the 1920s and it involved more than strict scientific considerations.[72] The discussion evaded the issue of how language contact phenomena created the type of linguistic continuum in this part of Europe that makes it possible to describe Catalan as a Gallo-Romance language, and Provençal as an Ibero-Romance language. Instead, both the German and the Spanish philologists insisted on pointing out the most radical grammatical differences between Catalan and Provençal. According to Guitarte, the problem originated from the then too common distinction between important and marginal European countries.[73] Guitarte argues that Meyer-Lübke tried to classify Catalan as a Gallo-Romance language believing that, in doing so, this speech community could claim the prestige of Provençal literature and the association with a European political powerhouse (France).[74] Amado Alonso objected to these arguments, claiming that historically and structurally Provençal belonged to the dialect continuum that includes Italian, Catalan, and Castilian.[75] Although theoretical issues were part of it, this controversy was also motivated by political and nationalistic concerns. In the identification and classification of these dialects, Catalan was assigned both a synchronic and political role as a buffer zone between Provençal and Spanish. The European cultural scale with which the Romanist operated assigned more social prestige to French language and tradition. The Hispanists sought to overturn this scale and reassert the status of Spanish.

Among the Center's other crowning achievements, we find *Revista de Filología Española* (1914), a successful journal that published some original works by its members and affiliates, such as Tomás Navarro Tomás's *Manual de pronunciación española* (1918), and translations of very important European linguistic texts, such as Meyer-Lübke's *Introducción al estudio de la lingüística romance* (1914). Through the edition and translation of Romance philology texts, Menéndez Pidal and his group were able to bring Hispanic philology up to date and adequately respond to trends in general linguistics. Since its inception, the *Revista* has won international recognition for the high quality of its scholarship.[76] Menéndez Pidal and his collaborators were also able to disseminate linguistic and cultural ideas and gain a legion of followers and supporters in Spain and abroad.

Menéndez Pidal also organized the Center's summer institute, which offered courses and seminars to foreigners dedicated to the teaching of Spanish. Menéndez Pidal referred to this program as a landmark event in the history of Hispanoamericanism.[77] Not only did the leading writers, philosophers, and philologists of Spain participate in the summer institute, but a select number of disciples, who were destined for academic posts in universities abroad, became lecturers or professors including Dámaso Alonso (Cambridge University), Federico de Onís (Columbia University), Antonio García Solalinde (University of Wisconsin), Samuel Gili Gaya (Middlebury College), and others.[78] Juan Gutiérrez Cuadrado (2007) referred to this project as the spread of linguistic Hispanism. In this climate, Menéndez Pidal carried out and promoted studies in the fields of Spanish literary tradition, the history of Spanish, and dialectology. Such studies provided Spanish intellectuals with opportunities to minimize the negative effects of the internal national crisis while simultaneously reaffirming the international image of Spain as a center of pan-Hispanic civilization. In a letter to Miguel de Unamuno Menéndez Pidal wrote in 1912:

> You believe that the best way to serve our country is by remaining in our posts as professors. But I believe that the best way to (rightfully) serve my nation's culture is by giving my all to my work at the Center of Historical Studies. There, I will be able to construct a piece of Spanish history which I shall then teach at the university tomorrow. Even if I were to become insane, I would not be able to teach this history, if did not exist... Therefore, I believe that the Center of Historical Studies, which is as much an official institution as any university, can do and has done more for Spanish culture than all the universities combined have done in the last three centuries.[79]

The Center's nation-building mission, of which Menéndez Pidal was fully aware, was what guaranteed the doctrinal orthodoxy.[80] Among all of them there was a strong commitment to the task of developing scientific studies in Spain for the greater glory of the nation.

Henríquez Ureña at the Center

At the Center, Menéndez Pidal created a school of philology with his first group of disciples, including Tomás Navarro Tomás, Federico de Onís and Américo Castro. By 1916, the Mexican Alfonso Reyes had also joined. Under his supervision and intellectual and moral authority, Menéndez Pidal was able to consolidate his role as founder of the Madrid school of philology, *La escuela de filología de Madrid*, which came to be recognized as such in approximately 1925.[81] Although not a homogeneous group, this school was bound by its members' absolute respect for its founder, a norm that characterized the behavior of the Center's researchers and prevented any form of criticism or departure from the school's fundamental doctrine.[82] While this is true, it is also true that Menéndez Pidal encouraged his students to pursue the study of new fields and endorsed new intellectual enterprises such as Henríquez Ureña's study of irregular verse, *La versificación irregular en la poesía castellana* (1920). Notably, the Spanish poet Enrique Diez Canedo (1897–1944) found it quite remarkable that such a "revolutionary" book was published by a conservative institution like the Center.[83]

There are many points of convergence and even disparities between Menéndez Pidal and Henríquez Ureña. It was after the start of this friendship and professional relationship with Menéndez Pidal that Henríquez Ureña began to sharpen his concept of a Hispanic-American culture, forged in the speech community. Contact between Henríquez Ureña and Menéndez Pidal first started in 1913: Henríquez Ureña had charged his brother Max with dispatching certain manuscripts and publications to Menéndez Pidal. Prior to his travels and studies in Spain, the Dominican intellectual was very familiar with Menéndez Pidal's philological and cultural work. Both scholars finally met in 1917 during Henríquez Ureña's first visit to Madrid. By then, Menéndez Pidal was well established as the leading scholar in philological and linguistic studies in the Hispanic world. For a while, Henríquez Ureña considered the possibility of relocating to Madrid. This city offered him the prospect of working along with a team of highly regarded intellectuals and reuniting with his closest friend, Alfonso Reyes; but, according to his biographers (Mateo 2001, Zuleta Álvarez 1996), the idea of earning only a minimal salary, along with fewer possibilities for professional advancement in Spain, discouraged him. On the other hand, Alfonso Reyes himself suggested that it was a personal crisis that prevented his friend and colleague from remaining in Spain.[84] Enrique Krauze suggests that Henríquez Ureña could not fathom how to overcome his marginal status as a Caribbean in European soil.[85] Unable to adapt to Spain, he returned to Minnesota in order to complete his doctorate and fulfill his teaching duties at the university.

In 1919, Henríquez Ureña was invited again to Spain. This time he remained in Madrid for a year in order to study and work at the Center under the sponsorship of Menéndez Pidal. At the Center, Henríquez Ureña worked as one of the editors of the *Revista* and cultivated friendships with Américo Castro and Tomás Navarro Tomás. Very little has been written about this substantially important period in Henríquez Ureña's intellectual and scholarly development. However, it is clear that editing and publishing his doctoral dissertation, *La versificación,* was one of his most important tasks. The book's prologue was written by Menéndez Pidal, an honor that helped to establish Henríquez Ureña's reputation as a scholar and as one of the original thinkers in the Hispanic world. During this second visit to Spain he also worked as one of the editors of the *Revista de Filología Española*. When the *Revista* was publicly criticized in Latin America, Henríquez Ureña came to its defense:

> I disagree with *Señor* Sanín Cano[86] that the objectives of the *Revista de Filología Española* are to discredit Latin American writers, bar them from publishing their work, and spread the notion that American speakers of Spanish are ruining the language... In Madrid, it is an open secret that the scholar Ramón Menéndez Pidal is not in the least responsible for the dictionaries published by the Academy.[87]

Henríquez Ureña expressed faith in that Menéndez Pidal's involvement would only result in the inclusion of more Americanisms in the Spanish Royal Academy's dictionary. In this defense, Henríquez Ureña was really waging battle on two fronts consisting of the Spanish Royal Academy's rejection of Americanisms and Latin Americans' distrust toward Spanish scholarship and intellectuals like Menéndez Pidal. Henríquez Ureña asserted that the journal's pages abounded with references to Bello and Cuervo and included among its contributors none other than the Mexican Alfonso Reyes.[88] These comments reveal Henríquez Ureña's admiration for Menéndez Pidal and his work and faith in the development of Hispanoamericanism. Henríquez Ureña strongly supported projects such as the *Revista* as a medium for advancing, in the Hispanic world, the study of language phenomena and understanding its diverse forms. Moreover, he believed that Menéndez Pidal, like Bello and Cuervo, was genuinely interested in the varieties of Spanish in the Americas. For that reason, he suggested to Latin American writers to send their work on any issue related to language and literature to Menéndez Pidal.[89] To Henríquez Ureña, the Spaniard's philological research was fundamental and needed to be incorporated for a proper account of linguistic Hispanoamericanism.

One cannot understand Henríquez Ureña's vision of Spain without taking into account Menéndez Pidal's influence. It was through Menéndez Pidal's inspirational and imposing philological monuments and theories that Henríquez Ureña then forged his vision of language, culture, and Spain. Both scholars also shared similarities in methodology. Like Menéndez Pidal, Henríquez Ureña found in literature the documentary base on which to reconstruct the history of Spanish and Hispanic civilization in the Latin American and Dominican contexts. They saw philology as a powerful means of combining studies on language, cultural history, and national identities. They both understood the history of language as well as literary history as part of a much greater historiographical project, documenting the most essential expressions of the past and preserving them as a road map for the future. We can appreciate Henríquez Ureña's interest in and admiration for Menéndez Pidal and his work in *En la orilla: mi España* (published in Mexico in 1922). Several passages in this book are dedicated to the appraisal and defense of the Madrid school and its director, Menéndez Pidal. To Henríquez Ureña, Menéndez Pidal and his group represented an elite group of intellectuals, "the new generation," that reaffirmed his *arcaica creencia* (old belief) that (high) culture saves nations.[90] As López Sánchez (2006) indicated, we find many points of connection between Menéndez Pidal's theoretical and methodological principles and Henríquez Ureña's initial linguistic investigations such as *Observaciones sobre el español en América* I (1921c). According to López Sánchez, these particular studies show the eagerness with which these researchers worked, scrutinizing the archaic features of Spanish, in order to affirm and justify Menéndez Pidal's concepts of traditionalism and cultural latency.[91] It was Menéndez Pidal, to paraphrase Gutiérrez Cuadrado (2007), who established the canon of linguistic Hispanism and organized its diffusion. In addition, Menéndez Pidal provided the theoretical base on which other Hispanic linguists began their studies of Spanish. For example, in Henríquez Ureña own account of Dominican Spanish we find traces of Menéndez Pidal's descriptive and explicatory statements on how the imposition of Castilian hegemony and the preservation of some linguistic archaisms were crucial to the development of Spanish in Iberia. For example, Menéndez Pidal wrote: "In our period of struggle for Castilian hegemony, archaisms such as the use of vowels in post-tonic or pre-tonic positions were prevalent in many regions. Even in Castile, until the first half of the twelfth century, we find archaisms such as *poblato* (village, modern Spanish *poblado*) in the written language of the educated."[92] Also consider the following statement by Menéndez Pidal: "New linguistic forms, even after gaining wide acceptance, do not have sufficient strength to displace the old forms that persist in the memory of the speakers."[93] Menéndez Pidal established a strict correlation between maintaining a political hegemony and the survival and spread of linguistic archaisms. We can clearly hear echoes of Menéndez Pidal in Henríquez Ureña's *Papa y batata: historia de dos palabras* (1938c), a text that includes an analysis of the evolution of the word *patata* (potato) in Spain:

> When did *papa* begin to displace the noun *patata?* Very early, judging by what happened in other [European] languages such as English by the end of the sixteenth century. Naturally, the similarity between roots and tubers also played a role in this process of change. In Spain, the coexistence of two forms, one beginning with b and the other with p, shows that there was a need to distinguish conceptually between the two objects, assigning to each one a specific noun. Thus, the adoption of the noun *patata* for the one belonging to the Solanaceae family was initially conditioned by a preference for the partial homophony created by *papa* . . . Parmentier's propaganda was indeed effective. And as often happens in cases of change in the Spanish language, Castile, the great dissident power, introduces the innovation.[94]

As in Menéndez Pidal's linguistic description in *Orígenes,* the researcher links the development of a particular linguistic form with the Castilian temperament. The personal beliefs, which emanated from careful reflection and collaboration with prestigious figures such as Menéndez Pidal, would also guide Henríquez Ureña's initial and subsequent approach to matters of language and culture in the contexts of Latin America and the Dominican Republic. To an extent, Menéndez Pidal was successful in engaging the Spanish and Latin American intellectual elite in what Del Valle (2002b) calls the project of constructing a "modern" Hispanic community.[95] *Hispanomamericanistas* from both sides of the Atlantic, working within different institutions and disagreeing with respect to the pan-Hispanic community's hierarchical structure, became involved in this project. During the course of the project, a number of polemic cultural and linguistic issues took center stage including the fear of the possible linguistic fragmentation of Spanish.

The Philological Institute of Buenos Aires

The Instituto de Filología de Buenos Aires (Philological Institute of Buenos Aires), modeled on Madrid's Center, was founded in 1923. Menéndez

Pidal and Ricardo Rojas, the Dean of the University of Buenos Aires, had created the initial vision for the Institute. Américo Castro was its first director; however, after a brief period he stepped aside and recommended the young Amado Alonso. In time, Amado Alonso and his collaborators transformed it into an internationally renowned center of research that was up-to-date with the trends in linguistics. In his inaugural address, Rojas alluded to one of the Institute's primary objectives, which was to resolve the controversy between Peninsular and American dialects of Spanish.[96] Although following the spirit of its model, under the directorship of Amado Alonso (1927–1946) and the collaboration of scholars such as Henríquez Ureña, the Institute developed its own image and character and rose to unprecedented international prominence as a center for Hispanic studies.[97] Yakov Malkiel attributed the Institute's success to Amado Alonso's "unique" personal charisma and effective management style.[98] Amado Alonso had trained in instrumental phonetics at Hamburg, and was well versed in historical grammar and dialectology. He brought to Argentina the nascent structural-functional linguistic theories of the time, by introducing and translating into Spanish fundamental texts, including Ferdinand de Saussure's *Course in General Linguistics* (1916), Karl Vossler's (1872–1949) *Philosophy of language* (1940), and Charles Bally's (1865–1947) *Le langage et la vie* (1913).

Amado Alonso (1943 and 1945) understood the profound differences between the old school of linguistics represented by August Schleicher and the new trends represented by Saussure's work. According to Amado Alonso, Saussure rejected Schleicher's conceptualization of language as an autonomous and self-regulated biological organism and replaced it with the idea of a language as an equally autonomous formal system, impervious to the individual communicative needs of its speakers.[99] Amado Alonso conceptualized these differences from a point of view that was opposed to Positivism. A few decades of reaction against Positivism prompted an evaluation of the limits of the two theories under consideration.[100] While Saussure expressed a view of language as a system that should be studied as a self-contained structure (*langue*) and separate from individual expression (*parole*), Amado Alonso, following Vossler's school of "linguistic idealism," emphasized the need to conceptualize language as a product of individual creation that hinges on the complicated life of a community.[101] Iorgu Iordan (1970) explains the difference between the two linguistic schools of thought. While Positivist linguists were dividing up grammar into phonology, morphology, syntax, et cetera, for a more convenient and systematic study of language, idealists thought that it was the "spirit" of language that constituted and integrated the sounds and words of sentences.[102] On one hand, Positivists conceptualized linguistic research as an end in itself. On the other, idealists were preoccupied with determining relations of causality between the facts of language.[103] This latter conceptualization of language became very influential among the new generation of linguists in Buenos Aires and to a certain extent determined their approach to the study of language.

Amado Alonso's best-known associate during these years was Henríquez Ureña. Through this association Henríquez Ureña acquired firsthand knowledge of some of these latest trends in linguistics. With the collaboration of important figures such as Lenz, the research team led by Amado Alonso and Henríquez Ureña carried out an important project that marked the inauguration of Latin American dialectology: a series of language studies entitled *Biblioteca de Dialectología Hispanoamericana*. In the first volume, Amado Alonso expressed that one of their main objectives was to aim to bring together all the scattered dialectological studies related to popular American Spanish and begin some new investigations.[104] The program for dialectological research that was developed at the Institute might have been a response to new trends in linguistics, but it was still guided by the desire to develop solutions to old problems in Hispanic linguistics.

Linguistic Polemics in Buenos Aires

The fear of linguistic fragmentation provoked interest in some of the lesser known characteristics of American Spanish and a vigilant attitude among some scholars. For example, Amado Alonso felt that, without the support of educated people and the proper reflection on language, young Argentineans were bound to propagate the myth of the uniquely Argentinean character of Buenos Aires speech.[105] For his part, Américo Castro had manifested some of his apprehensions as early as 1924. He gravely warned Argentineans of the likely assault on popular speech by immigrants' slang filled with words from the lexicon of uneducated speakers of dialects such as Genovese and mixed Spanish-Portuguese forms.[106] Again, in 1941, Castro complained about the absence of hierarchical values associated to literary traditions that could regulate linguistic practices in Argentina and put a halt to foreign influences. Both Castro and Amado Alonso attributed the linguistic irregularities, or what they called "linguistic chaos" in Buenos Aires to the plebeian tendencies of the period, a break from linguistic (and literary) tradition in Spanish America, and the slow rise of Argentina's stock as a colony, and the massive influx of immigrants.[107]

Castro and Amado Alonso particularly focused on the young and innovative generation of Argentine writers, whom they made partly responsible as the source and for the spread of irregularities in Buenos Aires speech. Amidst several ideological conflicts with different cultural groups, many of these local writers and intellectuals were indeed emphasizing the uniqueness of Spanish in Argentina: "We write poorly because our aim is not to be able to write well. We know our style is irregular, foul, and spontaneous. But we are understood by everyone, including the security guard up the corner."[108] Their argument was first elaborated by Luciano Abeille (1900) in his controversial book, *El idioma nacional de los argentinos*, and was based on the following convictions: (i) every autonomous nation is entitled to its own language; (ii) the national language must be based on a strictly Argentinean model (i.e., the *gaucho*); and (iii) Buenos Aires or *Porteño* speech, as the repository of democratic values and the revolutionary Argentinean character, must spread throughout the country. In contrast, some Spanish (and Argentinean) intellectuals (Capdevilla 1928, Costa Álvarez 1928) argued that such ideas contradicted the actual sociolinguistic landscape in Argentina and undermined social cohesiveness.

The Spaniards' linguistic apprehensions and the Argentineans' linguistic nationalism roused the attention of local observers like Jorge Luís Borges (1928, 1961) who maintained a relatively objective position throughout this controversy: "What insurmountable gap exists between Iberian Spanish and Argentinean speech? None, I believe, fortunately for our mutual comprehension. There is, however, a shade of differences, slight but particular nuances that represent our homeland."[109] To Borges, the so-called linguistic differences that alarmed the Spaniards and invigorated the Argentineans were not formal but simply stylistic. In his *Las alarmas del doctor Américo Castro* (1961), Borges responded with an insightful reflection on the use of the word "problem" in relation to language. Borges declared that the so-called linguistic problems affecting certain speech communities were the invention of language professionals who needed to justify their means of subsistence by telling others how to conduct their linguistic practice: "Our problems do not stem from dialects but from dialectological institutes. These institutions earn a living by condemning the same gobbledygook they manufacture."[110] We can infer from Borges's admonition that the chief preoccupation of those Spanish linguists working in Buenos Aires in the 1930s was the preservation of a particular linguistic norm. To Amado Alonso, there is no culture without norms and principles, just barbarism.[111] While Castro and Amado Alonso displayed different attitudes in Buenos Aires, they converged on some explanations. According to Amado Alonso, the disadvantages that Buenos Aires faced in relation to the Spanish America and Spain included its incredible demographic growth and its condition as colossal migrant camp: "In this maelstrom of activity, the tiny minority that cultivates the educated linguistic tradition is scattered and hardly taken into account."[112] Castro generally agreed with Amado Alonso's description with the following caveat. Castro believed that the alterations caused by immigrants are due less to their demographic pressure and habitual actions than to the internal social conditions of the host country and its inadequate self-image.[113] More specifically, according to Castro, the absence of ideal speakers in Buenos Aires was directly related to the lack of a hierarchical social structure in Argentina.[114] Elvira N. de Arnoux (2001) observed that in these views we can find echoes of Enlightenment thought as it had been formulated by Bello.[115] And in fact, Amado Alonso preferred to be identified with Bello rather than with his Iberian colleagues and mentors. A century earlier, Bello had described language as a "well-ordered system" and as a constituent of orderly and prosperous (civilized) societies and national states. Amado Alonso and Henríquez Ureña, to different degrees, were still working within the tradition of grammarians, philologist, and linguists who believed that it was possible to discipline the mind (and society) by rationalizing linguistic phenomena, regimenting language, preserving the norm, and rejecting illegitimate uses.

Viewing the situation from this perspective, Amado Alonso suggested possible ways to approach these linguistic issues. Among them was restoring linguistic hierarchy. The Academy,[116] in particular, represented the social institution most suited for sanctioning language use. In a series of statements, Amado Alonso suggested that the best way to contend with linguistic anarchy was a return to a previous linguistic order, akin to when courtly norms or the metropolis would presumably regulate sociolinguistic patterns: "Archaisms in literature always represent legitimate tradition, transmission, and continuity."[117] Adhering to previously established linguistic norms, albeit archaic, offered the best possibility for the transmission and continuity of the most adequate means of expressions.[118] Similar proposals would be considered in the discussion of the particular language "problems" of Spanish America, even with respect to questions of substrate influences in different dialects of Spanish.

The polemic regarding the peculiarities and status of Spanish in Buenos Aires is one particular context that gives meaning to Henríquez Ureña's work. Some of his own data were utilized to support the polemicists' counter arguments. Castro, for example, acknowledged that Henríquez Ureña, using Cuervo's views as a point of departure, had analyzed the use of the pronoun *vos* (you-singular) as a dialectological and historical problem in the *Revista de Filología Hispánica* (1921). In the same statement, Castro insinuated that Henríquez Ureña provided evidence against the acceptance of *vos* by the upper class in Buenos Aires.[119] Henríquez Ureña did, in fact, discuss the development and distribution of *voseo* (the use of *vos*), however, it was within the context of his initial stance against the theory of Andalusian origins.[120] Thus, Castro slightly mischaracterized Henríquez Ureña's description of *voseo*. With his respective studies, the Dominican sought to shed light on many of these linguistic issues but cautioned about the problem of generalizing too much with insufficient data.[121]

Key Questions in Hispanic Linguistics

Having reviewed the contributions and concerns of some of the principal figures in Hispanic linguistics and philology, we identify the following as the central themes in the development of the discipline: (i) the unity or possible fragmentation of Spanish, (ii) substratum influences in American Spanish, (iii) the peculiarities and status of American Spanish, and (iv) the question of the origins of Spanish (Andalusian versus polygenetic). In most cases, each of these key questions emerged in the work of Hispanic linguists who were articulating nationalism and Hispanoamericanism and defining the postcolonial relationship between former Latin American colonies and Spain.

As discussed earlier, the fragmentation debate consisted of a preoccupation by scholars with preserving the existing unity of Spanish. For Cuervo, Spain's loss of power and influence over the Hispanic nations, Latin Americans' disregard for Spanish literature and preference for French and English literary trends, the lack of consensus among Latin American and Spanish intellectuals, the lack of a pan-Hispanic linguistic norm, and the evolving nature of language represented obstacles to the preservation of the relative unity. Whether desired or not, Cuervo emphasized the linguistic conditions of Spanish in the Americas that would lead to fragmentation, for which there was an historical antecedent (the split of Latin). However, intellectuals such as Valera and Menéndez Pidal rejected his reasoning, claiming, among other things, that the correct image of the Spanish language, the Spanish nation, and the Hispanic community would preserve the linguistic unity.

After Lenz formulated his thesis of Spanish with Araucanian sounds in Chile, some linguists (Alonso 1939, Malmberg 1947, Rosenblat 1954, Wagner 1924) set out to refute or establish the limits of his statement. Ángel Rosenblat, for example, studied the distribution of population (Indian, black, white, and *mestizos*) in the different regions of Latin America in order to determine the degree of acculturation and possible substrate influence. The German-born Romance philologist Max Leopold Wagner (1880–1952) admitted that many of the Auracanian phonetic features described by Lenz were, in fact, Hispanic in origin. However, Wagner maintained that there were some exceptions such as the pronunciation of the consonant r, the prepalatal articulation of the consonant cluster tr, and the alveolar pronunciation of consonants d, t, n, s when in contact with r. Wagner went on to propose that there were influences in the lexicon from indigenous Caribbean languages. In contrast, Alonso declared that all of these supposed substrate features could be explained within the system of Spanish.[122] This tendency among Hispanic philologists to question or reject the validity of substratum theory dated back to the controversy on the classification of Catalan.

"The problem of language," as formulated by Alonso in the Buenos Aires context, focuses on certain aspects of language that were connected with aspects of social structure. Obviously, scholars like Amado Alonso, Castro, and Henríquez Ureña were interested in understanding theoretical issues and finding scientific solutions to sociolinguistic problems. For example, they sought to develop effective strategies and texts for teachers who were responsible for providing their students with tools that they needed (i.e., knowledge of standard Spanish plus the metalinguistic knowledge necessary for academic success) in order to be successful in their communities. However, they were also eager to participate in and settle particular conflicts in favor of a certain sociopolitical order, specific communities, and particular interests. In Amado Alonso's and Castro's discussion of Buenos Aires speech, we observe their specific attempts to settle local and international linguistic conflicts in order to banish the idea of a national language, other than traditional Spanish, determine who should control the linguistic (literary) market in Argentina, control the spread of Buenos Aires speech along the River Plate region (Montevideo, Uruguay), and prevent linguistic fragmentation as well as the spread of fragmentation theory.

American Spanish against the *Andalucismo* Machine

The question of the alleged Andalusian character of American Spanish is closely associated with the figure of Henríquez Ureña. The *andalucismo* debate began over opposing views on the origin and development of Spanish in the New World (Danesi 1977, Del Valle 1998, Guitarte 1958a, Izzo 1984). The traditional view proposed that American Spanish was a continuation of Spanish from Andalucia and not of the slightly different northern Peninsular varieties. As evidence, *andalucistas* pointed out that, like Andalusians, many American speakers of Spanish (i) merged the palatal consonants ll and y, pronouncing words such as *poyo* (stone bench) and *pollo* (chicken) as *pollo*; (ii) merged syllable-final l and r, pronouncing words such as *alma* (soul) and *arma* (weapon) as *alma*; (iii) abandoned the distinction between the alveolar s and interdental θ in favor of s, pronouncing words such as *casa* (home) and *caza* (hunt) as *casa*; and (iv) aspirated syllable-final /s/, pronouncing words such as *después* (after) as *dehpueh*. Presumably, these similarities between the two dialects were the result of the predominance of Andalusian settlers in America. But to the defenders of the diversity and category of "American Spanish," only a minority of settlers came from Andalucia. Furthermore, they argued that the features in question developed independently within each linguistic subsystem. This polemic reached its zenith in the 1920s and 1930s with Henríquez Ureña's and Alonso's contributions, which were developed over both linguistic and ideological grounds.

Henríquez Ureña's most important linguistic work includes *Observaciones sobre el español en América* I (1921c) and *El supuesto andalucismo de América* (1925a). These two articles were part of the well-known polemic sustained with Wagner on the genesis of American Spanish. Wagner, in his 1920 article *El español en America y el latín vulgar*, began by reformulating the question that had been already raised by Cuervo: To what extent is it possible to equate the split of Latin into the family of Romance languages to the allegedly possible rupture of Spanish into semiautonomous varieties? Pioneers such as Friedrich Hanssen, Menéndez Pidal,[123] and Navarro Tomás had not yet expressed formal views on the subject but were inclined in favor of highlighting unity by focusing on the strong mutual affinity of Andalusian and American dialects of Spanish and the supposed Andalusian demographic predominance in the New World.[124] However, these authors were only able to provide mostly incidental and impressionistic statements. Cuervo (1901b) had stated his belief in the equal demographic representation of all sections of Spain in the colonization of America. Wagner and the *andalucistas* claimed that American Spanish was an Andalusian dialect of Spanish. To Latin American scholars such as Henríquez Ureña, *andalucistas* ignored the wealth and significance of details concerning American Spanish.

Henríquez Ureña and Amado Alonso objected to the *andalucista* claim on philological and demographic grounds and advanced what came to be known as "the polygenetic theory," the belief that Spanish in the Americas developed its characteristics as a result of many (specifically) American conditions of development. Amado Alonso attempted to provide the linguistic evidence in support of Henríquez Ureña's argument, which was developed in a series of publications, including the three-part series *Observaciones sobre el español en América* (1921c, 1930b, and 1931). They both claimed that, while Spanish settlers brought an emergent *seseo* (use of the s sound instead of the θ variant) to America, the phenomenon developed amidst new social conditions and independently of the Peninsular linguistic norm. Henríquez Ureña utilized the available demographic evidence to show that the Spaniards who settled in America were from different points of origin and not predominantly from Andalusia:

> Before so much diversity, America's *andalucismo,* one of the most widely held beliefs, fails. This so called *andalucismo* exists, above all, in the lowland regions. It is the result of independent development and not of direct influence from southern Spain. The idea of *andalucismo* has worked its way into the debate inadvertently and where we least expect it. For example, Menéndez Pidal writes in *Gramática Histórica* on page eighty-seven: "characteristic of Andalusia, therefore American."[125]

In response to Henríquez Ureña's argument against this view of American Spanish, Wagner refined the *andalucista* hypothesis by proposing that all of southern Spain provided the speech forms in question to Spanish America. Henríquez Ureña countered that mere similarity between two dialects did not necessarily imply the descent of one from the other. In order to demolish what he called "the dialectological *andalucismo* machine in America," the Dominican dialectologist repeatedly tried to make his case on the authority of Cuervo and reiterated the Colombian's famous phrase "The entire Peninsula is represented in America's population."[126] The basic idea behind Henríquez Ureña's reformulation of Cuervo's phrase is that the Spaniards brought a number of varieties of Spanish to America that subsequently developed under new conditions and mixing among the settlers. However, as Guitarte points out, Cuervo's statement, read in its proper context, does not constitute an absolute rejection of the *andalucista* hypothesis, as Henríquez Ureña argued.[127] Guitarte observed that, in *El castellano en América,* Cuervo gave an account of the colonizers' diverse origins in order to simply show that many of them did not bring the Spanish spoken in Castile as their native language and not to necessarily make a case against *andalucismo*.[128] In fact, Cuervo did not have such a rigid concept of American Spanish. To him, the Spanish variety spoken by Americans was the result of language leveling, a koiné. According to Cuervo, although some Peninsular groups and provincialisms were more notable than others, mutual comprehension was the general rule.[129] Nevertheless, in several subsequent publications, Henríquez Ureña continued to mischaracterize the Colombian philologist's position, insisting that he had settled the question by establishing clear facts.[130] The Dominican pressed on, advancing the misconception that Cuervo had settled the question in favor of the *antiandalucistas* and meticulously assembled every piece of information that could be extracted from the early colonial chroniclers to prove Cuervo right. Many respected philologists such as Alwin Kuhn, Bertil Malmberg, and Serafim de Silva Neto accepted the *antiandalucista* position and eventually even Wagner came to embrace it.[131] Henríquez Ureña concluded that the Andalusians were not predominant during colonial times, and as a result they could not have imposed their dialect in America.

Guitarte[132] points out that Henríquez Ureña's insistence on Cuervo's alleged conclusion stems from an affective predisposition on the part of the Dominican. His position with respect to this linguistic debate was relatively consistent with his devotion toward his nineteenth-century intellectual predecessors from Latin America. While this is true, we must also remember that, at this juncture, Henríquez Ureña was still closely collaborating with the *Ateneo*[133] group that tried to establish the intellectual independence and unique character of Latin America. Henríquez Ureña's position in this debate was also consistent with the ideas and beliefs held by the modernist proponents of the original character of Latin America vis-a-vis those who postulated Spain as the principal source of culture and tradition in America. At a time when many Europeans and North Americans could not even fathom the concept of an autonomous Latin American culture while others tended to mythify it, *ateneistas* such as Alfonso Reyes and Henríquez Ureña dedicated a major portion of their work to establishing and expanding Latin American culture. Throughout this series of writings on the subject, Henríquez Ureña's stern tone is unequivocal. By demolishing the *andalucismo* machine, Henríquez Ureña and colleagues were hoping to undo the presumed inequality of Latin American nations in relation to Spain and this country's necessary cultural domination over them. In this enterprise, it is important to also keep in mind the significance of figures such as Cuervo and Bello for Latin American intellectuals. Henríquez Ureña found in the work of Bello, for example, the expression of a uniquely Latin American desire for cultural and intellectual independence:

> In a time of doubt and hope, when political independence had not yet been fully achieved, the peoples of Hispanic America declared themselves intellectually of age, made their own life their "proper study," and set out on the quest for self-expression. Our poetry, our literature, was to be a genuine expression of ourselves. Europe was old; here was a new life, a new world for freedom and enterprise and song. Such was the intent and meaning of the great Ode, the first of the *Silvas Americanas*, published by Andrés Bello in 1823.[134]

To Henríquez Ureña, Andrés Bello, Eugenio María de Hostos, and José Rufino Cuervo stood as symbols of the highest and most original form of intellectual achievement in Latin America. Bearing this in mind, Henríquez Ureña likely felt compelled to prove Cuervo right, at all cost, even with respect to claims that he wrongly attributed to the Colombian philologist. Henríquez Ureña's participation in this debate demonstrates the degree to which certain ideological *hispanoamericanista* positions and, more specifically, an intellectual climate determined the direction and outcome of some of Henríquez Ureña's linguistic investigations.

Henríquez Ureña's Linguistic Production

Henríquez Ureña's association with Amado Alonso and the Philological Institute of Buenos Aires resulted in a series of publications that constitute the bulk of the Dominican's linguistic and philological oeuvre. However, his contributions to language studies had already begun by the time he was at the Center in Madrid. Although, for the purpose of this study, I have divided his linguistic production into two major categories (American Spanish and Dominican Spanish), the major linguistic issues of each text always intersect with the central themes of linguistic Hispanoamericanism.

Interestingly, when Meyer-Lübke was making a case for substratum influence, proposing a classification of the Dominican dialect of Spanish as a Creole, one of the first scholars to take issue with this specific proposal was Henríquez Ureña (1919). "La lengua en Santo Domingo: rectificación a Meyer-Lübke," was in fact his first official foray into formal linguistic issues and polemics:

> In his Introduction to Romance Linguistics, translated into Spanish by *Don* Américo Castro as *Introducción al estudio de la lingüística romance* (1914: see pages. 37–38), Meyer-Lübke writes: "Thus we find black Spanish in Santo Domingo and Trinidad." This is a totally erroneous affirmation, at least with respect to Santo Domingo. It does not correspond with the facts. I have never seen this account published anywhere else. I can only explain this characterization as a result of an automatic but mistaken association with Haiti, which he had just described in previous [pages]. I must make this clarification not only because of the authority granted to Meyer-Lübke's book, but because Santo Domingo has also been omitted in Mr. Ford's recent and notable book, *Main Currents of Spanish* (1919) where he describes Spanish-speaking regions of America. This omission by the Harvard professor may have been motivated by Meyer-Lübke's mistaken assertion.[135]

Henríquez Ureña refuted the claim in the strongest possible terms and added that there was no documentary source for it:

There is no supporting evidence in any of the works cited by Meyer-Lübke in his book, not even, as we would expect in F. A. Coelho's *Dialectos románicos, ou neolatinos na Africa, Asia e América* (1881). Perhaps, the error comes from Baist's[136] "Die spanische Sprache," in *Grundiss d. romanischen Philologie*, compiled by Grober.[137]

Henríquez Ureña wanted to prevent the identification of the Dominican speech community with Creole languages, which were typically associated with "low cultures." In discussions regarding Creoles, this was almost always the immediate concern. For example, Lenz (1928) remarked that Papiamentu was a language of high culture, compared to other Creoles, which function as a means of communication between "low culture groups" such as blacks, Malay, Indian coolies, Chinese and "European groups" such as the Portuguese, Spanish, English, French, and Dutch.[138] Interest in Creole languages emerged at the end of the nineteenth century and the beginning of the twentieth century as the disciplines of folklore and philology converged. Iris Bachmann[139] (2007) has observed how tension began to invade certain quarters of the scientific community as some European linguists began to use the category of race as a descriptive tool. There was considerable debate regarding the extent to which researchers could determine African influences on Atlantic Creole languages. The positions ranged from the claim that there was no relevant influence besides a few lexical items to the contrary opinion that Creole languages clearly exhibited strictly African grammars. Henríquez Ureña adopted the former position. He repeatedly refuted the identification of Dominican Spanish with these low social prestige Creole languages.

As noticed in both the Catalan controversy and the Spanish Creole discussion, the image of Spanish became a major concern among Spanish and Latin American philologists, who wanted to change the negative views of their countries held by Europeans and North Americans.[140] There was also a change in their intellectual attitude. By then, they no longer first looked to greater Europe for scholarly authority. In fact, they felt it was their task to improve the Romanists' vision and theories of the Spanish-speaking world. According to Yakov Malkiel (1962), language studies had advanced so much in the Hispanic world that Hispanic researchers no longer felt compelled to simply adopt foreign theories and methodologies but were developing creative alternatives that they deemed more suitable for the realities of the Hispanic world.[141] Through many of these debates, Hispanists had come to form a close intellectual fellowship and were asserting their theoretical views. As they acquired better knowledge about the dialectal reality of the Spanish-speaking world, Hispanic scholars felt that it was time to abandon or at least reconsider substratum theory. The focus in research began to shift to specific phenomena (*seseo, yeísmo,* the leveling of liquids consonants r and l, etc.) and other theories *(andalucismo, antiandalucismo).*

While the majority of Henríquez Ureña's texts are not strictly theoretical, his article "El lenguaje" (1930) shows that he was familiar with the latest theoretical trends in linguistics and knew the importance of a sound theoretical-methodological apparatus. For example, in his discussion of Saussure, he emphasized the value of focusing on the systematicity of language and incorporating the advances of the linguistic science.[142] Even with the new linguistic trends and concepts at his disposal, Henríquez Ureña was adamant about not forgetting the old lessons from "the wise masters." He maintained solidarity with the old Madrid school, highly praising the latest work of its director, "Don" Ramón Menéndez Pidal.[143] While he certainly was able to elaborate key concepts and hone his skills as a language researcher during his tenure at the Institute in Buenos Aires, many different sources, experiences, and people contributed to Henríquez Ureña's development as a linguist.

Between 1938 and 1939, Amado Alonso and Henríquez Ureña published *Gramática castellana* (Volumes I and II), two landmark texts that helped cement a tradition of language teaching in Argentina and South America in the twentieth century. Specifically directed to language teachers and presented as a product of the latest advances in linguistics, the authors were also careful to frame their Grammar within the tradition of Bello.[144] They expressed their objective in the following terms: "The purpose of this pedagogy is for students to learn to speak and write their own language correctly, always reflecting their capacity for effective thinking."[145] These texts were a commercial and pedagogical success. Even though they were well received by intellectuals such as Borges, they still contributed to the linguistic polemic in Buenos Aires. As indicated previously, local intellectual figures reacted against the negative characterization of Buenos Aires speech.[146] It appears that Henríquez Ureña's role in this particular controversy was less prominent than Amado Alonso's.[147] While the Dominican was also moved by the same ideological concerns, he was more constrained in his description of the linguistic realities of the Buenos Aires of the 1920s and 1930s:

> We all agree that this variety of Spanish has undergone changes. Some changes are the result of natural evolution such as the variable use of *vos* and *tú* and its corresponding verbal forms. Other changes stem from the influence of indigenous languages, especially at the lexical level. The lexicon is also affected by popular literature and contact with immigrant languages. Thus, we find: Gallicisms such as *marrón, locatorio, es phrohibido* and Italianisms such as *yeta, pálpito, voy del medico,* [among others].[148]

In this particular case, Henríquez Ureña was more mindful of the interplay of diatopic, diastratic, and diaphasic variation and language contact situations, and more sensitive to the complexity of linguistic phenomena:

> As in Madrid, we find superimposed strata in Buenos Aires. For example, there are bilingual neighborhoods where Spanish is contaminated by Neapolitan or Yiddish. And there is Boca, a major site of the Lunfardo language, which has had a major impact on popular speech and is slowly but steadily reaching educated speech.[149]

Yet, as Arnoux (2001) argues, *Gramática castellana,* Amado Alonso's *El problema de la lengua en América* (1935) and Henríquez Ureña Narciso Binayan's pedagogical manual *El libro del idioma* (1927), outline a pedagogical program that is sociopolitical in nature. This program aimed at regulating people's reflections on language and language use, controlling the interplay of intellect and emotion, and persuading the public as to the value of linguistic unity and homogeneity in the culturally diverse Hispanic world.[150] In other words, these researchers were engaged in language planning. In these grammars and manuals, Arnoux argues, these scholars sought to create effective strategies as well as rational and logical discourse on language that would enable students, teachers, writers, and speakers to better deal with "the problem of language," or as Amado Alonso saw it, the profusion, extension, and "impunity of errors."[151] In Amado Alonso's view, language professionals had to intervene and develop ways to approach these diverging linguistic practices in the context of Buenos Aires. Obviously, Henríquez Ureña was very much attuned to all these sociolinguistic matters and sought to make his contribution.

In Henríquez Ureña's research on the history of American Spanish, we find the following central themes: *andalucismo* versus polygenesis, the dialectal zones of Spanish America, and the indigenous element as a determining factor in the American speech communities. In his treatment of these subjects we can delineate a sociopolitical conception of language. In other words, Henríquez Ureña viewed the linguistic sign as intricately connected to the extralinguistic environment in which social and political forces had an enormous impact. What was the nature of the extralinguistic environment that Henríquez Ureña used to explain linguistic facts? Throughout his entire linguistic work, the most important determining extralinguistic factor was the effect of high culture; specifically, it was the leading sociopolitical force in the history of a society. This concept of the linguistic form and view of language in history was prevalent among these language researchers in the Buenos Aires of the 1920s and 1930s. It is illustrated in Alonso's discussion of the social groups that are most able to intervene and solve important language problems, in which an argument is made in favor of the group with most cultural capital, "a small circle, made up of literary professionals, scientists, and the most gifted people."[152] According to Alonso, this social group is not only intellectually prepared for these tasks, but they also exhibit the only appropriate attitude toward sociolinguistic phenomena. In other words, they have a proper sense of the norm. In such a social landscape, docile speakers must allow this specialized group to operate unperturbed in the various linguistic domains. Amado Alonso described it in the following terms:

> The preexisting condition must be the active participation in society of that relatively prominent cultural group. The individuals that make up this group essentially consider literary principles a natural extension of thinking. The existence and participation of this core group are not enough ... The generalization of literariness requires certain permeability in the social spheres that surround the increasingly alienated but intellectually privileged social group. What was signified to in Latin as [*docilitas*] *enseñabilidad* (receptiveness to teaching), this permeability is nothing else but obedience. It is merely the external manifestation of a especially personal and responsive attitude towards linguistic phenomena; it means having a sense of the norm.[153]

This explanation reveals a specific language attitude on the part of the language specialist. This attitude, repeated and reformulated in various contexts, became Amado Alonso's and Henríquez Ureña's linguistic ideology, according to which language was also understood as a primary instrument in the symbolic domination of subordinate groups: "The speech habits of an educated man become the norm for everyone else, as long as they represent normality among the ruling social group."[154] Initially, these previous statements simply suggest that linguistic norm-setters can and should exert their influence over the practices of speakers. However, after further scrutiny and comparisons with other reflections on language, we observe the recurrence of certain principles (normality, educability, character, loyalty, effectiveness) that can be applied to language use and many related forms of social practice and that require the active leadership of the dominant group as well as the proper recognition by the dominated groups. Henríquez Ureña (1930) expressed similar ideas:

> Language is not only evolution but also perseverance. To the speakers, language is strictly a fixed system. Of course, it is conditioned by the surrounding social sphere and each person speaks according to his or her condition. When a society develops its culture and power, the language of the dominant groups spreads, multiplies, and becomes the object of desire for the people. Writing helps to fix it. Finally, grammars appear, helping to

institute what is considered the "best" model while the state imposes the norms through education. Thus, the language of the educated gains official status and becomes a substantial matter of [state].[155]

Again, read in isolation, Henríquez Ureña's reflection appears as the simple formulation of the sociolinguistic processes by which particular language forms are subject to selection, codification, and standardization. But when read in the context in which these language discourses emerged (e.g., in the context of linguistic polemics in Buenos Aires), we learn how they go beyond the realm of language.

Consider the following statement from Henríquez Ureña and his Argentinean colleague Narciso Binayan (1928) regarding the need to reject students' choice of discourse topics and use of certain language forms:

> The child, writing about these particular subjects, cannot but repeat clichés and phrases heard at home or in school, repeating them with the same degree of awareness that a parrot exhibits in its chatter. But the serious consequences of this go beyond good or bad writing. Even more serious are the effects it has on the formation of character. The teacher must recognize that the repetition of such errors constitutes a march towards insincerity. The result of which is a legalized system of lies which continually and pervasively interferes in the establishment of the child's connection to the world.[156]

These prevalent ideas represent the intellectual context and climate of opinion in which Amado Alonso, Castro, and Henríquez Ureña established their specific line of research, which was sociological and political in orientation. This linguistic idealism was represented by Benedetto Croce (1866–1952) and Karl Vossler, but also by Matteo Giulio Bartoli (1873–1946), Antonio Gramsci's teacher. While explaining language change, Bartoli employed notions of prestige and imitation, which were crucial to the development of Gramsci's concept of hegemony.[157]

Thus, in Henríquez Ureña's statements, we see an illustration of hegemony. Henríquez Ureña had this crucial role of history and social tradition in mind when he argued for the archaic nature of the lexicon and syntax of Dominican Spanish.[158] It is during the Argentine period (1935–1941) that Henríquez Ureña composed his classic text *El español en Santo Domingo* (ESD) and published it in the Institute's *Biblioteca de Dialectología Hispanoamericana*. This text is partially a compilation of previous studies (1919, 1933, 1937, and 1939) as well as a major description of the different components of the Dominican dialect and his views regarding the community's sociolinguistic configuration. Notably, Henríquez Ureña tries to explain the preservation of archaic Spanish in the Dominican Republic with reference to the four conditions that Amado

Alonso attributed to the deterioration of Spanish in Buenos Aires. In the Buenos Aires context, as we indicated earlier, these conditions included the plebeian tendencies of the period, a break from linguistic (and literary) tradition in Spanish America, the slow rise of Argentina's stock as a colony, and the massive influx of immigrants. Henríquez Ureña argues that it is the opposite conditions that are responsible for the Dominican Republic's presumably privileged sociolinguistic situation.

In sum, the body of concepts, hypotheses, proposals, affirmations, rejections, and contradictions in relation to Spanish, along with the evolution of his linguistic thought, places Henríquez Ureña at the threshold of structural linguistics. Like early structuralists, he explored the relationships between fundamental principles of language and literature upon which structural (mental, social, cultural) networks are built. However, in the study of linguistic phenomena, Henríquez Ureña also drew from the vast experience he gained from teaching, working, and living in so many different settings and from his participation in hotly contested debates, particularly the debates regarding the construction of the Hispanic community and the image of the Spanish language. Henríquez Ureña drew from the general climate of opinion established by all these different linguistic, intellectual, and political currents, which I have described. Therefore, it is necessary to situate Henríquez Ureña's linguistic work within the tradition of language studies in the Hispanic world, in order to understand his representations of Spanish in the Latin American and Dominican contexts. It is within this tradition that central sociolinguistic and ideological issues surrounding the use and status of Spanish in local and international contexts emerge. At different times in the history of Hispanic philology and Spanish linguistics, we encounter various efforts by scholars to mitigate or expand the effects of hegemony and the regime of knowledge called Hispanoamericanism. Henríquez Ureña is no exception. His approach to sociolinguistic issues clearly reflects positions in the ideological matrix comprised by this tradition.

5

Pedro Henríquez Ureña and the Whitening of Dominican Identity

> Nothing is *vital* for science; nothing can be. Its accepted propositions, therefore, are but opinions at most; and the whole list is provisional. The scientific man is not in the least wedded to his conclusions. He risks nothing upon them. He stands ready to abandon one or all as soon as experience opposes them. Some of them, I grant he is in the habit of calling *established truths*.
>
> Charles S. Peirce

> Reality is greater than what we can describe.
>
> Pedro Henríquez Ureña

Pedro Henríquez Ureña's characterization of Spanish in the Dominican Republic, as I show in this chapter, revolves around two themes. The first theme is the archaic nature of its lexicon and, the second, the scarcity of features of African origin. Through his focus on these themes, Henríquez Ureña produced an image of what he regarded as the standard Dominican dialect of Spanish in which its formal similarities with northern Peninsular varieties were highlighted and its consistency with the Spanish (Castilian[1] and Andalusian) base was affirmed. Spanish in the Dominican Republic is indeed a complex linguistic entity and as such a number of different approaches to its study could be emphasized. And in fact, other scholars, contemporaries of Henríquez Ureña, chose to focus on or at least further investigate other aspects of Caribbean varieties of Spanish (such as their African elements), or their uniqueness (as some Argentineans were doing with respect to their speech). In this chapter, in keeping with the approach to critical linguistic historiography and methodology outlined in Chapter 2, my focus will be less on the accuracy or inaccuracy of these alternative approaches and more on the question of *why* Henríquez Ureña chose to emphasize those particular features (archaisms and non-Africanness) and not others.

As the previous chapters have indicated, our analysis requires that we place the author in the precise historical context in which his work was being produced and Dominican identity was being constructed and reconstructed. The following cultural and racial categories and hierarchies are central to the present discussion: Hispanism versus Americanism, Hispanoamericanism versus Latinoamericanism, blackness versus whiteness, Dominicanness versus Haitianness.

Iconization as a Metalinguistic Device in Henríquez Ureña's Linguistic Texts

In Henríquez Ureña's linguistic texts we find several examples of indexical iconicity. At first glance, these passages appear to contain simple descriptions of linguistic forms and usage, but upon further scrutiny we observe that they also aim to reflect social and cultural categories, especially of racial and ethnic identity. In other words, Henríquez Ureña's descriptions highlight linguistic patterns while at the same time marking and pointing to racial and national boundaries. The following statement regarding the speech of the descendants of African slaves, originally made by Esteban Pichardo but often repeated by Henríquez Ureña, offers an example:

> Van Name cites observations made by the Dominican Esteban Pichardo, author of the first Dictionary of American provincialisms. According to Pichardo, the African-born blacks who were brought to Cuba used a mutilated and corrupted Spanish while their Cuban-born descendants spoke well like white natives.[2]

Addison Van Name (1868) was a scholar whose text *Contributions to Creole Grammar* has been said to represent the beginning of the scientific study of Creole languages. His reference to Pichardo lends more credibility to the line of argument pursued by Henríquez Ureña. But what I wish to highlight in this statement is the process by which the particular deployment of linguistic forms is used to determine membership in or distance from a racial group, region, or national identity.

The process of iconization as a metalinguistic and descriptive device appears very early in Henríquez Ureña's linguistic oeuvre. The first example is found in one of the last paragraphs of *La lengua en Santo Domingo* (1919). In this text, the author attempts to correct Wilhelm Meyer-Lübke's assertion that a black dialect was spoken in Santo Domingo. In this case,

Henríquez Ureña described syllable-final consonant deletion as the most characteristic phonetic feature of Caribbean dialects of Spanish.[3] While opening with a general linguistic description, he subsequently elaborates his explanation with more details: "The resurgence of this phenomenon in the Caribbean has been attributed to Andalusian influence, the warm climate, and the black population. Although the phenomenon is indeed more prevalent among illiterate blacks, we cannot easily determine if the cause is their race or their illiteracy."[4] At first he approaches the question hypothetically, but in the process of forming an argument, he begins to indexically link the selected linguistic phenomena with categories of identity:

> In Santo Domingo, African descendants are so far removed from their origins that Santo Domingo natives generally portray them, not necessarily as the worst speakers from the countryside, but as users of archaic speech such as: "*dende que lo vide hasta agora*" (since I last saw him until now).[5]

As we can see, Henríquez Ureña argues that the weakening of syllable-final consonants in the Dominican Republic cannot be attributed to people of African descent because its occurrence is conditioned by social factors and not race. But, in addition, he also argues against the possible African origins of syllable-final weakening by affirming that black Dominicans are often linguistically characterized by Dominican speakers as "rural" and "archaic." For Henríquez Ureña, as we soon learn from the relevant historical context, "rural" and "archaic" are discursively connected with "white." He makes this association explicit in Chapter 9 of *El español of Santo Domingo* (ESD) and also in earlier discussions of black speakers of Spanish, as in the earlier reference to Van Name and Pichardo. More importantly, however, Henríquez Ureña supports his linguistic reasoning in *La lengua en Santo Domingo* with reference to extralinguistic factors: the social images derived from the political and ideological landscape of the Dominican Republic at the turn of the century:

> Various reasons contributed to maintaining the purity of Spanish in Santo Domingo: one was the ever present dominance of families of Spanish ancestry; and culture also contributed, especially during colonial times. Colonial Santo Domingo was the site of schools, universities (founded first in the sixteenth century and again in the eighteenth century), convents, archdioceses, a Royal court, the printing press, and the theater. Pompously, its citizens called this capital city "the Athens of the New World." Also, literature has continuously flourished there for four centuries.[6]

Here, Henríquez Ureña establishes an immediate connection between language and social structure: one of the principal causes of the existence of "pure" Peninsular speech in the country is the social predominance of

Spanish families. In this text (as well as in ESD and in *La cultura y las letras coloniales*) he explicitly refers to the components of the social structure that underlie Spanish and its history in the Dominican Republic: family structure, social class, religion, and high culture. The link to ethnicity is initially elaborated by contrasting the Dominican sociolinguistic landscape with that of Haiti's: "The black race predominates there and most people speak a dialect derived from French. Haitians call it Patois or Creole. The other nation, Santo Domingo, was a Spanish colony."[7] This is a distinction that Henríquez Ureña makes repeatedly, as, for example, in his famous article on dialectal zonification: "The three Spanish Antilles (Cuba, Puerto Rico, and Dominican Republic, the old Spanish part of Santo Domingo)."[8] And again: "Dominican Spanish, in the popular as well as the standard form, is precisely more faithful to its European origins than any other Latin American variety."[9]

We find evidence of the process of iconization at work in several of Henríquez Ureña's linguistic writings, especially in passages in which he directly associates a linguistic feature with a social image or social activity that is not value-free. We find another example in some of his later linguistic publications such as "El enigma del aje" (1938a) in which he analyzes the evolution of and the confusion surrounding the indigenous word *aje* (sweet potato) and the African word *ñame* (yam) in the Spanish-speaking world and expresses causal connections with social patterns:

> Practically speaking for the Indians, and later for the Spaniards, there was a distinction between *aje* and *batata* as categories of food. After wider distribution in America, Guinean yam became associated with sweet potato as low quality food. Potato was considered a delicacy, similar to "the gentle marzipan." Meanwhile, as Las Casas wrote in *A short account of the destruction of the Indies*, sweet potato was considered fit only for the subjugated Indians, and *ñame* was thought of as "good sustenance" for the black slaves.[10]

The use and development of these particular loanwords in Spanish reflect the consumption patterns as well as the social hierarchies among Spaniards, Indians, and Africans. Furthermore, Henríquez Ureña claims that the confusion surrounding the use of the terms stems from the fact that the early colonial settlers did not care to establish a semantic distinction for items that they were not interested in consuming and the indigenous and African peoples were not linguistically equipped to do so in Spanish.[11] The explicatory validity and accuracy of this description is not under question here. We can accept the sociolinguistic fact that at any place and time social patterns correlate with linguistic variables. However, what attracts our attention is the process by which the words *aje* and *ñame* become iconically attached to cultural categories. Notably, the ideological character of the text rests in the fact that Henríquez Ureña does not expressly acknowledge that power differentials among these groups intervened in the borrowing and adaptation of these words. The process is presented as a natural occurrence.

At times, Henríquez Ureña's iconization originates in authors that he uses as evidentiary sources. For example, in section three of this article, he presents the colonial chronicler Fernando de Oviedo's treatment of the word *ñame*:

> The *ñame* that we find in the Hispaniola and other areas of this region is not native to these Indies. It arrived along with this bad breed of blacks. Thus, *ñame* is quite beneficial as good sustenance for these blacks, a rebellious lot, of whom there are more than we have a need for. These *ñames* resemble *ajes* but they are not the same. [12]

Moreover, Oviedo claimed: "*Ñame* is of very little value ... It is only fit for slaves and the servant class."[13] Oviedo established the history of *ñame* by briefly explaining its introduction in the Caribbean island by Africans. He described the role and function that the vegetable played in the community, while emphasizing the Africans' low status within the caste system and warning his readers that this group represented a threat. It is within this cultural scale of inferiority versus superiority that Oviedo tried to account for the categorical and linguistic differences between *aje* and *ñame*. Building on Oviedo's discussion, Henríquez Ureña concludes that speakers could not overcome the linguistic confusion and, as a result, the inferior word *ñame* displaced the word *aje* and became dominant. These passages reveal reflections on language and linguistic forms closely related to iconic images that are the result of ideological and social evaluations of groups and their situations. As evident in these lexico-semantic studies, Henríquez Ureña's diachronic understanding of Spanish relied substantially on data from the history of colonial immigration and settlement provided by Oviedo, Bartolome de Las Casas, and other colonial chroniclers.

One of the first instances of iconization of Spanish as loyalty to the Hispanic tradition in the Dominican Republic appears in the first few pages of ESD in the form of intriguing anecdotal evidence: "The Spanish poet García Lorca told me about a Dominican man he met on a ship headed for Spain. A former assistant to a Dominican President, this Dominican spoke Spanish splendidly! Do you know [,Lorca asked,] what he did as soon as we reached Spanish soil? He kissed the ground. Adolfo Salazar and I could not hold back our tears."[14] Here the focus of the observation is not so much on linguistic form as much as it is on style and distinctiveness.

The anecdote illustrates how the Spanish spoken by the Dominican traveler in this instance represents a unique variety of the language that surpasses the social, linguistic, and aesthetic expectations of the famous Spanish poet. The Martinican philosopher Frantz Fanon (2008) wrote that, for the Caribbean, admiration and recognition in the presence of the (European) other is of utmost importance.[15] To Henríquez Ureña, the Dominican's wonderful speech, defined and reported by Lorca and coupled with the speaker's subsequent actions (kissing the Spanish ground), also stands as a sign for the love, loyalty, and kinship Dominicans manifest toward Spain.

Iconization operates even in some cases in which linguistic forms function as sign-vehicles for sociohistorical meanings and evaluations. One example can be found in Henríquez Ureña's description of an adverbial comparative phrase in the chapter on morphology:

> ¡Más malo que Toussaint! (more evil than Toussaint): among the Dominican people, the name of Haiti's great liberator remains a symbol for the worst kind of atrocities that Spanish Santo Domingo has endured since the beginning of the nineteenth century.[16]

For many Dominicans, the image of Haiti, as we know from the discussion in Chapter 3, plays a crucial role in the definition of nation, language, and, as we can see here, even adverbial phrases. Nonetheless, for more in-depth analysis of the degree to which the semiotic-ideological processes of iconization and erasure operate in Henríquez Ureña, we must turn to the synchronic and diachronic analyses of Dominican Spanish found in his texts, especially in ESD.

Castilian Flavor and the Dominican Speech Community

In the text's brief prologue, Henríquez Ureña lays out the main tasks he wants to accomplish in ESD: (i) to prove that Spanish in the Dominican Republic is the most archaic dialect in the continent and a relatively unevolved dialect of Peninsular Spanish (ii) to correct the Dominican Rafael Brito's representation of Spanish in his *Diccionario de criollismos* as a radically distinct rural dialect of Spanish, and (iii) to obtain a record of the archaic speech before it begins to "naturally erode."[17] Chapters 1 through 4 of ESD provide a glimpse of the Dominican Republic in the context of the Caribbean region and an outline of important historical events that shaped the Dominican speech community, including its early colonial settlement, the foundation of cities, the early status of the Dominican Republic as a site of colonial power, and the sociolinguistic configuration. This last aspect, the sociolinguistic configuration of the Dominican Republic, is described along the following general lines: "Urban speech is uniform throughout the country, as we would expect in relation to general aspects of the standard language. However, we find divergence with respect to rural speech."[18] This introduction to the Dominican linguistic situation, while broad, highlights the main varieties for which Henríquez Ureña has to account, emphasizes the existing routes and modes of communication as well as the trends of demographic change, sketches the sociolinguist configuration, and identifies certain language contact zones such as the Haitian-Dominican border and the Samaná Peninsula. In this section, we also find the formulation of a number of dichotomies (e.g., diversity vs. homogeneity, variation vs. tradition) that will be crucial for fully understanding this text's serious implications.

Chapter 2 of ESD begins with a brief introduction to the main thesis and situates the Dominican Republic's speech community in relation to Latin America and a particular historical context. The author immediately presents the Caribbean, especially Santo Domingo, as a speech community characterized by "a strong Castilian flavor" in its lexicon and syntax and a mostly Andalusian influenced sound system:

> In relation to their traditional linguistic base, the Caribbean resembles Lima and Bogotá. In contrast to the rest of their respective nations, these two cities represent the highest degree of Castilian flavor in the Andes. Likewise, Santo Domingo exhibits a great deal of archaic features. This linguistic situation can be partially attributed to the fact that this island was the first site of Spanish settlement in America.[19]

At the beginning of Chapter 2, Henríquez Ureña clearly opposes *castellano* (Castilian) to *andaluz* (Andalusian). Thus, Dominican Spanish is characterized first and foremost for its Castilian flavor, which, it must be emphasized, is established by focusing on its lexicon and syntax. The author compares this variety synchronically with the Spanish of Bogotá and Lima, conservative dialects that enjoy greater prestige throughout Latin America. Through this association, he distances Dominican Spanish from its Caribbean counterparts that, still in our time,[20] occupy lower positions in the hierarchy of Spanish regional dialects. The emphasis on lexical and syntactic archaisms is a necessary part of the discourse that links the deployment of such linguistic forms to the expression of loyalty to Spain as opposed to Haiti or the United States and the cultural and linguistic heterogeneity that they potentially represent. After establishing this connection, Henríquez Ureña provides an initial diachronic explanation in support of his theory about the archaic nature of Spanish in the Dominican Republic:

> This is exactly what happened in Santo Domingo: during the first fifteen years following the Discovery, the relatively large core of the population established the linguistic base. To this initial foundational linguistic base, we

can add the contributions of *noveles* (new arrivals) and *chapetones* (urban dwellers from the Peninsula). However, the old (self-proclaimed) *baquianos* (indigenous name for "field scouts") must have greatly influenced the speech of the first settlers. This explains the survival in Santo Domingo of medieval words and other linguistic forms that had become archaic or at least obsolete by the sixteenth century.[21]

In order to establish the significance of the initial colonial settlement in Santo Domingo, Henríquez Ureña draws on a conception of a base that assumes the existence of an initial group of Spanish settlers who, with a few exceptions, exhibit no major regional, social, or dialectal differences. This conceptualization of a linguistic base is different than the one operating in his descriptions of Spanish in the Americas.[22] Nevertheless, he draws an image of a speech community that has resisted change because of a most important cultural characteristic, which from his cultural descriptions we learn is, loyalty to Spain and Hispanic tradition. After presenting his main argument, Henríquez Ureña provides further support for his theory with a statement from Cuervo: "We can affirm that Hispaniola was the first site of acclimatization for the Spanish language in America. Here it was that the language began to adapt to the new realities."[23] Indeed, according to Cuervo, Hispaniola, as the first Spanish colony in the New World, was a central point of communication between Spain and America and a key site in the establishment of linguistic norms. Henríquez Ureña offers Cuervo's characterization as supporting evidence of the preservation of an archaic variety that was established during the early stages of colonization in Hispaniola.

As stated, Chapters 1 through 4 of ESD draw a sketch of the historical circumstances that, according to Henríquez Ureña, explain the archaic nature of Spanish in the Dominican Republic. In accordance with tradition in Dominican historiography, he includes colonial heritage, intellectual tradition, the presence of powerful institutions, and linguistic pride among the most relevant historical factors that contributed to the initial configuration and subsequent development of the Dominican speech community: "While Santo Domingo was the capital of the Caribbean, pride in its privileges set the dignified tone which is characteristic of local speech."[24] Furthermore, Henríquez Ureña maintains that resistance to, first, Haitian domination and, second, U.S. occupation, led to the preservation and dominance of Hispanic cultural and linguistic tradition (i.e., archaic Spanish):

> Even after the indifference of the metropolis allowed the country to fall into foreign hands, it never gave up. For more than seventy years it fought

to preserve its Hispanic national character and cultural traditions from Spain... After proclaiming its independence with difficulty in 1821, it set out to resist the invasion and occupation by Franco-African Haiti in 1822. Dominicans put up a long and passive resistance to the foreign-speaking Haiti until 1844 when the resistance turned violent and independence was recovered. In 1861, it joins Spain again in an effort for annexation destined to fail in 1865. This attempt, however, was a ceremonious act which marked the end of contact with people of different spiritual roots. Therefore, the pride in its linguistic heritage, developed during colonial times, now reawakened in the desperate struggle for freedom, kept the language alive. The feeling of ferocious preservation persists in our time in light of the illegal and unprovoked invasion ordered by the United States government (1916–1922). Santo Domingo defends itself as it did one hundred years ago, resisting foreign linguistic influence and using the Spanish language as its only weapon and shield at home and abroad.[25]

According to Henríquez Ureña, in spite of the fact that Spain abandoned the eastern part of Hispaniola, its inhabitants resisted relinquishing Spanish and Hispanic tradition. The last statement, in this particular historical context, reveals a peculiar militarization and nationalization of the language consistent with formulas of Dominican national discourse and national imaginary. Nevertheless, subsequent isolation from Spain and the constant threat of foreign invasion spurred the leading Dominican social classes to preserve their Hispanic cultural and linguistic tradition until the twentieth century:

> As in Mexico and in Peru's great urban cultural center, Lima, another sign of linguistic and colonial influence is the use of the second person pronoun *tú* and its corresponding verbal forms... Another sign is the persistence of subjunctive future forms such as *hablare* (were to talk) and *hubiere* (were to be), which survive in Santo Domingo and are readily and effortlessly used by educated people, especially in writing.[26]

In his linguistic and cultural analyses of Dominican society, we find many references to "persistence" and "survival." As we explained in Chapter 3, Henríquez Ureña is providing this account at a time when serious tensions arose between the Dominican and Haitian governments and also at a time of intense Anglo-Caribbean immigration in the country. Thus, upon reflecting on the country's sociolinguistic history, he poses one of the questions that most troubled Dominican intellectuals and politicians in the 1930s: "Will this feeling of safe-guarding the nation weaken as a result of contact between the Dominican working class and the recently arrived

Caribbean immigrants?"[27] His initial answer to this question is not reassuring: "We cannot be certain that the intensity with which Dominicans previously opposed violent invasions will continue in light of these recent peaceful incursions."[28] Although he expressed doubt with respect to the restructuring of Dominican society at the turn of the century, his work on the history of Spanish and Hispanic culture provides proof of Dominicans' ability to preserve their national identity in the face of adverse conditions. Thus, the vision of this uncertain future provides a sense of the purpose, motivation, and conditions behind the theoretical and methodological processes of his work. Against the backdrop of the U.S. occupation and the perceived Haitian threat, Henríquez Ureña was compelled to address the interaction of language and race, the two most important subjects in the construction of national identity in the Dominican Republic.

Archaic Lexicon

As indicated, the lexicon becomes the first linguistic dimension and discursive site in which Henríquez Ureña begins his sociolinguistic study of Dominicans. Chapter 5 of ESD presents the main argument:

> Given the specifics of our country, Dominican Spanish is characterized by its archaic vocabulary. At the end of the nineteenth century and still today, among the educated, we can hear archaic expressions or soon to be archaic in relation to modern Spanish. Granted, we can find some of these archaic expressions in many parts of America. But no other country can rival Santo Domingo in usage.[29]

Thus, the archaic nature of the Dominican lexicon is manifest in the widespread use of words and expressions, most of which have become obsolete in other Spanish varieties. His documentary base is built on lexical forms that he collected mostly from written texts but also from oral speech. At times, in order to confirm their status as archaisms, he cross-references these forms with words that appear in the, until then, standard Spanish dictionaries, *Diccionario histórico de la lengua española* (1934) and Sebastian Covarrubias Orozco's *Tesoro de la lengua castellana o española* (1611), among others. In cases in which the archaic nature of these words is well known, he simply reproduces them: *catar, boto, brasil, galano, dizque, aína, celebro, mesmo, atanto, cuasi, dende*.[30] The following lexical entries provide a snapshot of the evidence on which his argument is grounded: "*acalenturado* [modern Spanish *febril*] (feverish); see *Rebusco de voces castizas* and the examples from Fray Alonso de Cabrera and Benito Pérez

Galdós in the *Diccionario histórico*."[31] Here is another description of typical archaisms, according to Henríquez Ureña:

> *Catar* [modern Spanish *mirar*] (to look): *cate usted*, the archaic Spanish equivalent of *mire usted qué cosa* (will you look at that!) ... By the end of the nineteenth century, I heard this expression a lot from old folks in Santo Domingo. According to Brito in his Dictionary, it still survives in rural areas. Although we find it in Auscabi, a compiler of gaucho speech in Argentina, Gonzalo Correas (176) had designated this idiom as outdated since the beginning of the seventeenth century.[32]

Among the list of words provided in his description of the lexicon in Chapter 5 of ESD we also find aguaje; apearse; arandelas, bregar; despacharse; dilatarse; gambado; guayar; prieto; privar en; rapapolvo; tíguere; tostón; vagamundo. Henríquez Ureña's lexicographical procedure involves cataloging the lexemes in alphabetical order, attributing a semantically archaic meaning, and documenting the occurrence of these words in Renaissance and Golden Age Spanish literature and among late nineteenth-century Dominican writers, or rural speakers. These descriptions appear under the headings voces del habla culta (standard linguistic forms), formas populares (popular linguistic forms), formas rurales (rural linguistic forms), and formas literarias (linguistic forms from literature). In the middle of Chapter 5, he introduces most of the popular archaic variants, including aguaitar (to watch) and alabancioso (boastful).[33] These forms are examples of archaisms that, although they may or may not have been attested in other Hispanic dialects, represent the true character of the Dominican lexicon.

We must note the importance and significance of (colonial) documentary sources for Henríquez Ureña and how he employs them. Throughout his description of the lexicon, Henríquez Ureña selects a series of words documented in the Dominican context and he attributes to these words the meaning given to them by the original Spanish colonizers: "*atajo* or *hatajo* 'recua,' 'caterva' (multitude of people); these words can be found in Pedro Cieza de León's *La crónica del Perú*, volume one, chapter nine, and in Alonso de Zuazo's *Colección de Ovalle*."[34] Interestingly, Alonso de Zuazo (1466–1539), a native of Segovia (according to Las Casas), was a Spanish lawyer, judge, and governor in New Spain under Hernán Cortés and in Santo Domingo (1524–1528 and 1531–1533). Another example of the particular use of documentary evidence is the discussion of the word *tostón*, whose meaning in Modern Caribbean Spanish is "a slice of fried plantain" but originally meant "a coin." Henríquez Ureña highlights that *tostón* (coin) is found in the writings of Cristóbal de Llerena (circa 1540–1606), a playwright and a hospital chaplain in Santo Domingo. It is reasonable to think that recourse to Peninsular documents from the sixteenth and seventeenth centuries was the only option available to someone demonstrating archaic Spanish structure, but colonial documentation also provided the most appropriate ethnographic lens for the ethnolinguistic discourse that Henríquez Ureña was framing.

The opening paragraph of ESD's Chapter 6 repeats the main argument and highlights the antiquity of a long list of proverbs and set phrases. Henríquez Ureña claimed that these proverbs and phrases were current in Dominican Spanish:

> One can hear thousands of these typically traditional phrases. Some have become archaic, while others are still used in every Spanish-speaking region. Many can be found in compilations of proverbs and phrases such as the one attributed to Marqués de Santillana which dates back to the fifteenth century. Other sources are Juan de Valdés's *Diálogo de la lengua* (1535) and the voluminous *Vocabulario de refranes y frases proverbiales*, written by Master Gonzalo Correas in the seventeenth century.[35]

Chapter 6 is a record of traditional linguistic folklore in Santo Domingo in which the author draws a strong connection between archaic speech, the northern Peninsular dialects, and a Dominican social group (peasants). In the Dominican national imaginary,[36] the rural population is thought to represent Dominicanness and was traditionally represented as predominantly white. Henríquez Ureña first makes a note of rural speakers' custom of transmitting traditional proverbs and set phrases, a practice that, in the broader context of his argument, highlights the relationship and proximity to Spanish in Spain:

> Another archaic feature is the conservation of proverbs, folk tales, prayers, remedy spells, romances, ballads, games, jokes, and riddles. The book of proverbs is enormous and was even larger by the end of the nineteenth century. The new generations are not as likely to use proverbs as "the old folks." But rural people preserve them and abundantly increase them. I remember hearing many traditional proverbs that can now be found in Correas's compilation from the fifteenth century, Juan de Valdés's *Diálogo de la lengua*, or *Quijote*.[37]

According to Henríquez Ureña, the old proverbs, which flourished in Spain in the fifteenth and sixteenth centuries, are not only abundantly preserved but they are also augmented by the Dominican rural population. What is remarkable here is Henríquez Ureña's emphasis on how widespread the proverbs are in the Dominican Republic and how they are linked to the prestigious Golden Age Spanish and the archive of Hispanic culture. For every entry, there is a reference that documents its source in Spanish tradition and dispels any notion of a possible unknown origin. The description of this and other related phenomena often includes references to the genealogy of a speech form or genre: "popular songs, unlike the ballad, have a long local tradition. As everywhere else in America, we can find the rural improvisational singers and the typical singing contests between improvisers."[38] In sum, Henríquez Ureña describes the Dominican lexicon as archaic, and through this feature, emphasizes how much it resembles a Peninsular variety spoken in, for example, the sixteenth century: "The typical Dominican exclamation!*Ofrézcome!* (Oh my God) was already in use by the sixteenth century; see Lope de Rueda's *La Eufemia*."[39] In the process of presenting this information, he indexically links this feature to social groups (i.e., Dominicans, Spaniards, Hispanics, educated class, rural speakers) and activities (i.e., speaking, uttering proverbs, writing, singing, playing word games) that reflect the nature of Dominican Spanish and its proximity to Peninsular dialects of Spanish.

Archaic Syntax

Henríquez Ureña's description of Dominican syntax is considerably shorter and limited in scope:

> Here is the typical syntax of standard Spanish. There are only a few irregularities related to agreement in the context of spatial and figurative proximity, which were already present in old Spanish. Some examples are: *la gente que estábamos allí* (the people [third person singular subject] that were [first person plural imperfect verbal form] there); *un reburujón de gente salían corriendo* (a crowd of people [third person singular subject] left [third person plural imperfect verbal form] running).[40]

He finds very little variation in the syntax and morphology of the Dominican variety with respect to general Spanish. However, in ESD as well as in an article entitled "Ello" (1939), Henríquez Ureña highlights the existence of archaic features such as the nonreferential pronoun *ello*, which is equivalent to the impersonal English pronoun "it," as opposed to the third person plural subject pronoun *ello* (they). Jacqueline Toribio (2000b) calls this linguistic phenomenon "the most intriguing and telling characteristic of the dialect."[41] Some analysts (González Tapia 2001, Jiménez Sabater 1975, Pérez-Leroux 1999) have focused on this phenomenon as a syntactic feature that characterizes innovation in Spanish in the Dominican Republic.

Following Marc-Olivier Hinzelin and Georg A. Kaiser (2007), I provide the following summary of Henríquez Ureña's explanation of the other uses of *ello* in the Dominican context. According to Henríquez Ureña, it is used as a concessive or an evasive response: "*Ello veremos* (it remains to be seen); *ello, quizás no viene* (maybe he or she will not come); *¿Es usted verde, azul o rojo? Ello, yo le diré; yo soy santiaguero* (Do you belong to the green, blue, or red political party? I'll tell you what: I am from Santiago)."[42] This nonreferential pronoun is also used to signify hesitation, probability, or acceptance: *¿Vas al pueblo?—Ello* (Are you going in to town?—It will depend); *¿Quiere bailar?—Ello* (Do you want to dance?—Yes, since you are asking).[43] It is also used in emphatic assertions: *¡Ello sí!* (Definitely yes!); *¡Ello no!* (Definitely no!).[44] According to Henríquez Ureña, these uses were extant for modern standard varieties of Spanish but were prevalent in Santo Domingo. He observes that *ello* appears frequently in Dominican Spanish as well as in other Hispanic dialects, but emphasizes its use in certain Dominican constructions that are atypical in the other contemporary dialects.[45] His characterization of this phenomenon is quite broad and generally limited to description of actual usage and explanation of its syntactic-semantic functions:

> The survival of *ello* as an impersonal subject, expletive pronoun, and as an overall linguistic fossil is an interesting phenomenon. It appears as the ritualized heading of a sentence. It began to appear as an unnecessary subject in phrases such as *Ello es así* (that's how it is). Then, it was used as the type of impersonal subject which is unnecessary in Spanish but typical in French, German, and English as in, for example, "it is good to be there."[46]

In tracing its history, Henríquez Ureña finds a relatively uninterrupted diachronic transmission of the phenomenon until the twentieth century. By then, he thinks that, with the exception of the (fossilized) Dominican variant, *ello* begins to disappear from everyday use and sounds archaic:

> After its continuous use for many centuries, since the early beginnings of Spanish, *ello* has begun to disappear from oral speech. It has become an archaic linguistic form, partially substituted by the demonstrative pronoun *eso* (that) or by noun phrases such as *el caso es que* (the case is that) or *la cosa es que* (the thing is that). Before, one would simply hear *ello es que*.[47]

While Henríquez Ureña's description of this phenomenon in his 1939 article is more detailed and explanatory, in ESD, it is subsumed by his demonstration of Dominican archaic Spanish. In fact, in both works, there is a tendency to focus on the fact that similarities exist between contemporary Dominican and Peninsular uses of *ello* in previous centuries:

> [In the Dominican Republic], *ello* survives as a linguistic fossil. In Spain, *ello* was, and perhaps it is still, utilized, for emphasis. Note the following examples from the seventeenth century, the eighteenth century and Quevedo's *Buscón*, respectively: *Ello has de casarte* (You must definitely get married); *Ello yo le vi* (I definitely saw him); and *Ello fue mucho dinero* (That was definitely a large sum of money).[48]

The repeated comparison of Dominicans' use of *ello* with the Peninsular Spanish variants from the seventeenth and the eighteenth centuries alerts us to the fact that Henríquez Ureña attempts to establish a solid connection between the archaic Spanish spoken in the Dominican Republic and the variety spoken in Spain.

Other prominent syntactic features described by Henríquez Ureña include infinitives and gerunds with pre-posed subjects: *al yo venir* (after my arrival); *sin tú decir nada* (without you revealing anything); and *en yo llegando* (as soon as I arrived).[49] He embedded the description of these and other linguistic forms within his argument in support of a distinctly archaic speech. Accordingly, Henríquez Ureña presents another phenomenon that is accounted for in previous stages of Spanish: the occurrence of clitic pronouns in indicative and subjunctive construction. Some examples are the following:

> *Llega y dícele* [modern Spanish *llega y le dice*] (She arrived and told him); *Clávale las espuelas al caballo y sale corriendo* [modern Spanish *Le cláva las espuelas al caballo y sale corriendo*] (He spurs the horse and begins racing). This is a typical structure, for which we find good examples in Cervantes's *La Señora Cornelia*.[50]

In this section, Henríquez Ureña also notes the incidence of pre-posed subject pronouns in infinitival phrases as well as gerunds and participles, as in, for example, *después de tú ido* (after you are gone).[51] To Henríquez Ureña, the tendency to place subject pronouns before infinitives and gerunds also has its origins in Spanish syntax, in which it was common to find these and other related phenomena:

> The use of double gerunds was not uncommon during the Spanish Golden Age. We find them in Santa Teresa or Quevedo. Writers that are masters of the Spanish language such as Emilia Pardo Bazán employ these structures, even though the majority of modern writers do not dare. The adjectival use of *ardiendo* (burning) and *hirviendo* (boiling) is a curious case because it was quite widespread: *lámpara ardiendo* (burning lamp).[52]

In his description of syntax, Henríquez Ureña argues that Dominican Spanish exhibits very little variation from other dialects. Yet he pays most attention to those Dominican syntactic forms that are rare in other contemporary dialects but commonly found in Santa Teresa, Quevedo, Cervantes, and other Spanish writers. Philologically, there is no denying that Henríquez Ureña was an excellent researcher. Yet, we cannot fail to observe how he goes out of his way to seek the archaic subtleties and rarities of Dominican Spanish. By emphasizing its archaic origin, Henríquez Ureña firmly grounds Dominican syntax in its Castilian base.

Dominicans' Pronunciation and Andalusian Phonetics

ESD includes three chapters (9 through 11) that examine the Dominican pronunciation of Spanish: "the sound system," "phonological variations," and "similarities with Andalusian phonetics." Framing his main argument again, Chapter 9 begins with a reformulation of the main thesis: "The lexicon and syntax of Dominican Spanish reveal a strong Castilian flavor, but its sound system, as I have said, resembles Andalusian phonology."[53] Regarding the phonology of Spanish in the Dominican context, Henríquez Ureña proposes three basic ideas: (i) Dominicans' pronunciation, just like in the rest of the Hispanic Caribbean, is remarkably similar to Andalusian pronunciation; (ii) high-class speech is manifestly different from lower-class speech; and (iii) with the possible exception of s deletion in syllable final position, there are no indigenous or African substrate influences. While these ideas may be uncontroversial (the Andalusian origin of *yeismo*, *seseo*, and s deletion or aspiration), in Henríquez Ureña's elaboration of some details, he introduces associations with racial and cultural categories and thus his statements acquire meanings that take us beyond the realm of language. One example involves the vocalization of liquids characteristic of the *Cibaeño* dialect in the Northern Dominican Republic:

> Consonants l and r can be realized as the vowel i as in the following examples: *comer* (to eat) is pronounced *comei*; *porque* (because) is pronounced *poique*; Isabel is pronounced Isabeil; *sueldo* (salary) is pronounced *sueido*; *conmigo* (with me) is perceived as *cormigo* and then is pronounced *coimigo*; abandonado (abandoned) is perceived as *abaldonado* and pronounced *abaidonao*. Communities which have experienced this change have experienced few others. It can be found in villages along the Cibao valley in the North, particularly in Santiago de los Caballeros, San Francisco de Macorís, and nearby areas but not in coastal Puerto Plata or Monte Cristi. It has also been found in the villages of Seibo in the South East. The phenomenon can be found among Puerto Rican rural people, who are generally white. Esteban Pichardo, in the introduction to his *Diccionario de voces cubanas*, documents this sound change among urban blacks in Cuba.[54]

As we can see, Henríquez Ureña starts with a simple description in which he highlights what happens to postvocalic r and l and contrasts linguistic forms such as *comer* and *porque* with comei and poique. However, directly following this description is an association to "peasants from the Cibao," "white Puerto Rican peasants," and "Cubans blacks." For the purposes of our analysis, we must highlight the following: "The phenomenon exists among rural people in Puerto Rico, who are generally white."[55] In this case, Henríquez Ureña attaches to a particular linguistic feature a social and ethnolinguistic identity that is, above all, white.

While addressing the details of some of these phonological phenomena under the heading *Indios y negros* in Chapter 12, Henríquez Ureña writes:

> In light of the disappearance of native Indian languages in the Caribbean in the sixteenth century, I do not think that we can raise the question of indigenous phonetic influence in the context of Dominican Spanish. That leaves us with the problem of African influence. Typically, some researchers point to the pronunciation of l instead of r or rr among blacks in Spanish America, particularly in Cuba, as proof of African linguistic influences. Although it has been documented in the Peninsular Leonés dialect, the reverse process (l instead of r) has also been attributed to African influences. This is even less likely. Neither of these pronunciations can be heard in Santo Domingo. The few existing cases of [r] becoming [l] that we do find involve words in which the change had already occurred in Spain. Also, there may be cases in which speakers imitate the Peninsular model. Or we may be dealing with phonetic dissimilation.[56] Some examples include: *celebro* (brain), *crisis* (crisis) which is pronounced *clises*, *climinal* (criminal), and others. The alternation between r and l only occurs in medial position in a word and it has been documented in Andalusian Spanish.[57]

In describing this process of lateralization of intervocalic r that results in the pronunciation of *cerebro* as *celebro*, the author rejects any suggestion of this feature's African origins and reverts again to drawing parallels to Peninsular Spanish. He proposes that the feature was an innovation that emerged in Spain. In addition, Henríquez Ureña discusses once more Pichardo's assumptions with respect to this phenomenon and its possible African origin. Pichardo, indeed, had attributed some phonetic features to the Cuban *bozales* (African-born blacks):

> Cuban-born blacks speak like white natives from any Cuban neighborhood. However, in Habana and Matanzas, some of the so-called *curros* (urban blacks) pronounce the vowel i instead of the consonants r and l. Note the following example: *poique ei niño puee considerai que es mejoi dinero que papei* (because the child can assume that money is better than paper).[58]

In his example, Pichardo contrasts the pronunciation of African-born, second language learners of Spanish *(bozales)* to that of Cuban-born blacks *(negros criollos)* and concludes that there are major differences. Yet, despite these differences Pichardo acknowledges that, with the exception of a few words that need translation, this *bozal* speech is mutually intelligible with Spanish.[59] Henríquez Ureña's reformulation of Pichardo's description, in contrast, augments the linguistic divide between these speech communities:

> Esteban Pichardo... contrasts the speech of black *criollos,* who speak like white natives, to the speech of *bozales,* who are recently arrived from Africa. According to Pichardo, the latter speak a broken and distorted Spanish. This dialect has no agreement in number, declension, or conjugation. Phonetically, they lack a strong r consonant; pronounce weak d consonants; replace ll with ñ, e with i, and g with v. In sum, the more recently arrived the African is, the worse jargon they speak.[60]

Having established these linguistic divides and cultural barriers between what we could call native speakers of these dialects (both white and nonwhite) and the African-born speakers, Henríquez Ureña does not seriously consider the possible African origins of these phonological phenomena. Besides being rare, *bozal* features are not found among native blacks, whose speech iconically reflects the linguistic patterns of white speech.[61]

After discarding the case for the African origin of rhotic (r sounds) and lateral (l sounds) merging, Henríquez Ureña weighs the possibility that nasalization (e.g., *yapa* pronounced as *ñapa,* and meaning "bonus") is a phenomenon produced by African influences. He concludes that the phenomenon is unlikely to have an African origin since it is also found in Spain where African influence would be difficult to explain:

> A more relevant case to consider is the change from y or ll to ñ... However, as a linguistic phenomenon, nasalization is not sufficiently systematic nor necessarily of African origin. It also exists in Spain. We find examples in Lamano from Salamanca: *yugo* (yoke) is pronounced *ñugo*... *pellizcar* (to pinch) is pronounced *peñiscar*... and *algaya* or *argaya* (wheat flower filament) is pronounced *argaña*. This last form had already appeared in Lope de Vega's *El vaquero de Moraña*.[62]

Henríquez Ureña considers nasalization in this context an unsystematic feature of Dominican Spanish, viewing it as a consequence of phonological change that had already occurred within the northern Peninsular dialect continuum. This view contrasts with some of his conclusions regarding indigenous substrate influences in American Spanish:

We cannot reject the possibility of indigenous linguistic influence in American Spanish simply because it is shown that the phenomenon under question exists in isolated areas in Spain. Can we not expect similar effects from different causes? The possible evolution of each phoneme moves within a limited set of constraints. Thus, coincidences of this type are frequent. Assuming that a phenomenon that occurs in Perú also occurs in Murcia, Spain, is it more logical to explain it as a Murcianism than as a Quechuism? Only when it has been documented that the phenomenon is widespread in Spain should we raise doubts about its local origin in America.[63]

Therefore, his position on nasalization in the Dominican dialect of Spanish is relatively consistent with one particular conceptualization of linguistic variation and change, according to which the possibilities of evolution for each phoneme are highly constrained by the linguistic system. In other words, phonetic change in the Dominican context is strictly limited to changes within the Spanish dialect continuum. Yet, it contradicts his view with respect to the nature of American Spanish and the influence of substrate and local conditions. This is a remarkable contradiction, but an understandable one in light of his overall arguments regarding the relationship between archaic Spanish in the Dominican context and the Hispanization of Dominicans, the ideological nature of his language representations, and the operation of processes such as iconization and erasure. His highly restrictive view of language change in the present context is consistent with his view on the similarity of Dominican pronunciation to Andalusian pronunciation.

Spanish, Hispanicness, and the Whitening of Dominican Identity

Thus far we have restricted our discussion to Henríquez Ureña's descriptive account of the lexicon, phonology, and syntax of Dominican Spanish but now we turn to an analysis of its implications. Therefore, we must integrate his analysis of Dominican history into his linguistic description. As Orlando Alba (1990) and Irene Pérez Guerra (1992) indicated, Henríquez Ureña's central argument (the linguistic archaism of Spanish in the Dominican context) determines the collection and selection of data in ESD. His treatment of the word *tostón* is a case in point. While Henríquez Ureña introduces its modern meaning, "a slice of fried plantain" (quite different from its sixteenth-century referent, a type of a coin), he chooses to emphasize the persistence of the original meaning in order to, once again, link present Dominican lexicon to its Spanish roots.[64] In contrast to the more descriptive and synchronic approach used by his compatriot and contemporary, the lexicographer and language purist Manuel Patín

Maceo in his book *Dominicanismos* (1940), Henríquez Ureña adopts a lexicographic strategy in which he insistently connects typically Dominican words to their Spanish Golden Age origin. In some cases, he points out that the lexeme in question is, in fact, a sociolinguistic or dialectal variable, but ends up only highlighting the prestige variant: "*crineja* or *crizneja*, in popular speech, *clineja*, which means *mechón de pelo* (hair braid). Las Casas wrote *crisneja* in his *Apologética*."[65] In contrast, in the case of the word *aguaje*, he neglects to mention its other meaning in Dominican popular speech: "the act of feigning." Thus, the popular lexicon is obscured because of the need to take into account the archaic lexicon that, in the context of the construction of Dominican national identity, has more sociolinguistic prestige and pragmatic significance.

As we noted, Henríquez Ureña's characterization of the dialect revolves around two central themes, the archaic nature of the lexicon and the scarcity of features of African origin. He articulates both with his specific concept of Dominican national identity that emerges throughout his Dominican linguistic and cultural writings: "Those who read my study on Dominican Spanish will find in *La cultura y las letras* many facts relevant to understanding the unique features of local speech."[66] The archaic Dominican lexicon, syntax, and Andalusian phonology are linked to the idea of a single cultural identity that is Hispanic and implicitly white: "The black race has never been prevalent there and the Spanish language remains pure."[67] Henríquez Ureña's principal conclusions with respect to Dominican Spanish as they appear in several of his cultural and linguistic texts are grounded in this pair of ideas: blacks never had a considerable presence in the country and the Dominican variety of Spanish remains pure and close to its origins.

> Regular importation of black slaves in the Dominican Republic occurred only until the first half of the sixteenth century. Thereafter, there were no resources to bring them in large numbers... We have no evidence of the arrival in the island, during the seventeenth and eighteenth centuries, of large shipments, as was indeed the case in more prosperous colonies. In the nineteenth century, there were even less.[68]

According to Henríquez Ureña, the Spanish settlers initially brought only a small number of African slaves to Hispaniola. Thus the shortage of blacks not only implies the numerical superiority of whites in the island's demographic development but also the lack of any African cultural trait: "The African element has not contributed a single distinctive feature."[69] In addition, a specific sociopolitical order or what he calls "patriarchal society"[70] contributed to the Hispanization of Dominicans and their cultural practices: "Coat of arms represented the Mendozas, Manriques and Guzmans, some of the many powerful Castilian families that lived in Santo Domingo neighborhoods."[71] And again, Henríquez Ureña notes: "In such a patriarchal society, numerous families organized around a male head and enjoyed peace."[72] Colonial society in Hispaniola was structured on the basis of these powerful family units whose members had control of the Church, the government, and the education system:

> For a long time, primary traditions have been preserved in the church, state institutions, and the university. Of them all, traditional culture survived well into the nineteenth century. Its vigor is attested by the influential impact of Dominican immigrants in Cuba after 1795. Manuel de la Cruz, the Cuban literary historian has called them civilizers.[73]

In this society, the transmission of Hispanic culture was so strong that it attracted people seeking an education from other parts of the continent. And later when Dominicans settled in other countries, they significantly shaped the local culture (as the Pichardos did, for example, in Cuba).[74] Henríquez Ureña maintains that this homogeneous culture and Hispanic identity developed relatively uncontested:

> There were few social prejudices during the colonial beginnings. Indeed, there were men of illustrious lineage or individuals who were, at least, distinguished gentlemen, all of whom founded families such as the Heredias, Mendozas, Guzmáns, Del Montes, Oviedos, and many others. Nevertheless, the gradual leveling of wealth, coupled with the democratic Spanish spirit, began erasing large social differences.[75]

In light of this demographically and predominantly Spanish Dominican society, Henríquez Ureña argues that, Spanish developed free from extra-Hispanic influences.[76] It is against this historical and cultural background of Dominican society that Dominican Spanish (its lexicon, syntax, and phonology) acquires the special meanings that index these social groups (i.e., the direct descendants of Spaniards as well as the few descendants of Africans) and their practices. Thus, in ESD, the ideas of an archaic lexicon and the demographic absence of blacks become icons representing the specificity of Dominican society and discursively whiten the national identity.

In Henríquez Ureña's characterization, the distinctive features of Dominican Spanish (i.e., the archaic lexicon and syntax) are linked to categories of identity (the original Spanish colonizers and their white Hispanic descendants). But even more directly than his description of the lexicon, his discussion of the laterization of intervocalic r and the reverse process (the replacement of l by r) among Dominican blacks minimizes the scope of the phenomenon[77] (we might refer to this as a pseudoerasure), locates it within the Hispanic linguistic tradition, and finally affirms the whitening of the black Dominican through the acquisition of white Dominicans' speech. In order to articulate Spanish and social groups in the Dominican Republic, Henríquez Ureña draws from these racial and cultural categories and proposes that there is a majority of purely archaic speakers in the Dominican Republic who are predominantly white. This is the fundamental idea that emerges out of the historical, cultural, and linguistic descriptions appearing in Henríquez Ureña's Dominican linguistic and cultural texts.

Erasure of Blackness

"From the beginning many of the slaves did not come directly from Africa. It is well known that they came from Spain, where they had been bought from the Portuguese and were already Hispanicized. Interestingly enough, the firsts groups of slaves were not all black. White slaves were also brought to America."[78] While acknowledging the fact that slaves were brought to Hispaniola, Henríquez Ureña claims that a substantial amount did not come directly from Africa but from Spain and suggests that they should have therefore undergone a process of acculturation in which they adopted the beliefs and practices of Spaniards. Furthermore, some slaves were, in fact, not just whitened Africans but actually were white Europeans. According to his reasoning, Dominicans, including the few black ones, are to be culturally and linguistically characterized by their non-Africanness:

> Similar to Puerto Rico in the nineteenth century, Dominican blacks were rarely pure. The perception of an africanized country, as many geographical accounts indicate, is due to our proximity to Haiti, formerly Saint Domingue. It is difficult to dispel such confusing notions. But more significant should be the fact that Dominican culture and letters were developed by *criollos* of European descent or mixed with indigenous elements. Some of these men of letters include Heredia, Núñez de Cáceres, Dávila, and Fernández de Castro.[79]

These assertions are part of the historical and cultural reasoning underlying Henríquez Ureña's major linguistic arguments with respect to Spanish in the Dominican Republic.

We find instances of erasure and iconization in Henríquez Ureña's early work on the Dominican dialect of Spanish. For example, in *La lengua en Santo Domingo*, he claims:

> The black race has never predominated in the Dominican Republic and the Castilian language remains pure. There has never been, nor is there now, a black dialect in the Republic. To the contrary, Santo Domingo belongs to that segment of America where the language remains closer to its Castilian roots.[80]

This is a remarkable minimization, if not a total erasure, of African heritage as a component of Dominican identity. But especially significant for our purpose are the presence and operation of mechanisms through which a particular linguistic ideology of national identity is produced and reproduced. The conjunction that links, on one hand, "The black race has never predominated" and, on other, "The Spanish language remains pure," does not establish a literal cause-effect relation between the two; however, the discursive disposition of these two statements clearly realizes the iconization of language that I have presented: blackness and "Spanish origins" are placed in opposite ends of the ethnolinguistic framework in which Dominican identity is embedded. This discursive construction is consistent with the nonblack ideology of national identity held by a large number of Dominican intellectuals and social agents. As we discussed in Chapter 3, members of the powerful Dominican educated classes have discursively constructed and monopolized national consciousness in the Dominican Republic. They have produced and reproduced a vision of the Dominican Republic as a nation defined solely by Hispanic tradition—measured in degrees of linguistic purity and whiteness. Naturally, in order for this vision to be consistent, dependable, and rational, its authors had to reject everything that complicated it, including Haitianness, Africanness, and blackness. Therefore, erasure became a vital ideological mechanism in the work of intellectuals such as Henríquez Ureña who assumed the task of drawing up the cultural and linguistic image of Dominicans.

We notice erasure in ESD in the scarcity of pages dedicated to the issue of African influence in Santo Domingo. Chapter 8 ("Exotic elements") contains seven pages and Chapter 12 ("Indians and blacks") only four pages. In contrast, the explanation of archaic Spanish extends over two long chapters (66 pages) and continues in other parts of the book. In addition, in instances in which Henríquez Ureña encounters a potential African substrate influence (Dominican diminutives fomed with -*ningo*), he declines to investigate it further. Instead, he provides an explanation of diminutives with the following caveat: "As in Castile, there are many cases of monosyllables and disyllabic segments containing diphthongs."[81] While the comparison between a series of diminutives from the Dominican and Peninsular varieties is allotted one paragraph, the ambiguous and passing reflection on Afro-Dominican diminutives is limited to a simple question: "Diminutives in rural speech such as *blandiningo* (a little soft), *chininingo* (very short), *poquiningo* (very few), *cerquininga* (very close). Could it be Africanish?."[82] More emphasis is given to the archaic diminutives and the alternative forms are de-emphasized.

Noticeably absent from this chapter on syntax is any discussion regarding another prominent syntactic feature of Dominican Spanish: double negation. As John Lipski (2005) noted, double negation is "overwhelmingly present in the vernacular speech of the Dominican Republic."[83] Here is one example of double negation: *nosotros no vamos, no* (we are not going). William Megenney (1990) and Armin Schwegler (1996) have studied the phenomenon in areas containing heavy Afro-American presence, including the Dominican Republic. Jiménez Sabater (1975) made the following observations:

> While not a genuine irregularity, sentences with double negation as well as double affirmation are typical in Dominican Spanish. See, for example: *yo no voy mañana, no* (I am not going tomorrow); *Pedro no es bruto, no* (Pedro is not stupid); *Ellos no están aquí, no* (They are not here); *Yo sí me quedo, sí* (I will stay).[84]

Jiménez Sabater attributes the semantic function of emphasis to this syntactic structure. According to Alba (2004), utterances with preverbal and postverbal negative markers such as *yo no sé decirle, no* (I don't know how to tell him) constitute "the type of syntactic construction that is very characteristic of Dominican Spanish. It has not been attested in any other Spanish-speaking country."[85] Alba proposes that this stigmatized construction is very common in the popular speech of low socioeconomic groups and frequently heard in spontaneous conversation.[86]

Schwegler (1996) states that double negation is a phenomenon that we can trace to Bantu languages. Lipski provides an example of the corresponding *ke* and *ko* structure in the Kikongo language: *ke besumba, ko* (they do not buy).[87] The Dominican writer Francisco Moscoso Puello (1936) had already documented this speech phenomenon in his novel *Cañas y bueyes: no son poquito, no* (they are not few).[88] A constant source of reference for Henríquez Ureña as well as other researchers, *Cañas y bueyes* is a novel about the sugar industry and the exploitation of the Dominican worker. For many researchers, it is rich source of speech samples from many of the varieties in the Dominican Republic. While he selected and highlighted numerous speech samples from this novel, Henríquez Ureña did not detect this phenomenon. In the absence of any documented Peninsular antecedent or counterpart, this peculiar syntactic phenomenon disappears from his description of Dominican Spanish. Erasure was such a prevalent process in the representation of the Dominican dialect of Spanish that he minimized and ignored some complex linguistic phenomena. In addition, it motivated his polemic intervention against other scholars who were trying to investigate the African-Dominican or Afro-Hispanic connection in the Caribbean.

Contesting Africanist Hypotheses

In Chapter 2, we considered the fact that, within any community, language ideologies are multiple and often in competition. In ESD, we perceive the presence of a dominant nationalistic and linguistic ideology as well as other competing ideologies. Specifically, in Chapter 8, Henríquez Ureña makes the reader aware of the existence of diverging views on the topic of African substrate influences. He polemically debates some of the ideas and hypotheses of his contemporaries such as the Cuban Fernando Ortiz (1881–1969) and the Dominican Carlos Larrazábal Blanco (1894–1989), questioning their theories of African influence in Cuba and the Dominican Republic.[89]

Fernando Ortiz

The Cuban anthropologist and ethnomusicologist Fernando Ortiz pioneered the study of African cultures in America. He had a different view of the possibilities for research in this field. For example, regarding the work of scholars such as Pichardo and Leo Wiener, Ortiz wrote:

> Wiener's and Pichardo's opinions should be sufficient for us to consider the word *conuco* (small plot of land) within the context of attested or hypothetical Africanisms. But in addition, we have a recent scholarly publication, a curiously interesting book, which attests to the African origins of this word... Although we must be careful with more shaky or inconclusive examples, Wiener's serious reputation as a Harvard professor and lexicographer must force us to pay attention. Indeed, we must recognize the possibility that African influences could have shaped the root of this word and, more importantly, determined its meaning and variation.[90]

Wiener was an important philologist and professor of Slavic languages at Harvard who, in his book *Africa and the Discovery of America* (1920), advanced the controversial idea that Africans reached America before Europeans and thought that he had correctly identified certain lexemes in the Americas that derived from African languages. Tuned in to these important scholarly discussions, Ortiz helped found the journals *Revista*

Bimestre Cubana, Archivos del Folklore de Cuba, and *Estudios Afrocubanos.* Since the publication of his first book, *Los negros brujos* (1906), Ortiz engaged in the study of not only the Afro-Cuban population and its contribution to Cuban society and history but also the linguistic development of this population.[91]

In an article entitled "Los afronegrismos de nuestro lenguaje" (Africanisms in our language), originally published in 1922 in *Revista Bimestre*, Ortiz shed some light on Cuba's sociolinguistic configuration and history: "Which *lingua franca* emerged in the plantations? It could have only been Spanish with a large number of imperfections. First of all, it must have been spoken with a *bozal* accent then a *criollo* accent, but never the same as in Castile."[92] Ortiz acknowledged the predominance of Spanish and the overall scarcity of African linguistic forms in Cuban speech, but went on to lament the lack of general interest in this subject by Cuban scholars. According to Ortiz, in Cuba like everywhere else, this lack of interest was tied to the, until then commonly held belief that

> Blacks only spoke a worthless jargon, made up of a handful of words, as Pliny simply put it two thousand years ago, *stridor non vox* (mere hissing noise). But this view is also the result of colonial apathy and contempt for the practices of slaves and the absence of those Church missionaries that patiently worked with Indians in the rest of the continent.[93]

Ortiz found it troubling that scholars did not explore the contributions of Africans in America. In Cuba, he encouraged scholars to break away from this paradigm and investigate African linguistic heritage. A sharp contrast emerges between Henríquez Ureña's position and Ortiz's perspective on the subject of African influence: "Over the centuries, first from Africa and more recently from nearby Jamaica and Haiti, the ethnic influence of black people, albeit under conditions of slavery and servitude, has never ceased in Cuba."[94] Ortiz specifically acknowledges the demographic impact of people of African descent in Cuba due to the Atlantic slave trade and immigration from the nearby islands of Jamaica and Haiti. One of the works in which he tried to remedy the lack of scholarship on people of African descent was *El glosario de afronegrismos* (1924). In this text's prologue Ortiz wrote:

> Many have always recognized that African influence pervades the lexicon of Latin American Spanish. Lexicographical studies of some breadth have provided examples of words that were brought by the slaves. Yet, we need more in-depth studies on the African linguistic heritage of Spanish-speaking nations. The subject is indeed tempting. But, in light of the missing direction and lack of proper direction, my main objective in this book is to open an avenue for Latin American linguistic research. So that these men of science,

devoted to the difficult study of language, can find a source of materials and, occasionally, the type of guidance that is empirically proven.[95]

Ortiz affirmed that there was widespread recognition of the lexical influence of Africans in the diverse Latin American dialects of Spanish and hoped that properly trained language scholars would pay more serious attention to these speech phenomena.

In contrast, Henríquez Ureña overlooked the need to reconsider some of the gaps in knowledge due to the scarcity of Afro-Hispanic studies. His contention was that, "surely" Ortiz's voluminous *Glosario* contained very few legitimate Africanisms:

> Certainly, the majority of the legitimate words do reveal African influence, especially those that denote origin, dances, and special instruments. But all the rest represent only suppositions. Granted, Ortiz provides a detailed study of all these hypotheses and possibilities, even the most preposterous ones, in order to accept or reject them and raise questions. Let us cite a few of these nouns that begin with the letter A and that denote origin: *ábalo, abaya, acocuá, achantí, augunga, apapá, arará*. The bulk of this vocabulary is unknown in Santo Domingo.[96]

In his chapter on Africanisms, Henríquez Ureña does not consider or include the following list of words from Ortiz's *Glosario* in the context of Dominican Spanish. Here, I reproduce a selected group with the English gloss where the modern Spanish variant is available:

> *bejuco* (foliage), *bemba* (big lips), *buche* (bloat), *burundanga* (foolish talk), *cicote* (foot odor), *cocotal* (coconut grove), *cocotazo* (knock on the head), *cocorícamo* (something strange), *cuaba* (kindling, also reprieve), *culeco* (carnavalesque), *chibirico* (bad or mischievous behavior), *chivo* (goat or suspicious), *embromar* (to bother), *fo* (phew), *fuñir* (to bother), *guarapo* (sugar cane juice), *guineo* (banana), *jabado* (very light skin), *mabí* (sugar cane drink), *macuto* (sack made out of straw material), *mengano* (an unidentified person), *mondongo* (intestine or tripe), *monigote* (big oaf), *ñáñara* (a skin rash), *taita* (father), *totuma* (inflammation), *zangano* (stupid), and *zape* (swoosh away).

Most of these words were not integrated into ESD's chapter on Africanisms because, according to the author, they were unheard of in the Dominican context. However, in recent fieldwork, I recorded all these words as part of the active vocabulary of an 80-year old informant from Santo Domingo.[97] Unlike Ortiz, Henríquez Ureña did not seek to explore those aspects of Dominican Spanish that diverged from its Peninsular base. We observe the same sharp contrast when we compare his work to that of his compatriot Carlos Larrazábal Blanco.

Carlos Larrazábal Blanco

Carlos Larrazábal Blanco is another scholar whose work on the subject has been influential. Henríquez Ureña's commentary on his work is limited to a few statements in two footnotes. For example, in footnote number four in Chapter 8, he writes: "Don Carlos Larrazábal Blanco deals with this subject in his *Vocabulario de afronegrismos*, published by the journal *Analectas*, in Santo Domingo, on February 1, 1935."[98] A contemporary of Henríquez Ureña, Larrazábal Blanco was born to Venezuelan parents in Santo Domingo. A graduate of Eugenio María Hostos's *Escuela Normal*, he went on to become a historian and a member of the Dominican Academy of History as well as the Dominican Academy of the Spanish Language. Like Henríquez Ureña, he spent many years living abroad. His exile was the result of deportation by the Trujillo regime, which claimed that he was a foreigner and not a Dominican citizen.[99]

The stark contrast between Henríquez Ureña's approach to the study of Dominican history and Larrazábal Blanco's is borne in this statement from his 1945 article entitled *Papeles de Familia*: "It is not only kings, bishops, presidents, and generals that make history through their required official duties. The common man and the family man also make history, shedding light on habits and customs from the past."[100] With these words, he heralded the beginning of the study of the practice of everyday life in the Dominican Republic and through his work inspired the Afro-Dominican research that proliferated after the fall of Trujillo. Although he had been researching and lecturing on Dominican history since the 1930s, his master work was not published until 1967: *Los negros y la esclavitud en Santo Domingo*. This text is considered a landmark in Afro-Dominican studies.[101] According to Larrazábal Blanco:

> In relation to the Hispanic cultural dimension that dominated the spiritual life of the colony, we must still recognize and distinguish between the Afro-Hispanic and Afro-Franco components. The Afro-Franco aspects of popular Dominican culture inevitably emerge from sharing a border, a palpitating and intense contact zone, which we cannot ignore. In addition, we must consider the continuous immigration of slaves that in some cases ran away from the French colony and founded communities [in the eastern part of the island] ... Both the Hispanic and French [Haitian] elements, each diluting into one another through different types of shared living experiences, largely

shaped the current Afro-Dominican cultural landscape. There are notable differences between the purely Haitian black and the pure Dominican black. But we do not have to go far in order to fully explain these differences. We need only to consider the surrounding social, political, and cultural circumstances.[102]

In addition to the role that Spaniards and their descendants played in the development of Dominican society, Larrazábal Blanco highlights contributions from Afro-Hispanic groups and Haitians. The author does not reduce the Haitian contribution to the border contact zones, but explains that it can be found throughout the Dominican territory and throughout different periods in the island's history.

In the same discussion, Larrazábal Blanco makes the following declaration: "In order to comprehend their full impact, cultural differences between two nations should be studied by comparing their masses and not their elites."[103] This statement sheds light on the different theoretical attitude and methodological approach between the two scholars. One selects a broader empirical base with which to work, while the other opts for a narrower scope. In the final section of Larrazábal Blanco's text ("Haitian influences"), he makes statements that were extremely rare among prior generations of Dominican historiographers and scholars:

> The Haitian influence has continued after the independence and still survives. This is evident not only along the border but throughout the country, in rural areas, villages, and cities... With a greater spiritual connection to their ancestral rituals, Haitians penetrate and influence Dominican society more than the less transculturated *cocolos*.[104] As proof of the existence of Haitian practices in Dominican culture, we provide interesting examples of voodoo rites and objects of witchcraft in a passage from Dr. Moscoso Puello's novel *Cañas y Bueyes*.[105]

Borrowing the concept coined by Ortiz, he proposes the existence of a particular process of Dominican-Haitian *transculturation*. In addition, his statement raises another interesting point of comparison: how the analyses of the same source of data yield different results. Larrazábal Blanco, as Lipski (2005) noted, was careful not to generalize too much from the data extracted from literary sources such as the novel *Cañas y bueyes*. Larrazábal Blanco cautioned: "The presence of Haitian Creole words in our folk tales does not necessarily imply African origin, as some might suppose."[106]

In contrast, Henríquez Ureña did not shy away from making broad generalizations and relied heavily on data from literary texts, some of which did not incorporate unusual words, idioms, or slang. In Chapter 8 of ESD,

Henríquez Ureña also cites *Cañas y bueyes* in reference to the arrival of migrant workers from Haiti and the English-speaking West Indies:

> This invasion is quickly *blackening* the country. It is estimated that there are more than 2,000 immigrants from the Antilles; the total population barely reaches a million and a half. Francisco Eugenio Moscoso Puello's interesting novel, *Cañas y bueyes,* portrays aspects of this invasion... Today the recent Caribbean fad of negro poetry that flourishes in Cuba and Puerto Rico with the works of Luís Pales Matos, Ramón Guirao, José Zacarías Tallet, Alejo Carpentier, Nicolás Guillén, Tomás Blanco, Emilio Ballagas, Marcelino Arozarena, and Vicente Gómez Kemp has reached Santo Domingo. The Negros in [the Dominican] Manuel Cabral's *Doce poemas negros* (1935) are primarily Haitians or *cocolos* from the English-speaking West Indies, because the ones that are native to Santo Domingo have less colorful customs... Arturo Pellerano Castro's old and wonderful *Criollas* are really *criollas* (natives); they speak of white women and *trigueñas* (light-skinned women).[107]

This passage, while not strictly dealing with linguistic matters, nonetheless reveals the powerful presence, in Henríquez Ureña's vision of the Dominican Republic, of an ideology of national identity in which, in keeping with the prevalent misconceptions of the time, racial hierarchies were reproduced and blackness erased. Although Henríquez Ureña does not define the word *trigueña* in this text, it is clear that he is referring to women of mixed race with light skin as opposed to darker skin *mulatas*. His writings reflect his hierarchy of female beauty. In *Memorias* (1909) he wrote the following about the daughters of upper class Haitian families: "Educated in Europe, they make up for their numerous physical defects with their multiple accomplishments."[108] In contrast: "The daughters of the owner of the house, seemed to me, better endowed than their cousins. They were finer. Almost all of them were blondes."[109] Certainly, to Henríquez Ureña, blackness was always foreign, a thing of *cocolos* and Haitians, and not part of what Larrazábal Blanco called "the current Afro-Dominican landscape."[110]

At the end of Chapter 16, Henríquez Ureña includes a list of Dominican toponyms *(Biafara, Bran, Sabana de Juan Bran, Pedro Bran)* of possible African origin but continues to make his case against African substrate influences.[111] He resumes his polemic with Larrazábal Blanco and places the burden of proof on the africanist researcher: "We would have to prove that the blacks who settled in what is today the Duarte Province came from the African Cape Coast."[112] And, as it happens consistently throughout ESD, the measure of proof is often times whether the term in question has a Hispanic antecedent or appears in a source such as Las Casas. In connection with *Los Minas,* the name of a historically black enclave in the city of Santo Domingo, Henríquez Ureña argues: "We cannot seriously consider the connection with the (paroxytone or proparoxytone?) noun of the tribe *Amina*. The fact is that it is an indigenous name, according to the irrefutable testimony of Las Casas in his *Apologética*."[113] In the same discussion, there is one instance in which Henríquez Ureña does concede that certain toponyms might be African in origin:

> *Biafara* (stream, small village, or hamlet): the etymology of this particular name does appear convincing. Mr. Larrazábal does show that *Biafara* blacks, who carried their tribe's name as their last names, did, in fact, live in Santo Domingo in the sixteenth and seventeenth centuries... *Bran* was the last name of blacks who originated from the tribe called by the same name... Mr. Larrazábal also includes *Camú*, which is too far removed from the (paroxytone?) word *Gami*. In the *Malinque* language, this word means "flood." [Larrazábal] merely points to this word, but in light of Las Casas testimony, we are forced to abandon African clues. We also have *can* (place), *ka* or *kan*, which in some African languages means "village." And indeed in Santo Domingo, since, at least, the eighteenth century, black encampments are called *can*. In sum, we have four names of certain or probable African origin and two which are possible Africanisms.[114]

Henríquez Ureña concludes that we can accept, with some degree of certainty, only four Afro-Dominican toponyms. Henríquez Ureña's elegant rebuff of Larrazabal Blanco's linguistic and toponymic analysis notwithstanding, we observe the reductive process of data on African expressions that we have been referring to as erasure. Although in this discussion Henríquez Ureña lends some veracity to Larrazábal Blanco's findings, we observe Henríquez Ureña's insistence that the proof is too minimal to overturn his own judgment or Las Casas's opinion, which forces us "to abandon African clues."[115] By comparing and contrasting the theoretical attitude and research of Ortiz and Larrazábal Blanco with that of Henríquez Ureña, we find more evidence of erasure in Henríquez Ureña's linguistic description.

Castilian Resistance to Babylonian Captivity

Henríquez Ureña reached five major conclusions with respect to the Dominican speech community. First, since there are few differences between educated and popular speech, Dominican Spanish is highly homogeneous. Second, the pronunciation is similar to Andalusian Spanish. Third, it is characterized by the preservation of lexical and syntactic archaisms, which, fourth, due to a process of linguistic fossilization, are markedly Castilian. Finally, Dominican Spanish is characterized the absence of Africanisms. What led him to these conclusions? Part of the answer can be found in ESD where specific linguistic forms are described within the context of a specifically Hispanic literary tradition. However, for the rest of the answer one must turn to the ideological context where the link between specific language forms, on one hand, and social hierarchies and cultural and racial categories, on the other, is not as obvious. Henríquez Ureña's characterization of Dominican Spanish must be considered in light of his affirmations in texts such as *La cultura y las letras* (1936) in which he links the forging of Dominican national consciousness to language maintenance in the struggle for independence from Haiti:

> Everything seemed to indicate that Spanish civilization was dead on Columbus's favorite island. But, no, the nation was not dead. The tenacious spirit of the Hispanic family survived among those that remained. Dominicans never mixed with the invaders. The small Castilian speech community would gather, separately, quietly, under that "Babylonian captivity," as the graduate Doña Ana de Osorio used to say.[116]

In a review of Emilio Rodríguez Demorizi's book on the history of Spanish in the Dominican Republic *(Vicisitudes de la lengua española en Santo Domingo)*, presumably, Henríquez Ureña's last published words on the subject, he highlights the following:

> Three types of languages coexist for a brief period during the sixteenth century: Spanish, indigenous languages, and African languages spoken by slaves. By 1600, only Spanish remained. Look at how many libraries began to appear all over! Núñez de Cáceres and Duarte see in the Spanish language a building block in the defense of the emerging nationality. Curiously enough, in 1844, Félix María del Monte wrote the war anthem against Haitians, avowing "Spaniards, take arms." Later, this war cry was changed to "Compatriots, take arms." In light of the imminent Haitian threat, the ephemeral Spanish reannexation (1861–1865) was certainly an enterprise for the defense of our Hispanicness. Indeed, the native color in literature appears with this awareness of the perseverance of the Spanish language. See Del Monte's *Cantos Dominicanos*.[117]

We must recognize the centrality of Hispanic tradition in Henríquez Ureña's understanding of the Dominican Republic's society and national consciousness. According to him, under the threat of cultural and linguistic extinction, Dominican *criollos* never allowed themselves to submit, collaborate, or mix with the invading Haitians (the only group of African ancestry in Hispaniola) and instead rallied around their

Hispanicness and the Spanish language in order to defeat the forces of change. In this and other similar statements, we can identify the continuity between linguistic descriptions and ideologies of ethnic and national identity that, as I have shown here, characterizes Henríquez Ureña's work. As pointed out before, the author himself alludes explicitly to some of these discursive continuities: his own linguistic and cultural production and the emphasis on the preservation of linguistic and cultural homogeneity in the Dominican Republic since its days as the first site of European settlement. However, only a language ideological approach allows us to fully unveil the ideological character of the apparently "natural" descriptions that emerge in Henríquez Ureña's linguistic production.

The case may be made that the absence of blacks and their linguistic practices in Henríquez Ureña's ESD may be attributed to the fact that they were largely unmapped. This claim is only partially true. The fact is that, while describing the anthropology and ethnography of the country, Enrique Deschamps (1906) had attested:

> Contrary to what happened in the case of the Indian race, the black race spread quickly, deriving considerable physical and moral advantages from their crossbreeding with the European and American races with which they came into immediate contact... Currently, the African race represents a sizeable portion of the Dominican population. Moreover, we find the group born out of mixed marriages with the Spanish race. And lastly, there is the racially pure African group.[118]

While Deschamps conformed to the myth of racial purity among the Spanish descendants, he acknowledged upfront the visible presence of Afro-Dominicans. Two decades before Deschamps recorded these observations, the poet Juan Antonio Alix (1833–1918) had observed the problem of racial erasure in Dominican society in his famous poem *El negro tras de la oreja* (Black behind the ear, 1884).[119] Indeed, there was, at some level, an awareness and discussion of the existence of Afro-Dominicans and of the complex racial composition of Dominican society.

In Pedro Henríquez Ureña's linguistic work we can discern the presence of much more than plain and simple dialectology. It is evident that, in his work, linguistic varieties are associated to racial positions. His knowledge of the linguistic reality of the island was unquestionably unprecedented and his familiarity with the Spanish language and its history admirable. And yet, his texts inevitably reveal a complex interaction between the apparently scientific and ideologically neutral vision of Dominican Spanish that he produced and contemporary discourses of national identity in which race was a central theme. In Henríquez Ureña's studies of Spanish in Santo Domingo, linguistic forms became iconically linked to social, racial, and cultural categories, and in their presence, an image of the nation emerged, a linguistic ideology that mirrors the white Hispanic identity that has dominated the discursive construction of the Dominican Republic since its historical emergence as an independent nation.

Conclusion

Tulio Halperín Donghi enjoys telling the following anecdote concerning Pedro Henríquez Ureña and the foundation of the Biblioteca Ayacucho in Venezuela in 1974: members of the founding committee—Latin American intellectuals from both the political left and the right—had reached an impasse with respect to their first series of Latin American classic works to be published that year. Amidst the building frustration, Enrique Anderson Imbert broke the stalemate by simply asking: "How about Don Pedro's list? Does anyone have Don Pedro's list?" He was referring to the famous list of classic texts that Henríquez Ureña compiled and carried around in his pocket for years, hoping to produce a tableau of Latin American literature. For Halperín Donghi, the most fascinating aspect of the episode, in which he himself participated, is how Henríquez Ureña had become a unifying figure for these ideologically diverse Latin American intellectuals. For me, it is the allure of the archive and the philological image of the past, which were embodied by Henríquez Ureña.

As we discussed in Chapter 4, Henríquez Ureña's linguistic work is clearly located within a scholarly tradition characterized by the following themes: the unity or possible fragmentation of Spanish, its substratum influences, the nature and status of the American varieties, and the question of the origins (Andalusian vs. polygenetic) of these varieties. During the first decades of the twentieth century, these themes were a privileged object of knowledge in the nascent field of Hispanic linguistics and, as I have argued, often emerged and developed in the work of linguists as discursive sites where national and continental identities were produced and disputed. Henríquez Ureña was no exception; his linguistic production addressed these complex issues in terms relevant to both Hispanoamericanism and Dominican nationalism.

Yet, there is still much to learn about the intellectual development of an individual whose career embraced so many different fields of knowledge. According to Rafael Gutiérrez Girardot (1978), it was not until 1945 that Henríquez Ureña achieved his "intellectual liberation" from Ramón Menéndez Pidal, Amado Alonso, and their brand of philology.[1] While this particular periodization is relative, Gutiérrez Girardot's point is well taken.

In the classic *Literary Currents in Hispanic America,* published during the latter part of his career, Henríquez Ureña considered the recent cultural gains of Latin Americans such as "a daring use of metaphor, a great variety of image association, and a free and living syntax."[2] In this text, there are additional signs that Henríquez Ureña's sociocultural ideas and historical notions had evolved, particularly regarding issues of race and the changing intellectual climate:

> At that time, racial theories emanating from European sources, dressed in what looked like a scientific garb, received serious consideration in Hispanic America. Now our attitude is changed. A realistic survey of the actual situation of the many races that mingle in Hispanic America has given us a simple and clear conviction: that no "racial problems" need exist in any community unless it wishes to create them... Our "racial problems" have been gradually reduced by habit and common sense to their cultural and economic grounds. The Indians, we know, have preserved a large part of their old cultures, in fusion with the meager portion of European civilization they have received. The Negroes, too, brought much of their tribal African cultures. In both cases, we were accustomed to look on such survivals as problems; we believed that our special development would be imperfect until the Indian and the Negro were thoroughly "Europeanized," until they had adopted the techniques and the habits that the industrial revolution compelled Europe and the United States to adopt. We know better now.[3]

After immersing himself for decades in the development of a theory of cultural and linguistic archaism that failed to account for black Dominicans and the cultural practices that resulted from their African ancestry and their unique historical experience, Henríquez Ureña seemed open to reconsidering his convictions and ideas of the intellectual climate and ideological matrix from which his previous work had emerged. Evidently, at this point in his career, he was embarking on another stage in his ideological evolution. In *Literary Currents in Hispanic America* as well as in other late essays, there are numerous references to issues of language, race, and identity that reveal a more nuanced view of the cultural and linguistic history of Latin American societies and a willingness to accept new frameworks for discussing cultural differences and plurality. Unfortunately, iconographers and iconoclasts continue to debate over the value of Henríquez Ureña's Dominicanness and the nature of his racial fears. Ultimately, they overlook the signs of Henríquez Ureña's ideological evolution, ignoring the more interesting questions and suggestions that he left us with at the end of his career, which include, What importance do we give to the sociocultural configuration and history of Dominicans in the study of Dominican Spanish? How do we approach sociolinguistic differences in the

Dominican context? Will the Hispanic base of the pan-Hispanic community be sufficiently wide and strong to support all the complex heteroglossic cultures of the Spanish-speaking world? Can Hispanism properly accommodate our linguistic and cultural realities? Do we continue to anchor Spanish on philological images of the past? How do the writings of scholars such as Pedro Henríquez Ureña speak to our current concerns? Do we, in fact, know better now?

Since the 1970s, the Dominican intellectual landscape has effectively been changing. In some intellectual contexts, we find reactions against previous ideological and discursive constraints and new explorations of previously erased subjects (e.g., the complicity between some Dominican intellectuals and state politics or the plurality of Dominican culture). While there is a considerable degree of ideological indifference in Dominican scholarship, the attitudes among scholars range from enthusiasm for the new research challenges to exasperation with having to deal with zones of contact, their origins, and their development. For example, in repetitive newspaper articles and essays, Manuel Núñez[4] rails against the special attention given to "hypothetical" African and Haitian elements by other scholars, whom he tries to radicalize by labeling them "idealizers" and "ideologues" of popular Dominican culture. Núñez insists on making a case against the tolerance of what he calls bad usage of Spanish, Spanglish, the "Haitianization" of the job market in the Dominican Republic, the "Hispanophobia" of some Dominican intellectuals, and the overall process of "de-Hispanization" of Dominican culture. On the other hand, we are encouraged by the work of Ciana Martínez Valdez, Irene Pérez Guerra and Jacqueline Toribio, all of whom, to different degrees, have sought to document and analyze the nature of linguistic contact between Haitians and Dominicans in the Dominican Republic.[5] In addition, we have the sobering work of Orlando Alba,[6] who charts the lexical and phonological changes in Dominican Spanish in relation to Dominicans' sociolinguistic insecurities and the impact of the media. For example, Alba explains how, in the lexical field of baseball, Dominicans first learn and adopt the anglicized variant such as *jonrón* (homerun) and *jonronear* (to hit a homerun) before they learn the available, if any, standard Spanish form (*cuadrangular, conectar un cuadrangular*).[7] Instead of blaming Dominicans for linguistic betrayal, Alba explains that this process of lexical borrowing responds to the communicative needs of the speech community. According to Alba, loan words go through a legitimate process of structural adaptation, thus receiving their "citizenship papers" in the expansion of the community's lexical field.[8]

Despite the emergence of new intellectual frameworks, we still find a monopoly not only on institutions but also on objects of study, and discourses of language, race, and national identity.[9] Just like the country's heteroglossic cultures, diverging points of views still succumb to the dogmas of homogeneism and essentialism, which produce various forms of oppression, discursive violence, and silence. Take, for example, the systematic and fierce denunciation, from various sectors of Dominican society, of the work of the Dominican human rights activist Sonia Pierre[10] on behalf of Haitian immigrants and their Dominican-born children. The misunderstanding and repudiation of all things Haitian by some Dominicans unfortunately contribute to a process of racial misrecognition and self-loathing. Even in the age of postnationalism, the prevalence of Europeanized Hispanism as the cultural and aesthetic standard forces many Dominicans to flee their own blackness, whiten their skin, and attempt to rein in their "wild" Spanish.

The relatively innovative ("free and living") syntax of Dominican Spanish is also a cause of anxiety for some Hispanists from both sides of the Atlantic. Every so often, we witness or read accounts of professors and teachers of Spanish who abhor the accelerated tempo of Dominican Spanish, the absence of s consonants in syllable-final position, and the speech varieties as well as the anti-languages associated with distinct identities (*cibaeño, cocolo, Dominican York, gay, jevito, palomo, rayaó, sureño,* and *tíguere,* among others). A look at the economic ground and cultural landscape in which these groups are embedded should alert us to the fact that their complex linguistic repertoires must correspond, in some degree, with their equally complex sociopolitical realities. We must, however, be careful not to idealize the features of popular Dominican Spanish or its usage. The effects of discursive violence can be found everywhere, even among speakers of minority dialects and minoritized sociolects who insist on "keeping it real"[11] at all costs and reject interlocutors unless they use the local code. Nonetheless, we must pose a fundamental question: should the ultimate goal of teachers of Spanish and language mavens be that their students adopt only the speech patterns, self-image, and linguistic loyalties of the most educated people in their respective societies? This question may not have a simple answer. But we may engage it to a greater advantage, provided we abandon our racial prejudices and resist the hegemonic impulses of power and truth regimes. If we could only desist from imposing our hierarchies upon our students and not force them to disengage from their most pressing sociopolitical realities! Perhaps then we could better guide them to study, understand, appreciate, and responsibly benefit from the treasures of Spanish-speaking cultures everywhere. In the end, I believe Pedro Henríquez Ureña was slowly embracing a similar perspective and calling for a renewed effort towards greater freedom.

Notes

Introduction

1. Edward Said, *Beginnings: Intention and Method* (New York: Columbia University Press, 1975), 6.
2. Pedro Henríquez Ureña, "La cultura y las letras coloniales en Santo Domingo," in *Obra dominicana*, ed. José Chez Checo (Santo Domingo: Sociedad Dominicana de Bibliófilos, 1988), 204. Unless otherwise noted, all translations from Spanish and French are mine.
3. Emilio Rodríguez Demorizi, "Vicisitudes de la lengua española en Santo Domingo," in *Lengua y folklore de Santo Domingo* (Santo Domingo: Universidad Católica Madre y Maestra, 1975), 14–16.
4. Joaquín Balaguer, "Discurso Pronunciado por el Presidente de la República Dominicana Joaquín Balaguer, en Ocasión de la Primera Cumbre Iberoamericana, Guadalajara, México, 1991," http://www.cip.cu/webcip/eventos/cumbre-ibero/cumbre1/discursos/ (accessed May 3, 2008).
5. I use the category of "Dominican Spanish"—instead of the longer phrase "the variety of Spanish in the Dominican Republic"—merely as a stylistic convenience in order to refer to phenomena related to the use of Spanish in the Dominican Republic. This stylistic choice applies to references to other dialectal varieties of Spanish.

Chapter 1

1. Pedro Henríquez Ureña, *Horas de estudio* (Paris: Ollendorf, 1910), 8.
2. Max Henríquez Ureña, "Hermano y maestro," in *Presencia de Pedro Henríquez Ureña: escritos sobre el maestro*, ed. Jorge Tena Reyes and Tomás Castro Burdiez (Santo Domingo: Editorial Ciguapa, 2001), 23.
3. Pedro Henríquez Ureña, *Memorias, diario, notas de viaje*, ed. Enrique Zuleta Álvarez (Mexico: Fondo de Cultura Económica, [1909] 2000), 32.
4. Ibid., 43.
5. Cited in Pedro Luis Barcia, *Pedro Henríquez Ureña y la Argentina* (Santo Domingo: Ediciones Ferilibro, 2006), 127.
6. Max Henríquez Ureña, "Hermano y maestro," in *Presencia de Pedro Henríquez Ureña: escritos sobre el maestro*, ed. Jorge Tena Reyes and Tomás Castro Burdiez (Santo Domingo: Editorial Ciguapa, 2001), 17.

7. Ibid., 41.
8. Pedro Henríquez Ureña, *Memorias, diario, notas de viaje,* ed. Enrique Zuleta Álvarez (Mexico: Fondo de Cultura Económica, [1909] 2000), 40.
9. Enrique Deschamps, *La República Dominicana: directorio y guía general* (Barcelona, Spain, 1906), 255–256.
10. Pedro Henríquez Ureña, *Memorias, diario, notas de viaje,* ed. Enrique Zuleta Álvarez (Mexico: Fondo de Cultura Económica, [1909] 2000), 82–84.
11. Guillermo Piña-Contreras, "El universo familiar en la formación intelectual de Pedro Henríquez Ureña," in *Presencia de Pedro Henríquez Ureña: escritos sobre el maestro,* ed. Jorge Tena Reyes and Tomás Castro Burdiez (Santo Domingo: Editorial Ciguapa, 2001), 348.
12. Cited in Alfredo Roggiano, *Pedro Henríquez Ureña en los Estado Unidos* (Mexico: Editorial Cultura, 1961), 89–90.
13. Ibid., 112.
14. Ibid., xl.
15. Ibid., XLVIII.
16. Ibid., XXXXX.
17. J. D. M. Ford, "A note from J. D. M. Ford on Pedro Henríquez Ureña," *Books Abroad* 21, 1 (1947): 31.
18. Alfredo Roggiano, *Pedro Henríquez Ureña en los Estado Unidos* (Mexico: Editorial Cultura, 1961).
19. Pedro Henríquez Ureña, "La influencia de la revolución en la vida intelectual de México," in *La utopía de América,* ed. Rafael Gutiérrez Girardot and Ángel Rama (Caracas: Biblioteca Ayacucho, [1925b] 1978), 370.
20. Javier Garciadiego, *Rudos contra científicos: La Universidad Nacional durante la Revolución Mexicana* (Mexico: el Colegio de México, 1996). The *Científicos* were a group of European-educated intellectuals from Mexico City. They were called *Científicos* (The Scientists) because of their strict subscription to Comte's scientific Positivism.
21. Cited in Sonia Henríquez Ureña de Hito, *Pedro Henríquez Ureña: apuntes para una biografía* (Mexico: Siglo XXI Editores, 1993), 47.
22. Pedro Henríquez Ureña, *Memorias, diario, notas de viaje,* ed. Enrique Zuleta Álvarez (Mexico: Fondo de Cultura Económica, [1909] 2000), 158.
23. Ibid., italics in the original.
24. Andrés L. Mateo, *Pedro Henríquez Ureña: errancia y creación* (Bogota: Taurus, 2001), 191–192; Silvio Torres-Saillant, "The Tribulations of Blackness: Stages in Dominican Racial Identity," *Callaloo* 23, 3 (2000): 1086–1111; Arcadio Díaz Quiñones, "Pedro Henríquez Ureña: Modernidad, diáspora y construcción de identidades," in *Modernización e identidades sociales,* ed. Gilberto Giménez and Ricardo Pozas H. (Mexico: Universidad Nacional Autónoma de México, 1994), 69.
25. Cited in Enrique Krauze, "El crítico errante: Pedro Henríquez Ureña," *Vuelta* 100 (March 1985): 20.
26. Samuel Ramos, "Pedro Henríquez Ureña," *Cuadernos Americanos* XXVIII, 4 (1946): 265.

27. Enrique Zuleta Álvarez, "La recepción crítica de la obra de Pedro Henríquez Ureña," in *Pedro Henríquez Ureña: ensayos*, ed. José Luis Abellán and Ana María Barrenechea (Madrid: Allca XX, 1998), 495.
28. Ibid., 522.
29. Rafael Gutiérrez Girardot, "El ensayo posmodernista: Pedro Henríquez Ureña," in *Presencia de Pedro Henríquez Ureña: escritos sobre el maestro*, ed. Jorge Tena Reyes and Tomás Castro Burdiez (Santo Domingo: Editorial Ciguapa, 2001a), 204.
30. Soledad Álvarez, *La Magna Patria de Pedro Henríquez Ureña* (Santo Domingo: Editorial Taller, 1981), 11.
31. Ibid., 79.
32. Rafael Gutiérrez Girardot, "Pedro Henríquez Ureña y la historiografía latinoamericana," in *Pedro Henríquez Ureña: ensayos*, ed. José Luis Abellán and Ana María Barrenechea (Madrid: Allca XX, 1998), 67.
33. Sergio Pitol, *De la realidad a la literatura* (Mexico: Ariel and Editorial Planeta Mexicana, 2002), 91.
34. Emilio Rodríguez Demorizi, *Breve panegírico de Pedro Henríquez Ureña* (Santo Domingo: Editora Taller, 1981), 5.
35. Emilio Rodríguez Demorizi, "Dominicanidad de Pedro Henríquez Ureña," in *Presencia de Pedro Henríquez Ureña: escritos sobre el maestro*, ed. Jorge Tena Reyes and Tomás Castro Burdiez (Santo Domingo: Editorial Ciguapa, 2001), 562.
36. Juan Jacobo de Lara, *Sobre Pedro Henríquez Ureña y otros ensayos* (Santo Domingo: UNPHU, 1982), 17.
37. Juan Jacobo de Lara, *Pedro Henríquez Ureña: su vida y su obra* (Santo Domingo: UNPHU, 1975), 232.
38. Carlos Federico Pérez y Pérez, "Nacionalismo y americanismo en Pedro Henríquez Ureña," in *El libro jubilar de Pedro Henríquez Ureña*, 2 vols., ed. Julio Jaime Julia (Santo Domingo: UNPHU, 1984), 361.
39. Soledad Álvarez, "La pasión dominicana de Pedro Henríquez Ureña," in *Pedro Henríquez Ureña: ensayos*, ed. José Luis Abellán and Ana María Barrenechea (Madrid: Allca XX, 1998), 625.
40. Fernando Valerio-Holguín, "Pedro Henríquez Ureña: el mulato intelectual poscolonial" (paper presented at the II International Conference on Caribbean Studies, University of Cartagena, Cartagena, Colombia, March 15–19, 2010).
41. Alfonso Reyes, "El criticón," in *Obras completas III* (Mexico: Fondo de Cultura Económica, 1995), 282.
42. See Leila Guerreiro's "Pedro Henríquez Ureña: el eterno extranjero" (2003), Victoria Núñez's dissertation, "Unpacking the Suitcases They Carried: Narratives of Dominican and Puerto Rican Migrations to the Northeastern United States" (2006) and Danny Mendez's dissertation "In Zones of Contact (Combat): Dominican Narratives of Migration and Displacements in the United States and Puerto Rico" (2008).
43. Arcadio Díaz Quiñones, "Pedro Henríquez Ureña: modernidad, diáspora y construcción de identidades," in *Modernización e identidades sociales*, ed.

Gilberto Giménez and Ricardo Pozas H. (Mexico: Universidad Nacional Autónoma de México, 1994), 65.
44. Enrique Krauze, "El crítico errante: Pedro Henríquez Ureña," *Vuelta* 100 (March 1985), 12.
45. Ibid., 23.
46. Tulio Halperín Donghi, *Vida y muerte de la república verdadera: 1910–1930* (Buenos Aires: Emecé, 1999), 115–116.
47. Eugenio Pucciarelli, *Pedro Henríquez Ureña, humanista* (Buenos Aires: Publicaciones del Centro de Estudios Filosóficos, 1984), 42.
48. Liliana Weinberg, "Pedro Henríquez Ureña: exilio y ensayo," http://www.ccydel.unam.mx/ensayo/pdf/fragmento/PHU%20Exilio%20ensayo.pdf (2002) (accessed June 12, 2007).
49. Ibid.
50. Arcadio Díaz Quiñones, "Pedro Henríquez Ureña: Modernidad, diáspora y construcción de identidades," in *Modernización e identidades sociales*, ed. Gilberto Giménez and Ricardo Pozas H. (Mexico: Universidad Nacional Autónoma de México, 1994), 79.
51. Arcadio Díaz Quiñones, *Sobre los principios: la tradición y los intelectuales caribeños* (Bernal, Argentina: Universidad Nacional de Quilmes Editorial, 2006), 252.
52. Juan M. Lope Blanch, *Estudios de lingüística hispanoamericana* (Mexico: Universidad Nacional Autónoma de México, 1989), 37.
53. Ibid., 34.
54. Carlisle González Tapia, *El pensamiento lingüístico de Pedro Henríquez Ureña* (Santo Domingo: Ciudad Universitaria, 1998), 13.
55. Ibid., 24–25.
56. Ibid., 28.
57. Ibid., 29.
58. Ibid., 76.
59. Ibid., 102.
60. Ibid., 168–170.
61. Edward Said, *Orientalism* (New York: Vintage Books, 1979), 132.
62. María Ángeles Álvarez Martínez, "Pedro Henríquez Ureña y la dialectología hispanoamericana," *La Torre* 3, 7–8 (1998): 178.
63. María Vaquero, "El español en América como problema en el siglo XX," *Revista de Estudios Hispánicos* 24, 1 (1997): 280.
64. Juan M. Lope Blanch, *Estudios de lingüística hispanoamericana* (Mexico: Universidad Nacional Autónoma de México, 1989), 36.
65. Ibid., 50.
66. Max Jiménez Sabater, *Más datos sobre el español dominicano de la República Dominicana* (Santo Domingo: Intec, 1975), 176.
67. Max Jiménez Sabater, "Enfoques sociolingüísticos sobre el español dominicano," *Scriptura* II (1981): 87.
68. Orlando Alba, *Estudios sobre el español dominicano* (Santiago, Dominican Republic: PUCMM, 1990), 212.
69. Ibid., 213.

70. Ibid., 214.
71. Irene Pérez Guerra, "La producción de tema lingüístico y filológico en la obra de Pedro Henríquez Ureña," in *Obras completas: estudios lingüísticos y filológicos,* vol. 4, ed. Irene Pérez Guerra (Santo Domingo: Editora Nacional, 2004), 9.
72. Irene Pérez Guerra, "Aportación a un tema en debate en el Caribe hispánico: el arcaísmo del español dominicano," in *Actas del II Congreso Internacional de Historia de la Lengua Española,* ed. M. Ariza et al., vol. 2 (1992): 485.
73. Ibid., 487–489.
74. Ibid., 490.
75. Juan Isidro Jimenes Grullón, *Pedro Henríquez Ureña, realidad y mito y otro ensayo* (Santo Domingo: Editorial Librería Dominicana, 1969), 11.
76. Ibid., 19.
77. Ibid., 24; ellipsis in the original.
78. Ibid., 137.
79. Ibid., 22.
80. Elvira N. de Arnoux, "Disciplinar desde la lengua: 'La gramática castellana' de Amado Alonso y Pedro Henríquez Ureña," in *Homenaje a Ofelia Kovacci,* ed. Elvira N. de Arnoux and Ángela Di Tullio (Buenos Aires: Eudeba, 2001), 72.
81. Guillermo Guitarte, "Cuervo, Henríquez Ureña y la polémica sobre el andalucismo de América," *Vox Románica* 17 (1958a): 368.
82. Beatriz Sarlo, "Pedro Henríquez Ureña: lectura de una problemática," in *Pedro Henríquez Ureña: ensayos,* ed. José Luis Abellán and Ana María Barrenechea (Madrid: Allca XX, 1998), 880.
83. Soledad Álvarez, *La Magna Patria de Pedro Henríquez Ureña* (Santo Domingo: Editorial Taller, 1981), 12.
84. Jean Franco, "El humanismo de Pedro Henríquez Ureña," in *Pedro Henríquez Ureña: ensayos,* ed. José Luis Abellán and Ana María Barrenechea (Madrid: Allca XX, 1998), 818.
85. González Tapia (1998), Pérez Guerra (2004), and Valdez (2008) have compiled the most definitive lists of Henríquez Ureña's linguistic works.

Chapter 2

1. Terry Eagleton, *Ideology: An Introduction* (London: Verso, 1991), 1.
2. Kathryn Woolard, "Language Ideology as a Field of Inquiry," in *Language Ideologies: Practice and Theory,* ed. B. Schieffelin, K. Woolard and P. Kroskrity (New York and Oxford: Oxford University Press, 1998), 8.
3. Francis Bacon, *The New Organon and Related Writings* (Indianapolis and New York: The Bobbs-Merrill Company, Inc., 1960) 47–48.
4. Francis Bacon, *The Essays or Counsels* (London: Penguin Books, 1985), 111.
5. Cited in Teun van Dijk, *Ideología y discurso: una introducción multidisciplinaria* (Barcelona: Ariel, 2003), 14.
6. Cited in Terry Eagleton, *Ideology: An Introduction* (London: Verso, 1991), 67.

7. Raymond Williams, *Marxism and Literature* (Oxford and New York: Oxford University Press, 1977), 55.
8. Terry Eagleton, *Ideology: An Introduction* (London: Verso, 1991), 89.
9. Raymond Williams, *Marxism and Literature* (Oxford and New York: Oxford University Press, 1977), 57.
10. Ibid., 62.
11. Teun van Dijk, "Discourse Analysis as Ideology Analysis," in *Language and Peace*, ed. C. Shaffner and A. Wenden (Aldershot: Dartmouth, 1995), 19.
12. Teun van Dijk, "Discourse, Knowledge and Ideology: Reformulating Old Questions and Proposing Some New Solutions," in *Communicating Ideologies: Multidisciplinary Perspectives on Language, Discourse and Social Practice*, ed. Martín Putz et al. (Frankfurt and Berlin: Peter Lang, 2002), 16.
13. Susan Phillips, "Language Ideologies in Institutions of Power: A Commentary," in *Language Ideologies: Practice and Theory*, ed. B. Schieffelin, K. Woolard and P. Kroskrity (New York and Oxford: Oxford University Press, 1998), 212.
14. Antonio Gramsci, *Selections from the Prison Notebooks of Antonio Gramsci*, ed. Quintin Hoare and Geoffrey Nowell Smith (New York: International Publishers, 1971), 57–58.
15. Pedro Henríquez Ureña, "La influencia de la revolución en la vida intelectual de México," in *La utopía de América*, ed. Rafael Gutiérrez Girardot and Ángel Rama (Caracas: Biblioteca Ayacucho, [1925b] 1978), 369.
16. Antonio Gramsci, *Selections from the Prison Notebooks of Antonio Gramsci*, ed. Quintin Hoare and Geoffrey Nowell Smith (New York: International Publishers, 1971), 245.
17. Ibid., 377.
18. Ibid.
19. Pedro Henríquez Ureña, "Seis ensayos en busca de nuestra expresión," in *Obras completas: estudios lingüísticos y filológicos*, vol. 4, ed. Irene Pérez Guerra (Santo Domingo: Editora Nacional, [1928] 2004), 409.
20. Cited in Peter Ives, *Language and Hegemony in Gramsci (Reading Gramsci)* (London and Ann Arbor: Pluto Press, 2004), 82.
21. Ibid., 349.
22. Antonio Gramsci, *Selections from the Prison Notebooks of Antonio Gramsci*, ed. Quintin Hoare and Geoffrey Nowell Smith (New York: International Publishers, 1971), 349.
23. Sara Mills, *Discourse* (London: Routledge, 2004).
24. Michel Foucault, *Discipline and Punish: The Birth of Prison*, trans. Alan Sheridan (New York: Random House, 1995), 26.
25. Ibid., 27.
26. Sara Mills, *Discourse* (London: Routledge, 2004), 32.
27. Michel Foucault, *Discipline and Punish: The Birth of the Prison*, trans. Alan Sheridan (New York: Random House, 1995), 27.
28. Ibid., 194.
29. Michel Foucault, *The Archeology of Knowledge and the Discourse on Language* (New York: Basic Books, 1994a), 216.

30. Michel Foucault, *The Order of Things: An Archeology of the Human Sciences* (New York: Vintage, 1994b), 87.
31. Pierre Bourdieu, *Language and Symbolic Power* (Cambridge, MA: Harvard University Press, 1991), 67; italics in the original.
32. V. N. Volosinov, *Marxism and the Philosophy of Language* (Cambridge, MA: Harvard University Press, 1986), 11.
33. Ibid., 15.
34. Susan Gal and Kathryn Woolard, "Constructing Languages and Publics: Authority and Representation," in *Languages and Publics: The Making of Authority*, ed. Susan Gal and Kathryn Woolard (Manchester: St. Jerome Publishing, 2001), 1.
35. José Del Valle, "Glotopolítica, ideología y discurso: categorías para el estudio del estatus simbólico del español," in *La lengua, ¿patria común? Ideas e ideologías del español*, ed. José del Valle (Madrid and Frankfurt: Iberoamericana and Vervuert, 2007), 20.
36. Kathryn Woolard, "Language Ideology as a Field of Inquiry," in *Language Ideologies: Practice and Theory*, ed. B. Schieffelin, K. Woolard and P. Kroskrity (New York and Oxford: Oxford University Press, 1998), 11.
37. Ibid.
38. Ibid., 14.
39. Paul V. Kroskrity, "Regimenting Languages: Language Ideological Perspectives," in *Regimes of Language: Ideologies, Polities and Identities*, ed. Paul V. Kroskrity (Santa Fe, NM: School of American Research Press, 2000), 3.
40. Ibid., 8.
41. Judith Irvine, "When Talk Isn't Cheap: Language and Political Economy," *American Ethnologist* 16 (1989): 248–267.
42. Jane Hill, " 'Today There is No Respect': Nostalgia, 'Respect' and Oppositional Discourse in Mexicano (Nahuatl) Language Ideology," in *Language Ideologies: Practice and Theory*, ed. B. Schieffelin, K. Woolard and P. Kroskrity (New York and Oxford: Oxford University Press, 1998).
43. Paul V. Kroskrity, "Regimenting Languages: Language Ideological Perspectives," in *Regimes of Language: Ideologies, Polities and Identities*, ed. Paul V. Kroskrity (Santa Fe, NM: School of American Research Press, 2000), 12.
44. Ibid., 19.
45. José Del Valle, "La lengua, patria común: política lingüística, política exterior y el post-nacionalismo hispánico," in *Studies on Ibero-Romance Linguistics. Dedicated to Ralph Penny*, ed. Roger Wright and Meter Ricketts (Newark, Delaware: Juan de la Cuesta, 2005), 12.
46. José Del Valle, "US Latinos, la Hispanofonía, and the Language Ideologies of High Modernity," in *Globalization and Language in the Spanish-Speaking World*, ed. Clare Mar-Moliero and Miranda Stewart (Hampshire, England: Palgrave Macmillan, 2006), 29.
47. Ibid., 29.
48. Paul V. Kroskrity, "Regimenting Languages: Language Ideological Perspectives," in *Regimes of Language: Ideologies, Polities and Identities*, ed. Paul V. Kroskrity (Santa Fe, NM: School of American Research Press, 2000), 18.

49. Jacqueline Toribio, "Nosotros Somos Dominicanos: Language and Self-Definition among Dominicans," in *Research on Spanish in the U.S.*, ed. Ana Roca (Somerville, MA: Cascadilla Press, 2000b), 261.
50. Paul V. Kroskrity, "Regimenting Languages: Language Ideological Perspectives," in *Regimes of Language: Ideologies, Polities and Identities*, ed. Paul V. Kroskrity (Santa Fe, NM: School of American Research Press, 2000), 18–19.
51. José Luis Blas Arroyo, *La sociolingüística del español: desarrollos y perspectivas en el estudio de la lengua en contexto social* (Madrid: Cátedra, 2006), 375.
52. Paul V. Kroskrity, "Regimenting Languages: Language Ideological Perspectives," in *Regimes of Language: Ideologies, Polities and Identities*, ed. Paul V. Kroskrity (Santa Fe, NM: School of American Research Press, 2000), 20–21.
53. Ibid., 21.
54. John Haiman, *Natural Syntax; Iconicity and Erosion* (New York: Cambridge University Press, 1985), 20.
55. Bruce Hawkins, "The Social Dimension of a Cognitive Grammar," in *Discourse and Perspective in Cognitive Linguistics*, ed. W. A. Liebert et al. (Amsterdam and Philadelphia: John Benjamins, 1997), 141.
56. Ibid., 31.
57. Ibid., 32.
58. Charles Sanders Peirce, *The Essential Peirce: Selected Philosophical Writings*, vol. 2 (Bloomington and Indianapolis: Indiana University Press, 1998), 13; italics in the original.
59. Ibid., 15.
60. William Hanks, "Indexicality," in *Key Terms in Language and Culture*, ed. Alessandro Duranti (Malden, Massachussetts: Blackwell, 2001), 119.
61. Michael Silverstein, "Shifters, Linguistic Categories, and Cultural Description," in *Meaning in Anthropology*, ed. Keith Basso and Henry Selby (Albuquerque: University of New Mexico Press, 1976), 27.
62. Charles Sanders Peirce, *The Essential Peirce: Selected Philosophical Writings*, vol. 2 (Bloomington and Indianapolis: Indiana University Press, 1998), 17. Peirce explained: "let us take as an example of a symbol the word 'loveth.' Associated with this word is an idea, which is the mental icon of a person loving another... 'Loveth' occurs in a sentence: Ezekiel loveth 'Huldah.' Ezekiel and Huldah must contain indices; for without indices it is impossible to designate what one is talking about... Now the effect of the word 'loveth' is that a pair of objects denoted by the pair of indices, Ezekiel and Huldah, is represented by the icon, or the image we have in our minds of a lover and his beloved."
63. Ibid., 19.
64. Michael Silverstein, "Shifters, Linguistic Categories, and Cultural Description," in *Meaning in Anthropology*, ed. Keith Basso and Henry Selby (Albuquerque: University of New Mexico Press, 1976), 30.
65. Kathryn Woolard, "Why Dat Now? Linguistic Anthropological Contributions to the Explanation of Sociolinguistic Icons and Change," *Journal of Sociolinguistics* 12, 4 (2007b): 432–452.

66. Judith Irvine and Susan Gal, "Language Ideology and Linguistic Differentiation," in *Regimes of Language: Ideologies, Polities and Identities*, ed. Paul V. Kroskrity (Santa Fe, NM: School of American Research Press, 2000), 37.
67. Kathryn Woolard, "Why Dat Now? Linguistic Anthropological Contributions to the Explanation of Sociolinguistic Icons and Change," *Journal of Sociolinguistics* 12, 4 (2007b): 432–452; Juan R. Valdez, "The Iconization of Dominican Spanish in Pedro Henríquez Ureña's Linguistic Texts," *Spanish in Context* 6, 2 (2009): 176–198.
68. Judith Irvine and Susan Gal, "Language Ideology and Linguistic Differentiation," in *Regimes of Language: Ideologies, Polities and Identities*, ed. Paul V. Kroskrity (Santa Fe, NM: School of American Research Press, 2000), 37.
69. Ibid., 39.
70. Ibid., 38.
71. Ibid., 46.
72. Ibid., 38.
73. Ibid., 47.
74. Ibid., 53.
75. Ibid., 55.
76. Ibid., 72.
77. Ibid., 76.
78. Ibid., 78.
79. Jan Blommaert and Jef Verschueren, "The Role of Language in European Nationalist Ideologies," in *Language Ideologies: Practice and Theory*, ed. B. Schieffelin, K. Woolard and P. Kroskrity (New York and Oxford: Oxford University Press, 1998), 194.
80. José Del Valle, "La lengua, patria común: política lingüística, política exterior y el post-nacionalismo hispánico," in *Studies on Ibero-Romance Linguistics. Dedicated to Ralph Penny*, ed. Roger Wright and Meter Ricketts (Newark, Delaware: Juan de la Cuesta, 2005), 18; emphasis in the original.
81. Joseph Errington, "Indonesian('s) Authority," in *Regimes of Language: Ideologies, Polities and Identities*, ed. Paul V. Kroskrity (Santa Fe, NM: School of American Research Press, 2000), 209.
82. Ibid., 211.
83. Elvira N. de Arnoux and Carlos R. Luis, *El pensamiento ilustrado y el lenguaje* (Buenos Aires: Eudeba, 2003), 8.
84. José Del Valle, "US Latinos, la Hispanofonía, and the Language Ideologies of High Modernity," in *Globalization and Language in the Spanish-Speaking World*, ed. Clare Mar-Moliero and Miranda Stewart (Hampshire: England: Palgrave Macmillan, 2006), 36.
85. See their website: (www.usefoundation.org).
86. Jacqueline Toribio, "Language Variation and the Linguistic Enactment of Identity among Dominicans," *Linguistics* 38, 5 (2000a): 1142.
87. "Glottopolitical," a label that is not widely used in the Anglo-Saxon tradition ("politics of language"), refers to the concrete impact of language planning

and language policies on linguistic behavior within a speech community. See Guespin and Marcellesi (1986).
88. Elvira N. de Arnoux, "Discursos sobre nación." PhD diss., Universidade Da Coruña (2007), 11.
89. Elvira N. de Arnoux and José Del Valle, "Las representaciones ideológicas del lenguaje: discurso glotopolítico y panhispanismo," *Spanish in Context* 7, 1 (2010): 17.
90. José del Valle and Luis Gabriel-Stheeman, "Lengua y mercado: el español en la era de la globalización económica," in *La batalla del idioma: la intelectualidad hispánica ante la lengua*, ed. José del Valle and Luis Gabriel-Stheeman (Frankfurt y Madrid: Vervuert and Iberoamericana, 2004c), 254.
91. Ibid., 260.
92. I am particularly referring to the perspective established by the Rouen school in France.
93. Elvira N. de Arnoux, "Discursos sobre nación," PhD diss., Universidade Da Coruña (2007), 13.
94. Louis Guespin and Jean-Baptiste Marcellesi, "Pour la Glottopolitique," *Langages* 83 (1986): 5–34.
95. Elvira N. de Arnoux, "El análisis del discurso en el pensamiento gramatical ilustrado: Jovellanos lector de Condillac," in *El pensamiento ilustrado y el lenguaje*, ed. Elvira N. de Arnoux and Carlos R. Luis (Buenos Aires: Eudeba, 2003), 67.
96. Konrad Koerner, *Professing Linguistic Historiography* (Amsterdam and Philadelphia: John Benjamins, 1995), 17–18.
97. Ibid., 17.
98. Ibid., 4.
99. Ibid., 21.
100. Paul Laurendeau, "Theory of Emergence: Towards a Historical-Materialistic Approach to the History of Linguistics," in *Ideologies of Language*, ed. John Joseph and Talbot Taylor (London: Routledge, 1990), 208.
101. Ibid., 210.
102. Ibid., 211; italics in the original.
103. Ibid., 212; italics in the original.
104. Ibid., 215; italics in the original.
105. Ibid., 215.
106. Ferdinand de Saussure, *Course in General Linguistics* (New York: MacGraw Hill, [1916] 1986), 232.
107. Ibid., 15–16.
108. Roy Harris, *Saussure and his Interpreters* (New York: New York University Press, 2001), 193.
109. Ibid., 193.
110. Ibid., 23.
111. Tony Crowley, *Language in History: Theories and Texts* (London: Routledge, 1996), 27.
112. Cited in Crowley.

113. Konrad Koerner, "Ideology in the 19th and 20th Century Linguistics," in *Language and Ideology: Theoretical Cognitive Approaches*, vol. 2, ed. René Dirven et al. (Amsterdam: John Benjamins, 2001), 255.
114. Paul T. Roberge, "The Ideological Profile of Afrikaans Historical Linguistics," in *Ideologies of Language*, ed. John Joseph and Talbot Taylor (London: Routledge, 1990), 131–132.
115. Ibid., 133.
116. Cited in José Del Valle, "Menéndez Pidal, National Regeneration, and Linguistic Utopia," in *The Battle over Spanish between 1800 and 2000: Language Ideologies and Hispanic Intellectuals*, ed. José Del Valle and Luis Gabriel-Stheeman (Madrid and Frankfurt: Iberoamericana and Vervuert, 2002b), 103; Del Valle's translation.
117. Konrad Koerner, "Ideology, 'Resonanzbedarf,' and Linguistic-Philological Scholarship," in *Communicating Ideologies: Multidisciplinary Perspectives on Language, Discourse, and Social Practice*, ed. Martin Pütz, JoAnne Neff-van Aertselaer and Teun van Dijk (Frankfurt: Peter Lang, 2004), 57.
118. José Del Valle, "Menéndez Pidal, National Regeneration, and Linguistic Utopia," in *The Battle over Spanish between 1800 and 2000: Language Ideologies and Hispanic Intellectuals*, ed. José Del Valle and Luis Gabriel-Stheeman (Madrid and Frankfurt: Iberoamericana and Vervuert, 2002b), 99.
119. Ibid., 100.
120. Susan Gal, "Linguistic Theories and National Images in Nineteenth Century Hungary," in *Languages and Publics: The Making of Authority*, ed. Susan Gal and Kathryn Woolard (Manchester: St. Jerome Publishing, 2001), 318.
121. Antonio Gramsci, *Selections from the Prison Notebooks of Antonio Gramsci*, ed. Quintin Hoare and Geoffrey Nowell Smith (New York: International Publishers, 1971), 350.

Chapter 3

1. Edwin Williamson, *The Penguin History of Latin America* (London: Penguin Books, 1992), 233.
2. Tulio Halperín Donghi, *Historia contemporánea de América Latina* (Madrid: Alianza Editorial, 1998), 276.
3. See Ángel Rama (1984), Halperín Donghi (1998), Williamson (1992).
4. Roberto Fernández Retamar, *Todo Calibán* (Concepción, Chile: Cuadernos Atanea, 1998), 64.
5. Julio Ramos, *Divergent Modernities: Culture and Politics in Nineteenth-Century Latin America* (Durham: Duke University Press, 2001), 57.
6. Ibid., 234–237.
7. Beatriz González Stephan, "Las disciplinas escriturarias de la patria: constituciones, gramáticas y manuales," *Estudios. Revista de Investigaciones Literarias* 3, 5, 1995: 28.

8. Andrés Bello, philologist, poet, and lawmaker, is a seminal figure whose work constitutes an important part of Latin American culture and history. See Chapter 4.
9. Julio Ramos, *Divergent Modernities: Culture and Politics in Nineteenth-Century Latin America* (Durham: Duke University Press, 2001), 56.
10. Michiel Baud, "Intelectuales, nación y modernidad en la República Dominicana," in *Relatos de nación: la construcción de identidades en el mundo hispánico*, ed. Francisco Colom González (Madrid and Frankfurt: Iberoamericana and Vervuert, 2005), 933.
11. Nicola Miller, *In the Shadow of the State: Intellectuals and the Quest for National Identity in Twentieth-Century Spanish America* (London: Verso, 1999).
12. Rafael Gutiérrez Girardot, *El intelectual y la historia* (Caracas: Fondo Editorial La Nave Va, 2001b), 30.
13. Eugenio María de Hostos, *Páginas dominicanas*, ed. Emilio Rodríguez Demorizi (Santo Domingo: Editora Taller, 1979), 40.
14. See Ángel Rama (1984) and Julio Ramos (2001).
15. Domingo Faustino Sarmiento, *Facundo: civilización y barbarie* (Madrid: Cátedra, 2005), 198.
16. Ángel Rama, *La ciudad letrada* (Hanover, NH: Ediciones del Norte, 1984), 32.
17. Beatriz González Stephan, "Las disciplinas escriturarias de la patria: constituciones, gramáticas y manuales," *Estudios. Revista de Investigaciones Literarias* 3, 5, 1995: 22.
18. Pedro Henríquez Ureña, *Literary Currents in Hispanic America* (Cambridge, MA: Harvard University Press, 1945), 117.
19. Eugenio María de Hostos, *Páginas dominicanas*, ed. Emilio Rodríguez Demorizi (Santo Domingo: Editora Taller, 1979), 88.
20. Julio Ramos, *Divergent Modernities: Culture and Politics in Nineteenth-Century Latin America* (Durham: Duke University Press, 2001), 204.
21. Pedro Henríquez Ureña, *Literary Currents in Hispanic America* (Cambridge, MA: Harvard University Press, 1945), 118.
22. Teresita Martínez-Vergne, *Nation and Citizen in the Dominican Republic, 1880–1916* (Chapel Hill: The University of North Carolina Press, 2005), 3.
23. Ibid., 6.
24. Henríquez Ureña borrowed this phrase *(carrera de constructor de la nación)* from Sarmiento. See Henríquez Ureña (*Literary Currents in Hispanic America* 137).
25. Pedro Henríquez Ureña, "La sociología de Hostos," in *Obras completas: escritos políticos, sociológicos y filosóficos*, vol. 4, ed. Manuel Núñez (Santo Domingo: Editora Nacional, [1905] 2004), 34.
26. See Mateo (2001) and Zea (1943).
27. José Portolés, *Medio siglo de filología española (1896–1952): Positivismo e idealismo* (Madrid: Cátedra, 1986), 32. *Krausismo* is a philosophy based on the ideas of the German thinker Karl Christian Friedrich Krause (1781–1832), but was developed in Spain mainly by Julián Sanz del Río (1814–1869) and

Francisco Giner de los Ríos (1839–1915). Mixed with elements of Positivism, Spanish *krausismo* proposed that humans were a reflection of natural and spiritual harmony that must be realized in their free and rational will. Hostos was a student of Sanz del Río in Spain.

28. Harry Hoetink, *The Dominican People 1850–1900: Notes for a Historical Sociology* (Baltimore and London: The Johns Hopkins University Press, 1982).
29. Pedro Henríquez Ureña, "La sociología de Hostos," in *Obras completas: escritos políticos, sociológicos y filosóficos,* vol. 4, ed. Manuel Núñez (Santo Domingo: Editora Nacional, [1905] 2004), 45.
30. Cited in Pedro Henríquez Ureña, ibid.
31. Ibid.
32. Ibid., 53.
33. *¡Escuela sin Dios!* ("Education without God") was one of their slogans.
34. Andrés L. Mateo, *Pedro Henríquez Ureña: errancia y creación* (Bogota: Taurus, 2001), 25. Although a conservative member of the clergy, Meriño, who was installed as President by the *Partido Liberal,* had initially given carte blanche to the Hostosian positivists and their reforms.
35. Eugenio María de Hostos, *Páginas dominicanas,* ed. Emilio Rodríguez Demorizi (Santo Domingo: Editora Taller, 1979), 173–174.
36. Julio Ramos, *Divergent Modernities: Culture and Politics in Nineteenth-Century Latin America* (Durham: Duke University Press, 2001), 43.
37. Mu-kien A. Sang, *Ulises Heureaux: biografía de un dictador* (Santo Domingo: Instituto Tecnológico de Santo Domingo, 1987), 1. In 1882, General Ulises Heureaux (1845–1889), a decisive figure in Dominican politics, rose to power. Heureaux, a black man of Haitian descent, was a soldier, initially a protégé of Gregorio Luperón, who later became President. His regime oversaw an extended period of relative peace and economic growth. Although initially a liberal government, the Heureaux regime became a dictatorship that catered to capitalist interests, the United States' imperialist designs, and the clergy's hope for control of education. Once liberal intellectuals became aware of Heureaux's attacks on positivist schools and the persistence of his dictatorship, they immediately opposed him.
38. Unhappy with the regime and the political conditions, Francisco Henríquez y Carvajal went into exile in Haiti. While still in exile, Francisco Henríquez y Carvajal advised and supplied arms to a group of political allies, who, from the border city of Montecristi, were conspiring, initially without much success, to overthrow Heureaux and planning for a future government. See Max Henríquez Ureña (2001).
39. Pedro L. San Miguel, *The Imagined Island: History, Identity and Utopia in Hispaniola* (San Juan and Santo Domingo: Isla Negra and La Trinitaria, 2005), 12–15.
40. Eugenio María de Hostos. *Obras completas* (La Habana: Cultural S.A., 1939), 132.
41. Jesús de Galíndez, *La era de Trujillo: un estudio casuístico de dictadura hispanoamericana* (Santo Domingo: Editora Taller, 1984), 197. Jesús de

Galíndez (1915–1956), a victim of the Trujillo regime, wrote about the complex Dominican-Haitian relations: "when I worked in the Ministry of Foreign Affairs in the Dominican Republic, I had the opportunity to confirm the existence of a secret room especially assigned for archiving files and documents related to Haiti. The Ministry's chief clerk secretly guarded the only key for this room. The existence of this secret archive shows how delicate the relations between the Dominican Republic and Haiti are to Dominicans."

42. Juan Pablo Duarte, along with Francisco del Rosario Sánchez (1817–1861) and Ramón Matías Mella (1816–1864), is considered one of the founding fathers of the Dominican Republic.
43. Cited in Jean Price-Mars, *La República de Haití y la República Dominicana* (Santo Domingo: Editora Taller, 2000), 43–44.
44. Franklin Knight, *The Caribbean: The Genesis of a Fragmented Nationalism* (New York and Oxford: Oxford University Press, 1990), 220.
45. Pedro L. San Miguel, *The Imagined Island: History, Identity and Utopia in Hispaniola* (San Juan and Santo Domingo: Isla Negra and La Trinitaria, 2005), 9.
46. Cited in Emilio Rodríguez Demorizi, "Vicisitudes de la lengua española en Santo Domingo," in *Lengua y folklore de Santo Domingo* (Santo Domingo: Universidad Católica Madre y Maestra, 1975), 17.
47. Roberto Cassá, *Historia social y económica de la República Dominicana*, vol. 1 (Santo Domingo: Editora Alfa y Omega, 1998), 154–155.
48. Pedro L. San Miguel, *The Imagined Island: History, Identity and Utopia in Hispaniola* (San Juan and Santo Domingo: Isla Negra and La Trinitaria, 2005), 10–11.
49. Jean Price-Mars, *La República de Haití y la República Dominicana* (Santo Domingo: Editora Taller, 2000), 80.
50. Roberto Cassá, *Historia social y económica de la República Dominicana*, vol. 2 (Santo Domingo: Editora Alfa y Omega, 1998), 44.
51. Martínez-Vergne (2005) contends that no such class existed in the Dominican Republic; however, Dominican historian Roberto Cassá (1998) believes otherwise; ibid.
52. It was during these years that Nicolás Ureña de Mendoza, Henríquez Ureña's maternal grandfather, began to distinguish himself. In 1853, after serving as the editor of *La Española Libre* (1846), he founded another important newspaper, *El Progreso*, a publication for the political, literary, and business sectors. As a journalist and later as a Senator, Nicolas's main preoccupation was national sovereignty and the fight against annexation to Spain. His political positions landed him in prison, where he was almost executed. See Piña-Contreras (2001).
53. Cited in Gérard Pierre-Charles, *El pensamiento sociopolítico moderno en el Caribe* (Mexico: Fondo de Cultura Económica, 1985), 155.
54. Frank Moya Pons, *The Dominican Republic: A National History* (New Rochelle, NY: Hispaniola Books, 1995), 207.
55. Roberto Cassá, *Historia social y económica de la República Dominicana*, vol. 2 (Santo Domingo: Editora Alfa y Omega, 1998), 81; Frank Moya Pons, *The*

Dominican Republic: A National History (New Rochelle, NY: Hispaniola Books, 1995), 206–207.
56. Roberto Cassá, "Nación y Estado en el pensamiento de Américo Lugo," in *Política, identidad y pensamiento social en la República Dominicana (Siglos XIX y XX)*, ed. Raymundo González et al. (Madrid and Santo Domingo: Doce Calles and Academia de Ciencias de la República Dominicana, 1999).
57. In 1866, inspired by the restoration war, Salomé began to publish her first poems. The constant themes of her poetry were patriotism, liberty and progress. Her poetry is directly linked to the epoch's political events. See Salomé Ureña's poem, *A la patria*.
58. See Hugo Tolentino Dipp (2004).
59. Cited in Gérard Pierre-Charles, *El pensamiento sociopolítico moderno en el Caribe* (Mexico: Fondo de Cultura Económica, 1985), 133.
60. Frank Moya Pons, *The Dominican Republic: A National History* (New Rochelle, NY: Hispaniola Books, 1995), 222; Roberto Cassá, *Historia social y económica de la República Dominicana*, vol. 2 (Santo Domingo: Editora Alfa y Omega, 1998), 24.
61. Roberto Cassá, *Historia social y económica de la República Dominicana*, vol. 2 (Santo Domingo: Editora Alfa y Omega, 1998), 126; Frank Moya Pons, *The Dominican Republic: A National History* (New Rochelle, NY: Hispaniola Books, 1995), 260.
62. Harry Hoetink, *The Dominican People 1850–1900: Notes for a Historical Sociology* (Baltimore and London: The Johns Hopkins University Press, 1982), 29.
63. Guillermo Piña-Contreras, "El universo familiar en la formación intelectual de Pedro Henríquez Ureña," in *Presencia de Pedro Henríquez Ureña: escritos sobre el maestro*, ed. Jorge Tena Reyes and Tomás Castro Burdiez (Santo Domingo: Editorial Ciguapa, 2001), 319.
64. Frank Moya Pons, *The Dominican Republic: A National History* (New Rochelle, NY: Hispaniola Books, 1995), 174.
65. Pedro Henríquez Ureña, "La sociología de Hostos," in *Obras completas: escritos políticos, sociológicos y filosóficos*, vol. 4, ed. Manuel Núñez (Santo Domingo: Editora Nacional, [1905] 2004), 48.
66. Enrique Deschamps, *La República Dominicana: directorio y guía general* (Barcelona, Spain, 1906), 265–266.
67. Ibid., 266.
68. Frank Moya Pons, *The Dominican Republic: A National History* (New Rochelle, NY: Hispaniola Books, 1995), 322.
69. Frank Moya Pons, *The Dominican Republic: A National History* (New Rochelle, NY: Hispaniola Books, 1995), 329; Roberto Cassá, "Nación y Estado en el pensamiento de Américo Lugo," in *Política, identidad y pensamiento social en la República Dominicana (Siglos XIX y XX)*, ed. Raymundo González et al. (Madrid and Santo Domingo: Doce Calles and Academia de Ciencias de la República Dominicana, 1999), 121–123.
70. Cited in Emilio Carilla, *Pedro Henríquez Ureña, Signo de América* (Santo Domingo: Publicaciones de La Universidad Nacional Pedro Henríquez Ureña, 1988), 88.

71. Ibid., 89.
72. Cited in Alfredo Roggiano, *Pedro Henríquez Ureña en los Estado Unidos* (Mexico: Editorial Cultura, 1961), 68.
73. Ibid., 72.
74. Eugenio María de Hostos, "El cholo," http://www.ensayistas.org/antologia/XIXA/hostos/hostos2.htm [1870] (accessed April 4, 2007).
75. José Martí, "Nuestra América," *La Revista Ilustrada de Nueva York*, http://www.analitica.com/bitbiblioteca/jmarti/nuestra_america.asp [1891] (accessed January 15, 2007).
76. Jean Muteba Rahier, "The Study of Latin-American 'Racial Formations': Different Approaches and Different Contexts," *Latin-American Research Review*, 39, 3 (2004): 283.
77. Ibid.
78. Julio Ramos, *Divergent Modernities: Culture and Politics in Nineteenth-Century Latin America* (Durham: Duke University Press, 2001), 259.
79. Michiel Baud, "Intelectuales, nación y modernidad en la República Dominicana," in *Relatos de nación: la construcción de identidades en el mundo hispánico*, ed. Francisco Colom González (Madrid and Frankfurt: Iberoamericana and Vervuert, 2005), 935–936.
80. Teresita Martínez-Vergne, *Nation and Citizen in the Dominican Republic, 1880–1916* (Chapel Hill: The University of North Carolina Press, 2005), 5.
81. Carlos Dobal, "Hispanidad y dominicanidad," *Eme Eme* 12, 71 (1984): 89.
82. Silvio Torres-Saillant, "The Tribulations of Blackness: Stages in Dominican Racial Identity," *Callaloo* 23, 3 (2000): 1090.
83. Pedro Henríquez Ureña, *En la orilla: mi España* (Mexico: Cultura, 1922), 15.
84. Jorge Luis Borges, "Prólogo," in *Obra crítica*, ed. Emma Susana Sperantti Piñero (Mexico and Buenos Aires: Fondo de Cultura Económica, 1960).
85. Cited in Emilio Carilla, *Pedro Henríquez Ureña, Signo de América* (Santo Domingo: Publicaciones de La Universidad Nacional Pedro Henríquez Ureña, 1988), 25.
86. Pedro Henríquez Ureña, "Carta a Alfonso Reyes," in *Epistolario íntimo, 1906–1946*, ed. Juan Jacobo de Lara (Santo Domingo: UNPHU, 1981), 288–289.
87. Andrés L. Mateo, *Pedro Henríquez Ureña: errancia y creación* (Bogota: Taurus, 2001), 245.
88. Pedro Henríquez Ureña, "La antigua sociedad patriarcal de las Antillas: modalidades arcaicas de la vida en Santo Domingo durante el siglo XIX," in *Obra dominicana*, ed. José Chez Checo (Santo Domingo: Sociedad Dominicana de Bibliófilos Inc, [1932c] 1988), 503.
89. Pedro Henríquez Ureña, *El español en Santo Domingo* (Santo Domingo: Taller, [1940] 1975), 90.
90. Diony Durán, *Literatura y sociedad en la obra de Pedro Henríquez Ureña* (La Habana: Letras Cubanas, 1994), 11.
91. Emilio Rodríguez Demorizi, *Lengua y folklore de Santo Domingo* (Santo Domingo: Universidad Católica Madre y Maestra, 1975), 17.

92. Cited in Roberto Cassá, "Nación y Estado en el pensamiento de Américo Lugo," in *Política, identidad y pensamiento social en la República Dominicana (Siglos XIX y XX)*, ed. Raymundo González et al. (Madrid and Santo Domingo: Doce Calles and Academia de Ciencias de la República Dominicana, 1999), 123.
93. Américo Lugo, "Discurso inaugural del Ateneo Dominicano," in *Obras escogidas*, vol. 1 (Santo Domingo: Ediciones de la Fundación Corripio, 1993), 254.
94. Cited in Meindert Fennema, "Hispanidad y la identidad nacional de Santo Domingo," in *Política, identidad y pensamiento social en la República Dominicana (Siglos XIX y XX)*, ed. Raymundo González et al. (Madrid and Santo Domingo: Doce Calles and Academia de Ciencias de la República Dominicana, 1999), 213.
95. Enrique Deschamps, *La República Dominicana: directorio y guía general* (Barcelona, Spain, 1906), 253–254.
96. Ibid.
97. Manuel Matos Moquete, *La cultura de la lengua* (Santo Domingo: Biblioteca Nacional, 1986), 46.
98. Ibid., 55.
99. Ibid., 62.
100. Pedro Henríquez Ureña, "Carta a Max," in Familia Henríquez Ureña, *Epistolario*, vol. 1 (Santo Domingo: Secretaría de Estado de Educación, Bellas Artes y Cultos, 1996), 181.
101. Gérard Pierre-Charles, *El pensamiento sociopolítico moderno en el Caribe* (Mexico: Fondo de Cultura Económica, 1985), 143.
102. Andrés L. Mateo, *Pedro Henríquez Ureña: errancia y creación* (Bogota: Taurus, 2001), 184.
103. Pedro Henríquez Ureña, "La República Dominicana," in *Obras completas: escritos políticos, sociológicos y filosóficos*, vol. 4, ed. Manuel Núñez (Santo Domingo: Editora Nacional, [1917] 2004), 301–302.
104. This group includes luminaries such as José Gabriel García (1834–1910), Manuel de Jesús Galván (1834–1910), Federico García Godoy (1857–1924), and Américo Lugo (1870–1952).
105. Teresita Martínez-Vergne, *Nation and Citizen in the Dominican Republic, 1880–1916* (Chapel Hill: The University of North Carolina Press, 2005), 17–18.
106. Ibid., 21.
107. Andrés L. Mateo, *Mito y cultura en la era de Trujillo* (Santo Domingo: Editora Manatí, 2004).
108. Jacqueline Toribio, "Language Variation and the Linguistic Enactment of Identity among Dominicans," *Linguistics* 38, 5 (2000a): 267.
109. Michiel Baud, "Intelectuales, nación y modernidad en la República Dominicana," in *Relatos de nación: la construcción de identidades en el mundo hispánico*, ed. Francisco Colom González (Madrid and Frankfurt: Iberoamericana and Vervuert, 2005), 950.

110. Jesús de Galíndez, *La era de Trujillo: un estudio casuístico de dictadura hispanoamericana* (Santo Domingo: Editora Taller, 1984), 197.
111. José Cordero Michel, *Análisis de la era de Trujillo: informe sobre la República Dominicana, 1959* (Santo Domingo: Editora de la UASD, 1975), 32–33.
112. Ramiro Guerra Sánchez, *Azúcar y población en las Antillas* (La Habana: Imprenta Nacional de Cuba, 1927), 209.
113. Manuel Matos Moquete, *La cultura de la lengua* (Santo Domingo: Biblioteca Nacional, 1986), 30.
114. Ibid., 28.
115. Ibid.
116. See Joan Resina (2005) and Lía Schwartz (2002).
117. Fredrick Pike, *Hispanismo, 1898–1936: Spanish Conservatives and Liberals and Their Relations with Spanish America* (Notre Dame: University of Notre Dame Press, 1971), 1.
118. Isidro Sepúlveda Muñoz, *El sueño de la Madre Patria: hispanoamericanismo y nacionalismo* (Madrid: Marcial Pons, 2005), 13.
119. It is also useful to distinguish the agents who are ideological proponents of these movements ("Hispanoamericanistas" who construct unitary visions for political purposes) from the people who specifically specialize in the study of language and literature in the Spanish-speaking world ("hispanistas" or "americanistas"). In the description of this and other related phenomena, I adopt Sepulveda's terminology.
120. José Del Valle and Luis Gabriel-Stheeman, *La batalla del idioma: la intelectualidad hispánica ante la lengua* (Frankfurt and Madrid: Vervuert and Iberoamericana, 2004b), 24.
121. *Ariel* is a meditation on the nature of civilizations, in which Rodó contrasts two forms of society symbolized by Ariel and Caliban, characters from Shakespeare's The Tempest (1623). The latter represents the United States, a utilitarian society where the unguided appetites of the masses results in a new barbarism. Ariel, on the other hand, represents a civilization where an enlightened ruling elite subordinates material urges to reason and spiritual concerns.
122. Pedro Henríquez Ureña, *Memorias, diario, notas de viaje*, ed. Enrique Zuleta Álvarez (Mexico: Fondo de Cultura Económica, [1909] 2000), 66.
123. Pedro Henríquez Ureña, "Ariel," in *Obras completas: escritos políticos, sociológicos y filosóficos*, vol. 4, ed. Manuel Núñez (Santo Domingo: Editora Nacional, [1904] 2004), 58.
124. Ibid., 63.
125. Ibid.
126. Ibid., 58.
127. Louis-Jean Calvet, *Lingüística y colonialismo: Breve tratado de glotofagia* (Buenos Aires: Fondo de Cultura Económica, 2005), 270.
128. Hernán Pérez de Oliva (1494–1533) was a Spanish humanist and writer.
129. Pedro Henríquez Ureña, *En la orilla: mi España* (Mexico: Cultura, 1922), 150–151.

130. Manuel Ugarte (1875–1951) was an Argentine author and member of the socialist party who spent many years working for the unity of Latin America.
131. Cited in Sonia Henríquez Ureña de Hito, *Pedro Henríquez Ureña: apuntes para una biografía* (Mexico: Siglo XXI Editores, 1993), 83.
132. José Rafael Vargas, *El nacionalismo de Pedro Henríquez Ureña* (Santo Domingo: Editora de la UASD, 1984), 162.
133. José Vasconcelos, *La raza cósmica* (Costa Rica: Editorial Fundación-UNA, [1925] 1999), 78.
134. The theories of Gregor Mendel explained the inheritance of traits according to particular laws.
135. Pedro Henríquez Ureña, "Raza y cultura," in *La utopía de América*, ed. Rafael Gutiérrez Girardot and Ángel Rama (Caracas: Biblioteca Ayacucho, [1933b] 1978), 12.
136. Ibid., 12.
137. Ibid., 13.
138. Pedro Henríquez Ureña, "La utopía de América," in *La utopía de América*, ed. Rafael Gutiérrez Girardot and Ángel Rama (Caracas: Biblioteca Ayacucho, [1933a] 1978), 5.
139. Pedro Henríquez Ureña, "El descontento y la promesa," in *La utopía de América*, ed. Rafael Gutiérrez Girardot and Ángel Rama (Caracas: Biblioteca Ayacucho, [1926] 1978), 38.
140. He even challenged his mentor Menéndez Pidal's position in this debate (see the next chapter).
141. Carlos Rama, *Historia de las relaciones culturales entre España y la América Latina: Siglo XIX* (Mexico: Fondo de Cultura Económica, 1982), 111.
142. See Pérez Cabral (1967).

Chapter 4

1. William Dwight Whitney, *The Life and Growth of Language: An Outline of Linguistic Science* (New York: Dover Publications, Inc., 1979), 5.
2. Konrad Koerner, *Professing Linguistic Historiography* (Amsterdam and Philadelphia: John Benjamins, 1995), 65.
3. William Dwight Whitney, *The Life and Growth of Language: An Outline of Linguistic Science* (New York: Dover Publications, Inc., 1979), 4.
4. Edward Said, *Orientalism* (New York: Vintage Books), 132.
5. James M. Anderson, "Historical Linguistics," in *The Linguistics Encyclopedia*, ed. Kirsten Malmkjaer (London and New York: Routledge, 2001), 194. Neogrammarians held that phonetic laws were similar to laws of nature (or the physical sciences) in their consistency of operation. Neogrammarian ideas, best represented by Hermann Paul's *Principles of the History of Language*, first published in 1880, are seen by many in the twentieth century as the movement that started scientific linguistics in Europe.
6. Ferdinand de Saussure, *Course in General Linguistics* (New York: MacGraw Hill, [1916] 1986), 6.

7. José Portolés, *Medio siglo de filología española (1896–1952): Positivismo e idealismo* (Madrid: Cátedra, 1986), 45.
8. Yakov Malkiel, *Linguistics and Philology in Spanish America: A Survey (1925–1970)* (The Hague and Paris: Mouton, 1972), 15.
9. Ibid., 15.
10. Andrés Bello, *Gramática de la lengua castellana destinada al uso de los americanos* (Madrid: Editorial EDAF, [1847] 2001), 32.
11. Ibid., 31.
12. Cited in Belford Moré, "The Ideological Construction of an Empirical Base: Selection and Elaboration Andrés Bello's Grammar," in *The Battle over Spanish between 1800 and 2000: Language Ideologies and Hispanic Intellectuals,* ed. José Del Valle and Luis Gabriel-Stheeman (Madrid and Frankfurt: Iberoamericana and Vervuert, 2002), 74.
13. Andrés Bello, *Gramática de la lengua castellana destinada al uso de los americanos* (Madrid: Editorial EDAF, [1847] 2001), 35.
14. Andrés Bello, "Discurso de instalación de la Universidad de Chile," in *Obras completas: opúsculos literarios y críticos,* ed. Miguel Luis Amunátegui (Santiago: Impresora Pedro G. Ramírez, 2005), 315.
15. Andrés Bello, *Gramática de la lengua castellana destinada al uso de los americanos* (Madrid: Editorial EDAF, [1847] 2001), 33.
16. Ibid., 33.
17. Guillermo Guitarte, "Un concepto de la filología hispanoamericana: la base del español en América," *La Torre* 3, 7–8 (1998): 426.
18. Pedro Henríquez Ureña, *Literary Currents in Hispanic America* (Cambridge, MA: Harvard University Press, 1945), 103.
19. Amado Alonso, "Pedro Henríquez Ureña, investigador," in *Presencia de Pedro Henríquez Ureña: escritos sobre el maestro,* ed. Jorge Tena Reyes and Tomás Castro Burdiez (Santo Domingo: Editorial Ciguapa, 2001), 357.
20. Esteban Pichardo, *Diccionario provincial casi razonado de voces y frases cubanas* (La Habana: Editorial de Ciencias Sociales, [1836] 1985), 1–2.
21. Carlos Rama, *Historia de las relaciones culturales entre España y la América Latina: Siglo XIX* (Mexico: Fondo de Cultura Económica, 1982), 126.
22. Fernando Antonio Martínez, "Lexicography," in *Current Trends in Linguistics IV: Ibero-American and Caribbean Linguistics,* ed. Thomas Sebeok (The Hague and Paris: Mouton, 1968), 91.
23. Esteban Pichardo, *Diccionario provincial casi razonado de voces y frases cubanas* (La Habana: Editorial de Ciencias Sociales, [1836] 1985), 3.
24. Ibid., 2–7.
25. Ibid., 9.
26. Humberto López Morales, "Introducción," in *Vocabulario de Puerto Rico,* ed. Humberto López Morales (Madrid: Arco Libros, 1999), 7.
27. Ibid.
28. Augusto Malaret, *Vocabulario de Puerto Rico,* ed. Humberto López Morales (Madrid: Arco Libros, 1999), 11.
29. Carlos Rama, *Historia de las relaciones culturales entre España y la América Latina: Siglo XIX* (Mexico: Fondo de Cultura Económica, 1982), 116.

30. See, for example, Malaret's (1942) *Por mi patria y por mi idioma.*
31. Juan de Arona, *Diccionario de peruanismos,* volumes 1 and 2 (Lima: Biblioteca Peruana, [1882] 1975), 22–23.
32. Pedro Henríquez Ureña, "Rufino José Cuervo," in *La utopía de América,* ed. Rafael Gutiérrez Girardot and Ángel Rama (Caracas: Biblioteca Ayacucho, 1978), 276–277.
33. On the basis of this rejection, Henríquez Ureña sought to convince his contemporaries that Cuervo had formally expressed his views against *andalucismo.*
34. Rufino José Cuervo, "Castellano popular y castellano literario," in *Obras,* vol. 1, ed. Fernando A. Martínez (Bogota: Instituto Caro y Cuervo, [1901a] 1987), 736.
35. Guillermo Guitarte, "El camino de Cuervo al español de América," in *Philologica Hispaniensia: in Honorem Manuel Álvar,* vol. 1, ed. Julio Fernández Sevilla et al. (Madrid: Gredos, 1983), 248.
36. Rufino José Cuervo, "El castellano en América," in *Obras,* vol. 1, ed. Fernando A. Martínez (Bogota: Instituto Caro y Cuervo, [1901b] 1987), 205–206.
37. Ibid., 206.
38. Ibid.
39. José Del Valle, "Historical Linguistics and Cultural History: The Polemic between Rufino José Cuervo and Juan Valera," in *The Battle over Spanish between 1800 and 2000: Language Ideologies and Hispanic Intellectuals,* ed. José Del Valle and Luis Gabriel-Stheeman (London and New York: Routledge, 2002a), 95.
40. Ibid., 100.
41. Ramón Menéndez Pidal, *La unidad del idioma* (Madrid: Instituto Nacional del Libro, 1944), 7.
42. José Del Valle, "Menéndez Pidal, National Regeneration, and Linguistic Utopia," in *The Battle over Spanish between 1800 and 2000: Language Ideologies and Hispanic Intellectuals,* ed. José Del Valle and Luis Gabriel-Stheeman (London and New York: Routledge, 2002b), 132.
43. Rufino José Cuervo, "Castellano popular y castellano literario," in *Obras,* vol. 1, ed. Fernando A. Martínez (Bogota: Instituto Caro y Cuervo, [1901a] 1987), 419.
44. Ibid.
45. José Del Valle, "Historical Linguistics and Cultural History: The Polemic between Rufino José Cuervo and Juan Valera," in *The Battle over Spanish between 1800 and 2000: Language Ideologies and Hispanic Intellectuals,* ed. José Del Valle and Luis Gabriel-Stheeman (Madrid and Frankfurt: Iberoamericana and Vervuert, 2002a), 102.
46. Rufino José Cuervo, "El castellano en América," in *Obras,* vol.1, ed. Fernando A. Martínez (Bogotá: Instituto Caro y Cuervo, [1901b] 1987), 13.
47. Guillermo Guitarte, "El camino de Cuervo al español de América," in *Philologica Hispaniensia: in Honorem Manuel Álvar,* vol. 1, ed. Julio Fernández Sevilla et al. (Madrid: Gredos, 1983), 2.

48. Rufino José Cuervo, "El castellano en América," in *Obras*, vol. 1, ed. Fernando A. Martínez (Bogotá: Instituto Caro y Cuervo, [1901b] 1987), 296.
49. Yakov Malkiel, *Linguistics and Philology in Spanish America: A Survey (1925–1970)* (The Hague and Paris: Mouton, 1972), 17.
50. Helmut Hatzfeld, "Hispanic Philology in Latin America," *The Americas* 3 (1947): 352.
51. Ibid.
52. Rudolph (Rodolfo) Lenz, *El español en Chile*, ed. Amado Alonso and Raimundo Lida (Buenos Aires: Biblioteca de Dialectología Hispanoamericana, [1891] 1940), 224.
53. Guillermo Guitarte, "Un concepto de la filología hispanoamericana: la base del español en América," *La Torre* 3, 7–8 (1998): 417.
54. Ibid., 424.
55. Rudolph (Rodolfo) Lenz, *El español en Chile*, ed. Amado Alonso and Raimundo Lida (Buenos Aires: Biblioteca de Dialectología Hispanoamericana, [1891] 1940), 10.
56. Ibid., 223.
57. Guillermo Guitarte, "Un concepto de la filología hispanoamericana: la base del español en América," *La Torre* 3, 7–8 (1998): 423–424.
58. Pedro Henríquez Ureña, *En la orilla: mi España* (Mexico: Cultura, 1922), 88.
59. Ibid.
60. José Del Valle, "La historificación de la lingüística histórica: los orígenes de Ramón Menéndez Pidal," *Historiographia Lingüística XXIV* 1, 2 (1997): 183.
61. Ramón Menéndez Pidal, *Manual elemental de gramática histórica española* (Madrid: Librería General de Victoriano Suárez, [1904] 1925), 143.
62. José Del Valle, "La historificación de la lingüística histórica: los orígenes de Ramón Menéndez Pidal," *Historiographia Lingüística XXIV* 1, 2 (1997): 186.
63. Ramón Menéndez Pidal, *Manual elemental de gramática histórica española* (Madrid: Librería General de Victoriano Suárez, [1904] 1925), 2.
64. Ibid., 8.
65. Ramón Menéndez Pidal, *Orígenes del español: estado lingüístico de la península ibérica hasta el siglo XI* (Madrid: Espasa-Calpe, [1926] 1964), 93.
66. Ibid., 302.
67. José María López Sánchez, *Heterodoxos españoles: el Centro de Estudios Históricos, 1910–1936* (Madrid: Marcial Pons Ediciones de Historia, 2006), 336.
68. Ramón Menéndez Pidal, *Orígenes del español: estado lingüístico de la península ibérica hasta el siglo XI* (Madrid: Espasa-Calpe, [1926] 1964), 486.
69. José del Valle, "Menéndez Pidal, National Regeneration, and Linguistic Utopia," in *The Battle over Spanish between 1800 and 2000: Language Ideologies and Hispanic Intellectuals*, ed. José Del Valle and Luis Gabriel-Stheeman (London and New York: Routledge, 2002b), 122.
70. Ramón Menéndez Pidal, *Orígenes del español: estado lingüístico de la península ibérica hasta el siglo XI* (Madrid: Espasa-Calpe, [1926] 1964), 529.

71. José Del Valle, "Menéndez Pidal, National Regeneration, and Linguistic Utopia," in *The Battle over Spanish between 1800 and 2000: Language Ideologies and Hispanic Intellectuals*, ed. José Del Valle and Luis Gabriel-Stheeman (London and New York: Routledge, 2002b), 81.
72. Guillermo Guitarte, *Siete estudios sobre el español de América* (Mexico: Universidad Nacional Autónoma de México, [1958b] 1983), 365.
73. Ibid.
74. Ibid.
75. Amado Alonso, *Estudios lingüísticos: temas españoles* (Madrid: Gredos, 1951), 104–105.
76. Steven Hess, *Ramón Menéndez Pidal* (Boston: Twayne Publishers, 1982), 8.
77. Cited in José Ignacio Pérez Pascual, *Ramón Menéndez Pidal: ciencia y pasión* (Valladolid, Spain: Junta de Castilla y León, 1998), 129.
78. Ibid., 130.
79. Ibid., 133.
80. José María López Sánchez, *Heterodoxos españoles: el Centro de Estudios Históricos, 1910–1936* (Madrid: Marcial Pons Ediciones de Historia, 2006), 15.
81. Yakov Malkiel, "Filología española y lingüística general," http://cvc.cervantes.es/obref/aih/pdf/01/aih_01_009.pdf (1962) (accessed May 8, 2007).
82. José Portolés, *Medio siglo de filología española (1896–1952): Positivismo e idealismo* (Madrid: Cátedra, 1986), 112.
83. Cited in Juan Jacobo de Lara, *Sobre Pedro Henríquez Ureña y otros ensayos* (Santo Domingo: UNPHU, 1982), 201.
84. In a letter to Julio Torri, Alfonso Reyes wrote: "I have a distressingly sad memory of Pedro. He seemed to be in a constant state of somnambulism... What do we do about him? We have suggested that he can come and work in Spain. There are very few possibilities, but we can find them. But he refuses in definite horror." Cited in Enrique Krauze, "El crítico errante: Pedro Henríquez Ureña," *Vuelta* 100 (March 1985): 16.
85. Ibid.
86. Baldomero Sanín Cano (1861–1957) was a professor, journalist, diplomat and member of the Colombian Language Academy who criticized the *RAE*.
87. Pedro Henríquez Ureña, "En defensa de la Revista," in *Obras completas: estudios lingüísticos y filológicos*, vol. 4, ed. Irene Pérez Guerra (Santo Domingo: Editora Nacional, [1921b] 2004), 57.
88. Ibid., 58.
89. Ibid., 59.
90. Pedro Henríquez Ureña, *En la orilla: mi España* (Mexico: Cultura, 1922), 19.
91. José María López Sánchez, *Heterodoxos españoles: el Centro de Estudios Históricos, 1910–1936* (Madrid: Marcial Pons Ediciones de Historia, 2006), 337.
92. Ramón Menéndez Pidal, *Orígenes del español: estado lingüístico de la península ibérica hasta el siglo XI* (Madrid: Espasa-Calpe, [1926] 1964), 511–512.
93. Ibid., 517.

94. Pedro Henríquez Ureña, "Papa y batata: historia de dos palabras," in *Para la historia de los indigenismos,* ed. Pedro Henríquez Ureña (Buenos Aires: Biblioteca de Dialectología Hispanoamericana, 1938c), 140.
95. José Del Valle, "Menéndez Pidal, National Regeneration, and Linguistic Utopia," in *The Battle over Spanish between 1800 and 2000: Language Ideologies and Hispanic Intellectuals,* ed. José Del Valle and Luis Gabriel-Stheeman (Madrid and Frankfurt: Iberoamericana and Vervuert, 2002b), 98.
96. Frida Weber de Kurlat, "Pedro Henríquez Ureña en el Instituto de Filología de Buenos Aires," in *El libro jubilar de Pedro Henríquez Ureña,* vol. 1, ed. Julio Jaime Julia (Santo Domingo: UNPHU, 1994), 1.
97. Helmut Hatzfeld, "Hispanic Philology in Latin America," *The Americas* 3 (1947): 347; José Polo, *Epistemología del lenguaje e historia lingüística: momentos de su desarrollo bibliográfico en el ámbito hispanohablante* (Madrid: Gredos, 1986), 144.
98. "A. Alonso typified, to the Argentine intelligentsia, the progressive, versatile, new-styled philologist, where the straight-classicist Hanssen had been a mouthpiece for cumbersome, old-style philology and Lenz had represented the stringent line of unadulterated linguistic inquiry (slightly reminiscent in his unyielding austerity of L. Bloomfield)" (Malkiel, Linguistics and Philology 19).
99. Amado Alonso, "Prologo a la edición española," in *Curso de lingüística general de F. Saussure,* trans. Amado Alonso (Buenos Aires: Losada, 1945).
100. José Portolés, *Medio siglo de filología española (1896–1952): Positivismo e idealismo* (Madrid: Cátedra, 1986), 99–100.
101. Amado Alonso, "Prefacio," in *Filosofía del lenguaje de K. Vossler,* trans. Amado Alonso (Buenos Aires: Losada, 1943), 12.
102. Iorgu Iordan, *An Introduction to Romance Linguistics: Its Schools and Scholars* (Oxford: Basil Blackwell, 1970), 86–87.
103. Ibid.
104. Amado Alonso, "Rodolfo Lenz y la dialectología hispanoamericana," in *El español en Chile,* ed. Amado Alonso (Buenos Aires: Biblioteca de Dialectología Hispanoamericana, 1940), 11.
105. Amado Alonso, *El problema de la lengua en América* (Madrid: Espasa-Calpe, 1935), 48.
106. Américo Castro, "Introducción," *Boletín del Instituto de Filología* 1 (1923).
107. Américo Castro, *La peculiaridad lingüística rioplatense y su sentido histórico* (Buenos Aires: Losada, 1941), 24; Amado Alonso, *El problema de la lengua en América* (Madrid: Espasa-Calpe, 1935), 40–41.
108. Cited in John King, *Sur: A Study of the Argentine Literary Journal and its Role in the Development of a Culture (1931–1970)* (Cambridge: Cambridge University Press, 1986), 27.
109. Jorge Luis Borges, *El idioma de los argentinos* (Buenos Aires: M. Gleizer, 1928), 186.
110. Jorge Luis Borges, *Otras inquisiciones* (Madrid: Alianza Editorial, 1961), 37.
111. Amado Alonso, *El problema de la lengua en América* (Madrid: Espasa-Calpe, 1935), 75.

112. Ibid., 139.
113. Américo Castro, *La peculiaridad lingüística rioplatense y su sentido histórico* (Buenos Aires: Losada, 1941), 24–25.
114. Ibid., 27.
115. Elvira N. de Arnoux, "Disciplinar desde la lengua: 'La gramática castellana' de Amado Alonso y Pedro Henríquez Ureña," in *Homenaje a Ofelia Kovacci,* ed. Elvira N. de Arnoux and Ángela Di Tullio (Buenos Aires: Eudeba, 2001), 53.
116. Amado Alonso, *El problema de la lengua en América* (Madrid: Espasa-Calpe, 1935), 43.
117. Ibid., 26.
118. Ibid., 25–31.
119. Américo Castro, *La peculiaridad lingüística rioplatense y su sentido histórico* (Buenos Aires: Losada, 1941), 29.
120. Pedro Henríquez Ureña, "Observaciones sobre el español en América I," in *Obras completas: estudios lingüísticos y filológicos,* vol. 4, ed. Irene Pérez Guerra (Santo Domingo: Editora Nacional, [1921c] 2004), 87.
121. Ibid., 61.
122. Amado Alonso, "Examen de la teoría indigenista de Rodolfo Lenz," *Revista de Filología Hispánica* 1 (1939): 284–289.
123. Ramón Menéndez Pidal, "Sevilla frente a Madrid: algunas precisiones sobre el español de América," in *Miscelánea homenaje a Andrés Martinet, Estructuralismo e Historia III,* ed. Diego Catalán (Madrid: La Laguna, [1941] 1962), 134–135. While Menéndez Pidal had expressed some idea regarding the subject in his *Gramática,* he formally expressed his views in "Sevilla frente a Madrid" (1941). In this work, he claimed that, by accepting the phonological *ceceo-seseo* simplification from the kingdom of Seville, transatlantic Spanish received a "distinctive Andalusian flavor."
124. Pedro Henríquez Ureña, "El supuesto andalucismo de América," in *Obras completas: estudios lingüísticos y filológicos,* vol. 4, ed. Irene Pérez Guerra (Santo Domingo: Editora Nacional, [1925c] 2004), 97.
125. Pedro Henríquez Ureña, "Observaciones sobre el español en América I," in *Obras completas: estudios lingüísticos y filológicos,* vol. 4, ed. Irene Pérez Guerra (Santo Domingo: Editora Nacional, [1921c] 2004), 62.
126. Rufino José Cuervo, "El castellano en América," in *Obras,* vol. 1, ed. Fernando A. Martínez (Bogota: Instituto Caro y Cuervo, [1901b] 1987), 215.
127. Guillermo Guitarte, *Siete estudios sobre el español de América* (Mexico: Universidad Nacional Autónoma de México, [1958b] 1983), 377.
128. Ibid., 376.
129. Rufino José Cuervo, "El castellano en América," in *Obras,* vol. 1, ed. Fernando A. Martínez (Bogota: Instituto Caro y Cuervo, [1901b] 1987), 553.
130. Pedro Henríquez Ureña, "Observaciones sobre el español en América III," in *Obras completas: estudios lingüísticos y filológicos,* vol. 4, ed. Irene Pérez Guerra (Santo Domingo: Editora Nacional, [1931] 2004), 123.
131. Guillermo Guitarte, *Siete estudios sobre el español de América.* Mexico: Universidad Nacional Autónoma de México, [1958b] 1983.

132. Ibid., 388.
133. See Robert Conn (2002).
134. Pedro Henríquez Ureña, *Literary Currents in Hispanic America* (Cambridge, MA: Harvard University Press, 1945), 3–4.
135. Pedro Henríquez Ureña, "La lengua en Santo Domingo," in *Obras completas: estudios lingüísticos y filológicos*, vol. 4, ed. Irene Pérez Guerra (Santo Domingo: Editora Nacional, [1919] 2004), 49.
136. F. A. Coelho was Portugal's pioneer linguist who conducted research on Asian Portuguese creoles. He also outlined Portuguese phonology in "Sobre a lingua Portuguessa" (1871) and "A lingua Portuguesa: Nocoes de Glotologia Geral e Especial Portuguesa" (1881). Gottfried Baist (1853–1920) was a Hispanic philologist from Germany. His monumental Spanish historical grammar was published by the Romance scholar Gustav Grober (1844–1911).
137. Pedro Henríquez Ureña, "La lengua en Santo Domingo," in *Obras completas: estudios lingüísticos y filológicos*, vol. 4, ed. Irene Pérez Guerra (Santo Domingo: Editora Nacional, [1919] 2004), 49.
138. Rudolph (Rodolfo) Lenz, *El papiamento: la lengua criolla de Curazao* (Santiago: Los Anales de La Universidad de Chile, 1928), 13.
139. Iris Bachmann, "Negertaaltje or Volkstaal: The Papiamentu Language at the Crossroads of Philology, Folklore and Anthropology," *Indiana* 24 (2007): 88; see also Mühleisen (2009).
140. "The idea that a Creole language exists in this region is false. Mr. Henríquez Ureña has noted the mistake made by Meyer-Lübke by attributing Santo Domingo a Afro-Hispanic dialect." Augusto Malaret, *Vocabulario de Puerto Rico*, ed. Humberto López Morales (Madrid: Arco Libros, 1999), 11.
141. Yakov Malkiel, "Filología española y lingüística general," http://cvc.cervantes.es/obref/aih/pdf/01/aih_01_009.pdf (1962) (accessed May 8, 2007).
142. Pedro Henríquez Ureña, "El lenguaje," in *Obras completas: estudios lingüísticos y filológicos*, vol. 4, ed. Irene Pérez Guerra (Santo Domingo: Editora Nacional, [1930] 2004), 105.
143. Ibid., 107.
144. Amado Alonso and Pedro Henríquez Ureña, *Gramática castellana*, vol. 1 (Buenos Aires: Losada, 1938), 7.
145. Ibid., 18.
146. Elvira N. de Arnoux, "Disciplinar desde la lengua: 'La gramática castellana' de Amado Alonso y Pedro Henríquez Ureña," in *Homenaje a Ofelia Kovacci*, ed. Elvira N. de Arnoux and Ángela Di Tullio (Buenos Aires: Eudeba, 2001), 55.
147. Ibid., 54.
148. Alonso, Amado and Pedro Henríquez Ureña. *Gramática castellana*, volumes 1 and 2 (Buenos Aires: Losada, 1938), 112–113.
149. Ibid., 113.
150. Ibid., 53.
151. Amado Alonso, *El problema de la lengua en América* (Madrid: Espasa-Calpe, 1935), 72.

152. Ibid., 32.
153. Ibid., 68–69.
154. Ibid., 73.
155. Pedro Henríquez Ureña, "El lenguaje," in *Obras completas: estudios lingüísticos y filológicos,* vol. 4, ed. Irene Pérez Guerra (Santo Domingo: Editora Nacional, [1930] 2004), 115.
156. Cited in Elvira N. de Arnoux, "Disciplinar desde la lengua: 'La gramática castellana' de Amado Alonso y Pedro Henríquez Ureña," in *Homenaje a Ofelia Kovacci,* ed. Elvira N. de Arnoux and Ángela Di Tullio (Buenos Aires: Eudeba, 2001), 68.
157. Peter Ives, *Language and Hegemony in Gramsci (Reading Gramsci)* (London and Ann Arbor: Pluto Press, 2004), 87.
158. Pedro Henríquez Ureña, "El idioma español y la historia política en Santo Domingo," in *Obras completas: estudios lingüísticos y filológicos,* vol. 4, ed. Irene Pérez Guerra (Santo Domingo: Editora Nacional, [1937] 2004), 239.

Chapter 5

1. At the time Henríquez Ureña was writing, the term *castellano* was used to designate the entire Spanish language and not, as we do today, simply referring to a subset of the language. In most cases Henríquez Ureña's use of *castellano* can be translated as "Spanish," except in a few instances when he is specifically distinguishing northern from southern Peninsular varieties.
2. Pedro Henríquez Ureña, "Observaciones sobre el español en América I," in *Obras completas: estudios lingüísticos y filológicos,* vol. 4, ed. Irene Pérez Guerra (Santo Domingo: Editora Nacional, [1921c] 2004), 65.
3. Pedro Henríquez Ureña, "La lengua en Santo Domingo," in *Obras completas: estudios lingüísticos y filológicos,* vol. 4, ed. Irene Pérez Guerra (Santo Domingo: Editora Nacional, [1919] 2004), 50.
4. Ibid., 51.
5. Ibid. The modern Spanish versión would be: *desde que lo vi hasta ahora.*
6. Ibid.
7. Ibid., 50.
8. Pedro Henríquez Ureña, "Observaciones sobre el español en América I," in *Obras completas: estudios lingüísticos y filológicos,* vol. 4, ed. Irene Pérez Guerra (Santo Domingo: Editora Nacional, [1921c] 2004), 63.
9. Ibid., 65.
10. Pedro Henríquez Ureña, "El enigma del aje," in *Para la historia de los indigenismos,* ed. Pedro Henríquez Ureña (Buenos Aires: Biblioteca de Dialectología Hispanoamericana, 1938a), 194–195.
11. Ibid., 195.
12. Ibid., 183.
13. Ibid., 195.

14. Pedro Henríquez Ureña, *El español en Santo Domingo* (Santo Domingo: Taller, 1975), 46.
15. Frantz Fanon, *Black Skin, White Masks* (New York: Grove Press, 2008), 186. According to Fanon, the Caribbean is "hungry for reassurance."
16. Pedro Henríquez Ureña, *El español en Santo Domingo* (Santo Domingo: Taller, 1975), 178.
17. Ibid., 8.
18. Ibid., 37–39.
19. Ibid., 41.
20. See Peter Bajarkman (1989) and Ana Celia Zentella (2002).
21. Pedro Henríquez Ureña, *El español en Santo Domingo* (Santo Domingo: Taller, 1975), 41.
22. Pedro Henríquez Ureña, "Observaciones sobre el español en América I," in *Obras completas: estudios lingüísticos y filológicos,* vol. 4, ed. Irene Pérez Guerra (Santo Domingo: Editora Nacional, [1921c] 2004), 61–62.
23. Pedro Henríquez Ureña, *El español en Santo Domingo* (Santo Domingo: Taller, 1975), 41.
24. Ibid., 47.
25. Ibid., 47–48.
26. Ibid., 48–49.
27. Ibid., 48.
28. Ibid.
29. Ibid., 55–56.
30. Ibid., 55.
31. Ibid., 57.
32. Ibid., 60.
33. Ibid., 71–75, 76–81.
34. Ibid., 59.
35. Ibid., 95.
36. See Michiel Baud (1995).
37. Ibid., 108.
38. Ibid., 116.
39. Ibid., 118.
40. Ibid., 225.
41. Jacqueline Toribio, "Nosotros Somos Dominicanos: Language and Self-Definition among Dominicans," in *Research on Spanish in the U.S.,* ed. Ana Roca (Somerville, MA: Cascadilla Press, 2000b), 254.
42. Cited in Marc-Olivier Hinzelin and Georg A. Kaiser, "El pronombre 'ello' en el léxico del español dominicano," in *Language Contact and Language Change in the Caribbean and Beyond,* ed. Wiltrud Mihatsch and Monika Sokol (Frankfurt: Peter Lang, 2007), 172.
43. Pedro Henríquez Ureña, *El español en Santo Domingo* (Santo Domingo: Taller, 1975), 228.
44. Ibid.

45. Pedro Henríquez Ureña, *El español en Santo Domingo* (Santo Domingo: Taller, 1975), 226–228.
46. Ibid., 226.
47. Pedro Henríquez Ureña, "Ello," *Revista de Filología Hispánica* 1, no. 3 (1939): 209.
48. Pedro Henríquez Ureña, *El español en Santo Domingo* (Santo Domingo: Taller, 1975), 227–229.
49. Ibid., 230–231.
50. Ibid., 228–229.
51. Ibid., 230.
52. Ibid., 232.
53. Ibid., 136.
54. Ibid., 149.
55. Ibid.
56. This is the phonological process in which one sound becomes different from a neighboring sound.
57. Pedro Henríquez Ureña, *El español en Santo Domingo* (Santo Domingo: Taller, 1975), 168.
58. Esteban Pichardo, *Diccionario provincial casi razonado de voces y frases cubanas* (La Habana: Editorial de Ciencias Sociales, [1836] 1985), 12.
59. Ibid., 11.
60. Pedro Henríquez Ureña, *El español en Santo Domingo* (Santo Domingo: Taller, 1975), 168.
61. Ibid.
62. Ibid., 168–169.
63. Pedro Henríquez Ureña, "Observaciones sobre el español en América II," in *Obras completas: estudios lingüísticos y filológicos*, vol. 4, ed. Irene Pérez Guerra (Santo Domingo: Editora Nacional, [1930b] 2004), 120.
64. Pedro Henríquez Ureña, *El español en Santo Domingo* (Santo Domingo: Taller, 1975), 67.
65. Ibid., 57.
66. Pedro Henríquez Ureña, "La cultura y las letras coloniales en Santo Domingo," in *Obra dominicana*, ed. José Chez Checo (Santo Domingo: Sociedad Dominicana de Bibliófilos Inc., [1936] 1988), 199.
67. Pedro Henríquez Ureña, "La lengua en Santo Domingo," in *Obras completas: estudios lingüísticos y filológicos*, vol. 4, ed. Irene Pérez Guerra (Santo Domingo: Editora Nacional, [1919] 2004), 50.
68. Pedro Henríquez Ureña, *El español en Santo Domingo* (Santo Domingo: Taller, 1975), 132.
69. Pedro Henríquez Ureña, "La lengua en Santo Domingo," in *Obras completas: estudios lingüísticos y filológicos*, vol. 4, ed. Irene Pérez Guerra (Santo Domingo: Editora Nacional, [1919] 2004), 50.
70. Pedro Henríquez Ureña, "La antigua sociedad patriarcal de las Antillas: modalidades arcaicas de la vida en Santo Domingo durante el siglo XIX,"

in *Obra dominicana,* ed. José Chez Checo (Santo Domingo: Sociedad Dominicana de Bibliófilos Inc, [1932c] 1988), 504.
71. Pedro Henríquez Ureña, "La cultura y las letras coloniales en Santo Domingo," in *Obra dominicana,* ed. José Chez Checo (Santo Domingo: Sociedad Dominicana de Bibliófilos Inc., [1936] 1988), 202.
72. Pedro Henríquez Ureña, "La antigua sociedad patriarcal de las Antillas: modalidades arcaicas de la vida en Santo Domingo durante el siglo XIX," in *Obra dominicana,* ed. José Chez Checo (Santo Domingo: Sociedad Dominicana de Bibliófilos Inc, [1932c] 1988), 506.
73. Pedro Henríquez Ureña, "La cultura y las letras coloniales en Santo Domingo," in *Obra dominicana,* ed. José Chez Checo (Santo Domingo: Sociedad Dominicana de Bibliófilos Inc., [1936] 1988), 201–202.
74. Ibid., 202.
75. Pedro Henríquez Ureña, "La antigua sociedad patriarcal de las Antillas: modalidades arcaicas de la vida en Santo Domingo durante el siglo XIX," in *Obra dominicana* (Santo Domingo: Sociedad Dominicana de Bibliófilos Inc, [1932c] 1988), 507.
76. Pedro Henríquez Ureña, *El español en Santo Domingo* (Santo Domingo: Taller, 1975), 250.
77. The replacement of l by r (rotacism) is quite spread in the southern region of the Dominican Republic. See Jiménez Sabater (1975).
78. Pedro Henríquez Ureña, *El español en Santo Domingo* (Santo Domingo: Taller, 1975), 132–133.
79. Ibid., 134.
80. Pedro Henríquez Ureña, "La lengua en Santo Domingo," in *Obras completas: estudios lingüísticos y filológicos,* vol. 4, ed. Irene Pérez Guerra (Santo Domingo: Editora Nacional, [1919] 2004), 430.
81. Pedro Henríquez Ureña, *El español en Santo Domingo* (Santo Domingo: Taller, 1975), 193.
82. Ibid.
83. John Lipski, *A History of Afro-Hispanic Language* (Cambridge: Cambridge University Press, 2005), 258.
84. Max Jiménez Sabater, *Más datos sobre el español dominicano de la República Dominicana* (Santo Domingo: Intec, 1975), 170.
85. Orlando Alba, *Como hablamos los dominicanos: un enfoque sociolingüístico* (Santo Domingo: Grupo León Jimenes, 2004), 143.
86. Ibid.
87. John Lipski, "A New Perspective on Afro-Dominican Spanish: The Haitian Contribution," http//:www.personal.psu.edu/faculty/j/m/jml34/afrodom.pdf (1994) (accessed October 25, 2006).
88. Francisco Moscoso Puello, *Cañas y bueyes* (Santo Domingo: La Nación, 1936), 45.
89. Pedro Henríquez Ureña, *El español en Santo Domingo* (Santo Domingo: Taller, 1975), 130.
90. Fernando Ortiz, *El glosario de afronegrismos* (La Habana: Imprenta el Siglo XX, 1924), 141–142.

91. See Ortiz (1939).
92. Fernando Ortiz, "Los afronegrismos de nuestro lenguaje," in *Etnia y sociedad,* ed. Isaac Barreal (La Habana: Editorial de Ciencias Sociales, 1993), 98.
93. Ibid., 99.
94. Fernando Ortiz, "La cubanidad y los negros," *Estudios Afrocubanos* 3 (1939): 7.
95. Fernando Ortiz, *El glosario de afronegrismos* (La Habana: Imprenta el Siglo XX, 1924), 13.
96. Pedro Henríquez Ureña, *El español en Santo Domingo* (Santo Domingo: Taller, 1975), 132.
97. Pura Roque (my grandmother), in discussion with the author, Santo Domingo, September 2007. Also see Alejandro and Castro (2005).
98. Pedro Henríquez Ureña, *El español en Santo Domingo* (Santo Domingo: Taller, 1975), 131.
99. Andrés L. Mateo, *Mito y cultura en la era de Trujillo* (Santo Domingo: Editora Manatí, 2004), 99.
100. Carlos Larrazábal Blanco, "Papeles de Familia," *Clio* 13 (1945): 13.
101. See Américo Moreta Castillo (2003).
102. Carlos Larrazábal Blanco, *Los negros y la esclavitud en Santo Domingo* (Santo Domingo: La Trinitaria, [1967] 1998), 180–181.
103. Ibid., 181.
104. *Cocolo* is a term used by Dominicans, Puerto Ricans and, to a lesser extent, Cubans in order to refer to immigrants and black people from the English-speaking Antilles and North America. See Juan Valdez (2007).
105. Carlos Larrazábal Blanco, *Los negros y la esclavitud en Santo Domingo* (Santo Domingo: La Trinitaria, [1967] 1998), 182–183.
106. Ibid., 191.
107. Pedro Henríquez Ureña, *El español en Santo Domingo* (Santo Domingo: Taller, 1975), 133, italics in the original.
108. Pedro Henríquez Ureña, *Memorias, diario, notas de viaje,* ed. Enrique Zuleta Álvarez (Mexico: Fondo de Cultura Económica, [1909] 2000), 54.
109. Ibid., 56.
110. Carlos Larrazábal Blanco, *Los negros y la esclavitud en Santo Domingo* (Santo Domingo: La Trinitaria, [1967] 1998), 181.
111. Pedro Henríquez Ureña, *El español en Santo Domingo* (Santo Domingo: Taller, 1975), 213.
112. Ibid., 213–214.
113. Ibid., 214.
114. Ibid.
115. Ibid.
116. Pedro Henríquez Ureña, "La cultura y las letras coloniales en Santo Domingo," in *Obra dominicana,* ed. José Chez Checo (Santo Domingo: Sociedad Dominicana de Bibliófilos Inc., [1936] 1988), 276.
117. Pedro Henríquez Ureña, "Reseña de 'Vicisitudes de la lengua española en Santo Domingo' por Emilio Rodríguez Demorizi," in *Obra dominicana,* ed.

José Chez Checo (Santo Domingo: Sociedad Dominicana de Bibliófilos Inc., [1944] 1988), 499.
118. Enrique Deschamps, *La República Dominicana: directorio y guía general* (Barcelona, Spain, 1906), 73–74.
119. Cited in Ginetta Candelario, *Black Behind the Ears: Dominican Racial Identity from Museums to Beauty Shops* (Durham: Duke University Press, 2007), 1–2. The poem begins: "since nowadays there are so many/whom this dismays/I will employ my modest pen/to offer all a lesson/for in our Nation/this will not do/that was in old Spain/or so I heard as a youngster/but nowadays what abounds/is 'the black behind the ear.'" Alix's poems are also well recognized for his imitations of regional Dominican dialects and Haitians' pidginized Spanish.

Conclusion

1. Rafael Gutiérrez Girardot, "Prólogo," in *La utopía de América,* ed. Rafael Gutiérrez Girardot and Ángel Rama (Caracas: Biblioteca Ayacucho, 1978).
2. Pedro Henríquez Ureña, *Literary Currents in Hispanic America* (Cambridge, MA: Harvard University Press, 1945), 191.
3. Ibid., 195.
4. See his speech of acceptance into the Dominican Academy of the Spanish Language, included in the Academy's 2004 Bulletin, especially pages 147, 177, 186–187.
5. See Irene Pérez Guerra (1989) and Barbara Bullock and Jacqueline Toribio (2008).
6. Orlando Alba, *La identidad lingüística de los dominicanos* (Santo Domingo: La Trinitaria, 2009).
7. Ibid., 144.
8. Ibid., 147. In a different context, Ricardo Otheguy and Naomi Lapidus (2005) have also explained lexical borrowing in contact situation as a process of adaptation and functional restructuring of cognitive loads.
9. Odalís Pérez (2005).
10. Solange (Sonia) Pierre, who recently won "The International Women of Courage" award, has been fighting anti-Haitian discrimination and bringing attention to issues of statelessness since the age of 13, when she was arrested for being the spokesperson for protesting sugarcane cutters. See "A rights advocate divides Dominicans," *New York Times,* September 29, 2007; "Hillary Clinton, Sonia Pierre y Michelle Obama," *Hoy,* March 20, 2010.
11. Kathryn Woolard, "La autoridad lingüística del español y las ideologías de la autenticidad y el anonimato," in *La lengua, ¿patria común? Ideas e ideologías del español,* ed. José Del Valle (Madrid and Frankfurt: Iberoamericana and Vervuert, 2007), 132. According to Woolard, *keepin' it real* is one example of the language ideology of *authenticity,* which primarily values language as the particular, private, an authentic expression of a localized group, for example, the speakers of African-American Vernacular English (AAVE).

References

Abeille, Luciano. *El idioma nacional de los argentinos*. Buenos Aires: Biblioteca Nacional, [1900] 2005.

Alba, Orlando. "A propósito de la identidad lingüística dominicana." *Eme Eme* 12, no. 72 (1984): 31–43.

———. *Como hablamos los dominicanos: un enfoque sociolingüístico*. Santo Domingo: Grupo León Jimenes, 2004.

———. *La identidad lingüística de los dominicanos*. Santo Domingo: La Trinitaria, 2009.

———. *Estudios sobre el español dominicano*. Santiago, Dominican Republic: PUCMM, 1990.

Alejandro, Paulino and Aquiles Castro. *Diccionario de cultura y folklore dominicano*. Santo Domingo: ABC Editorial, 2005.

Alix, Juan Antonio. *Décimas*. Santo Domingo: Imprenta de J. R. Vda. García, [1884] 1927.

Alonso, Amado. *Castellano, español, idioma nacional*. Buenos Aires: Imprenta y Casa Editora Coni, 1938.

———. *El problema de la lengua en América*. Madrid: Espasa-Calpe, 1935.

———. *Estudios lingüísticos: temas españoles*. Madrid: Gredos, 1951.

———. "Examen de la teoría indigenista de Rodolfo Lenz." *Revista de Filología Hispánica* 1 (1939): 313–350.

———. *La identidad lingüística de los dominicanos*. Santo Domingo: La Trinitaria, 2009.

———. "La subagrupación románica del catalán." *Revista de Filología Española* XIII, no. 1 (January-March 1926): 225–261.

———. "Pedro Henríquez Ureña, investigador." In *Presencia de Pedro Henríquez Ureña: escritos sobre el maestro*, edited by Jorge Tena Reyes and Tomás Castro Burdiez. Santo Domingo: Editorial Ciguapa, 2001.

———. "Prefacio." In *Filosofía del lenguaje de K. Vossler*, translated by Amado Alonso. Buenos Aires: Losada, 1943.

———. *Problemas de dialectología hispanoamericana*. Buenos Aires: Instituto de Filología, 1930.

———. "Prólogo a la edición española." In *Curso de lingüística general de F. Saussure*, translated by Amado Alonso. Buenos Aires: Losada, 1945.

———. "Rodolfo Lenz y la dialectología hispanoamericana." In *El español en Chile*, edited by Amado Alonso. Buenos Aires: Biblioteca de Dialectología Hispanoamericana, 1940.

Alonso, Amado and Pedro Henríquez Ureña. *Gramática castellana,* volumes 1 and 2. Buenos Aires: Losada, 1938.
Álvarez, Soledad. *La Magna Patria de Pedro Henríquez Ureña.* Santo Domingo: Editorial Taller, 1981.
———. "La pasión dominicana de Pedro Henríquez Ureña." In *Pedro Henríquez Ureña: ensayos,* edited by José Luis Abellán and Ana María Barrenechea. Madrid: Allca XX, 1998.
Álvarez Martínez, María Ángeles. "Pedro Henríquez Ureña y la dialectología hispanoamericana." *La Torre* 3, no. 7–8 (1998): 177–185.
Anderson, Benedict. *Imagined Communities: Reflections on the Origins and Spread of Nationalism.* London and New York: Verso, 1983.
Anderson, James. M. "Historical Linguistics." In *The Linguistics Encyclopedia,* edited by Kirsten Malmkajaer. London and New York: Routledge, 2001.
Anderson Imbert, Enrique. "La filosofía de Pedro Henríquez Ureña." *Revista Sur* 355 (1984): 5–19.
———. "Notas sobre Pedro Henríquez Ureña." In *Presencia de Pedro Henríquez Ureña: escritos sobre el maestro,* edited by Jorge Tena Reyes and Tomás Castro Burdiez. Santo Domingo: Editorial Ciguapa, 2001.
Arnoux, Elvira N. de. *Análisis del discurso: modos de abordar materiales de archivo.* Buenos Aires: Santiago Arcos, 2006.
———. "Disciplinar desde la lengua: 'La gramática castellana' de Amado Alonso y Pedro Henríquez Ureña." In *Homenaje a Ofelia Kovacci,* edited by Elvira N. de Arnoux and Ángela Di Tullio. Buenos Aires: Eudeba, 2001.
———. "Discursos sobre nación," PhD diss., Universidade Da Coruña, 2007.
———. "El análisis del discurso en el pensamiento gramatical ilustrado: Jovellanos lector de Condillac." In *El pensamiento ilustrado y el lenguaje,* edited by Elvira N. de Arnoux and Carlos R. Luis. Buenos Aires: Eudeba, 2003.
———. "La Glotopolítica: transformaciones de un campo disciplinario." In *Lenguajes: teorías y prácticas,* edited by Elvira N. de Arnoux. Buenos Aires: Gobierno de la Ciudad de Buenos Aires, Instituto Superior del Profesorado, 2000.
Arnoux, Elvira N. de and Carlos R. Luis. *El pensamiento ilustrado y el lenguaje.* Buenos Aires: Eudeba, 2003.
Arnoux, Elvira N. de and José Del Valle. "Las representaciones ideológicas del lenguaje: discurso glotopolítico y panhispanismo." *Spanish in Context* 7, no. 1 (2010): 1–24.
Arona, Juan de. *Diccionario de peruanismos,* volumes 1 and 2. Lima: Biblioteca Peruana, [1882] 1975.
Arquistain, Luis. *La agonía antillana: el imperialismo yanqui en el Caribe.* Madrid: Espasa-Calpe, 1928.
Ashley, Leonard R. N. "Language and Identity in Cuba Today." *Geolinguistics* 28 (2002): 22–33.
Bachmann, Iris. "Negertaaltje or Volkstaal: The Papiamentu Language at the Crossroads of Philology, Folklore and Anthropology." *Indiana* 24 (2007): 87–105.
Bacon, Francis. *The Essays or Counsels, Civil and Moral.* London: Penguin Books, 1985.

———. *The New Organon and Related Writings*. Indianapolis and New York: The Bobbs-Merrill Company, Inc., 1960.

Bajarkman, Peter C. "Radical and Conservative Hispanic Dialects: Theoretical Accounts and Pedagogical Implications." In *American Spanish Pronunciation*, edited by P. Bajarkman and R. Hammond. Washington: Georgetown University Press, 1989.

Bakhtin, Mikhail. *The Dialogic Imagination*, edited by Michael Holquist. Austin: University of Texas Press, 1981.

Balaguer, Joaquín. "Discurso Pronunciado por el Presidente de la República Dominicana Joaquín Balaguer, en Ocasión de la Primera Cumbre Iberoamericana, Guadalajara, México, 1991," http://www.cip.cu/webcip/eventos/cumbre-ibero/cumbre1/discursos/ (accessed May 3, 2008).

———. *La isla al revés: Haití y el destino dominicano*. Santo Domingo: Librería Dominicana, 1983.

Barbour, Stephen. "Nationalism, Language, Europe." In *Language and Nationalism in Europe*, edited by Stephen Barbour and Cathie Carmichael. Oxford: Oxford University Press, 2000.

Barcia, Pedro Luis. *Pedro Henríquez Ureña y la Argentina*. Santo Domingo: Ediciones Ferilibro, 2006.

Barrera Enderle, Victor. *De la amistad literaria: ensayo sobre la genealogía de una amistad: Alfonso Reyes, Pedro Henríquez Ureña, 1906–1914*. Mexico: Universidad Autónoma de Nuevo León, 2006.

Baud, Michiel. "Intelectuales, nación y modernidad en la República Dominicana." In *Relatos de nación: la construcción de identidades en el mundo hispánico*, edited by Francisco Colom González. Madrid and Frankfurt: Iberoamericana and Vervuert, 2005.

———. *Peasants and Tobacco in the Dominican Republic*. Knoxville: University of Tennessee Press, 1995.

Bauman, Richard. *Let Your Words Be Few: Symbolisms of Speaking and Silence among Seventeenth Century Quakers*. New York: Cambridge University Press, 1983.

Bauman, Richard and Charles Briggs. "Poetics and performance as critical perspectives on language and social life." *Annual Review of Anthropology* 19 (1990): 59–88.

Becker, Carl Lotus. *The Heavenly City of the Eighteenth Century Philosophers*. New Haven: Yale University Press, 1932.

Bello, Andrés. "Discurso de instalación de la Universidad de Chile." In *Obras completas: opúsculos literarios y críticos*, edited by Miguel Luis Amunátegui. Santiago: Impresora Pedro G. Ramírez, 2005.

———. *Gramática de la lengua castellana destinada al uso de los americanos*. Madrid: Editorial EDAF, [1847] 2001.

Blas Arroyo, José Luis. *La sociolingüística del español: desarrollos y perspectivas en el estudio de la lengua en contexto social*. Madrid: Cátedra, 2006.

Blommaert, Jan and Jef Verschueren. "The Role of Language in European Nationalist Ideologies." In *Language Ideologies: Practice and Theory*, edited by B. Schieffelin, K. Woolard and P. Kroskrity. New York and Oxford: Oxford University Press, 1998.

Borges, Jorge Luis. *El idioma de los argentinos*. Buenos Aires: M. Gleizer, 1928.

———. "Las alarmas del doctor Américo Castro." In *Otras inquisiciones*, edited by Jorge Luis Borges. Madrid: Alianza Editorial, 1961.

———. "Prólogo." In *Obra crítica*, edited by Emma Susana Sperantti Piñero. Mexico and Buenos Aires: Fondo de Cultura Económica, 1960.

Bourdieu, Pierre. *Language and Symbolic Power*. Cambridge, MA: Harvard University Press, 1991.

Brito, Rafael. *Diccionario de criollismos*. San Francisco de Macorís, Dom. Rep.: Imprenta ABC de C. F. de Moya, 1930.

Bucholtz, Mary. "The Whiteness of Nerds: Superstandard English and Racial Markedness." *Journal of Linguistic Anthropology* 11, no. 1 (2001): 84–100.

Bullock, Barbara and Jacqueline Toribio. "Kreyol Incursions into Dominican Spanish: The Perception of Haitianized Speech among Dominicans." In *Bilingualism and Identity: Spanish at the Crossroads with Other Languages*, edited by Mercedes Niño-Murcia and Jason Rothman. Philadelphia: John Benjamins, 2008.

Calvet, Louis-Jean. *Lingüística y colonialismo: Breve tratado de glotofagia*. Buenos Aires: Fondo de Cultura Económica, 2005.

Candelario, Ginetta. *Black Behind the Ears: Dominican Racial Identity from Museums to Beauty Shops*. Durham: Duke University Press, 2007.

Capdevilla, Arturo. *Babel y el castellano*. Buenos Aires: Losada, [1928] 1940.

Carilla, Emilio. "El tema esencial de Pedro Henríquez Ureña." *Thesaurus* 35 (1980): 124–135.

———. *Pedro Henríquez Ureña, Signo de América*. Santo Domingo: Publicaciones de La Universidad Nacional Pedro Henríquez Ureña, 1988.

Cassá, Roberto. *Historia social y económica de la República Dominicana*, volumes 1 and 2. Santo Domingo: Editora Alfa y Omega, 1998.

———. "Nación y Estado en el pensamiento de Américo Lugo." In *Política, identidad y pensamiento social en la República Dominicana (Siglos XIX y XX)*, edited by Raymundo González et al. Madrid and Santo Domingo: Doce Calles and Academia de Ciencias de la República Dominicana, 1999.

Castro, Américo. "Introducción." *Boletín del Instituto de Filología* 1 (1923).

———. *La peculiaridad lingüística rioplatense y su sentido histórico*. Buenos Aires: Losada, 1941.

Castro-Klaren, Sara and John Charles Chasteen. *Reading and Writing the Nation in Nineteenth Century Latin America*. Baltimore and London: The Johns Hopkins University Press, 2003.

Centeno Añeses, Carmen. "Lengua, identidad nacional, posmodernidad." *Revista de Estudios Hispánicos* 26, no. 2 (1999): 217–237.

Chevalier, J. C. and P. Encrevé. "La création des revues dans les années '60s." *Langue Française* 63 (1984): 57–102.

Colom González, Francisco, ed. *Relatos de nación: la construcción de las identidades nacionales en el mundo hispánico*, volumes 1 and 2. Madrid: Iberoamericana and Vervuert, 2005.

Conn, Robert T. *The Politics of Philology: Alfonso Reyes and the Invention of the Latin American Tradition*. London: Associated University Presses, 2002.

Cordero Michel, José. *Análisis de la era de Trujillo: informe sobre la República Dominicana, 1959.* Santo Domingo: Editora de la UASD, 1975.

Costa Álvarez, Arturo. *El castellano en la Argentina.* Buenos Aires: Talleres de la Escuela San Vicente de Paúl, 1928.

Crowley, Tony. *Language in History: Theories and Texts.* London: Routledge, 1996.

Cuervo, Rufino José. *Apuntaciones críticas sobre el lenguaje bogotano.* Bogotá: Imprenta de Echeverría Hermanos, 1876.

———. "Castellano popular y castellano literario." In *Obras,* vol. 1, edited by Fernando A. Martínez. Bogota: Instituto Caro y Cuervo, [1901a] 1987.

———. *Diccionario de construcción y régimen de la lengua castellana.* Bogotá Instituto Caro y Cuervo, [1886] 1953.

———. "El castellano en América." In *Obras,* vol. 1, edited by Fernando A. Martínez. Bogota: Instituto Caro y Cuervo, [1901b] 1987.

Danesi, Marcel. "The case for andalucismo re-examined." *Hispanic Review* 45 (1977): 181–193.

De Cuypere, Ludovic and Klaas Willems. "Introduction: Naturalness and Iconicity in Language." In *Limiting the Iconic: From Metaphorical Foundations to the Creative Possibilities of Iconicity in Language,* edited by Klaas Willems and Ludovic De Cuypere. Amsterdam and Philadelphia: John Benjamins, 2008.

Del Valle, José. "Andalucismo, poligénesis y koineización: dialectología e ideología." *Hispanic Review* 66, no. 2 (1998): 132–149.

———. "Glotopolítica, ideología y discurso: categorías para el estudio del estatus simbólico del español." In *La lengua, ¿patria común? Ideas e ideologías del español,* edited by José del Valle. Madrid and Frankfurt: Iberoamericana and Vervuert, 2007.

———. "Historical Linguistics and Cultural History: The Polemic between Rufino José Cuervo and Juan Valera." In *The Battle over Spanish between 1800 and 2000: Language Ideologies and Hispanic Intellectuals,* edited by José Del Valle and Luis Gabriel-Stheeman. Madrid and Frankfurt: Iberoamericana and Vervuert, 2002a.

———. "La historificación de la lingüística histórica: los orígenes de Ramón Menéndez Pidal." *Historiographia Lingüística* XXIV, no. 2 (1997): 175–196.

———. "La lengua, patria común: política lingüística, política exterior y el postnacionalismo hispánico." In *Studies on Ibero-Romance Linguistics. Dedicated to Ralph Penny,* edited by Roger Wright and Meter Ricketts. Newark, Delaware: Juan de la Cuesta, 2005.

———. "Menéndez Pidal, National Regeneration, and Linguistic Utopia." In *The Battle over Spanish between 1800 and 2000: Language Ideologies and Hispanic Intellectuals,* edited by José Del Valle and Luis Gabriel-Stheeman. London and New York: Routledge, 2002b.

———. "Menéndez Pidal, la regeneración nacional y la utopía lingüística." In *La batalla del idioma: la intelectualidad hispánica ante la lengua,* edited by José del Valle y Luis Gabriel-Stheeman. Frankfurt y Madrid: Vervuert and Iberoamericana, 2004.

———. "Monoglossic Policies for a Heteroglossic Culture: Misinterpreted Multilingualism in Modern Galicia." *Language and Communication* 20 (2000): 105–132.

———. "US Latinos, la Hispanofonía, and the Language Ideologies of High Modernity." In *Globalization and Language in the Spanish-Speaking World*, edited by Clare Mar-Moliero and Miranda Stewart. Hampshire, England: Palgrave Macmillan, 2006.

Del Valle, José and Luis Gabriel-Stheeman, *The Battle over Spanish between 1800 and 2000: Language Ideologies and Hispanic Intellectuals*. Madrid and Frankfurt: Iberoamericana and Vervuert, 2002.

———. "Codo con codo: la comunidad hispánica y el espectáculo de la lengua." In *La batalla del idioma: la intelectualidad hispánica ante la lengua*, edited by José del Valle y Luis Gabriel-Stheeman. Frankfurt y Madrid: Vervuert and Iberoamericana, 2004a.

———. *La batalla del idioma: la intelectualidad hispánica ante la lengua*. Frankfurt and Madrid: Vervuert and Iberoamericana, 2004b.

———. "Lengua y mercado: el español en la era de la globalización económica." In *La batalla del idioma: la intelectualidad hispánica ante la lengua*, edited by José del Valle and Luis Gabriel-Stheeman. Frankfurt y Madrid: Vervuert and Iberoamericana, 2004c.

———. "Nacionalismo, hispanismo y cultura monoglósica." In *La batalla del idioma: la intelectualidad hispánica ante la lengua*, edited by José del Valle y Luis Gabriel-Stheeman. Frankfurt y Madrid: Vervuert and Iberoamericana, 2004d.

Deschamps, Enrique. *La República Dominicana: directorio y guía general*. Barcelona, Spain, 1906.

Díaz Quiñones, Arcadio. *Sobre los principios: la tradición y los intelectuales caribeños*. Bernal, Argentina: Universidad Nacional de Quilmes Editorial, 2006.

———. "Pedro Henríquez Ureña: modernidad, diáspora y construcción de identidades." In *Modernización e identidades sociales*, edited by Gilberto Giménez and Ricardo Pozas H. Mexico: Universidad Nacional Autónoma de México, 1994.

Diez, Friedrich. *Grammatik der romanischen sprachen*. Bonn: E. Weber, 1882.

Dobal, Carlos. "Hispanidad y dominicanidad." *Eme Eme* 12, no. 71 (1984): 89–97.

Durán, Diony. *Literatura y sociedad en la obra de Pedro Henríquez Ureña*. La Habana: Letras Cubanas, 1994.

Eagleton, Terry. *Ideology: An Introduction*. London: Verso, 1991.

Errington, Joseph. *Linguistics in a Colonial World: A Story of Language, Meaning, and Power*. Malden, MA and London: Blackwell, 2008.

———. "Indonesian('s) Authority." In *Regimes of Language: Ideologies, Polities, and Identities*, edited by Paul V. Kroskrity. Santa Fe, NM: School of American Research Press, 2000.

Familia Henríquez Ureña. *Epistolario*, volumes 1 and 2. Santo Domingo: Secretaría de Estado de Educación, Bellas Artes y Cultos, 1996.

Fanon, Frantz. *Black Skin, White Masks*. New York: Grove Press, 2008.

Febres, Laura. *Pedro Henríquez Ureña, crítico de América*. Caracas: Ediciones la Casa de Bello, 1989.

Fennema, Meindert. "Hispanidad y la identidad nacional de Santo Domingo." In *Política, identidad y pensamiento social en la República Dominicana (Siglos XIX y XX)*, edited by Raymundo González et al. Madrid and Santo Domingo: Doce Calles and Academia de Ciencias de Dominicana, 1999.

Fernández Retamar, Roberto. *Todo Calibán.* Concepción, Chile: Cuadernos Atanea, 1998.
Ford, J. D. M. "A Note from J. D. M. Ford on Pedro Henríquez Ureña." *Books Abroad* 21, no. 1 (1947): 31–38.
———. *Main Currents of Spanish Literature.* New York: H. Holt and Company, 1919.
Foucault, Michel. *The Archeology of Knowledge and the Discourse on Language.* New York: Basic Books, 1994a.
———. *Discipline and Punish: The Birth of the Prison,* translated by Alan Sheridan. New York: Random House, 1995.
———. *The Order of Things: An Archeology of the Human Sciences.* New York: Vintage, 1994b.
Franco, Jean. "El humanismo de Pedro Henríquez Ureña." In *Pedro Henríquez Ureña: ensayos,* edited by José Luis Abellán and Ana María Barrenechea. Madrid: Allca XX, 1998.
Gal, Susan. "Codeswitching and Consciousness in the European Periphery." *American Ethnologist* 14 (1987): 637–653.
———. "Linguistic Theories and National Images in Nineteenth Century Hungary." In *Languages and Publics: The Making of Authority,* edited by Susan Gal and Kathryn Woolard. Manchester: St. Jerome Publishing, 2001.
———. "Multiplicity and Contention among Language Ideologies: A Commentary." In *Language Ideologies: Practice and Theory,* edited by B. Schieffelin, K. Woolard and P. Kroskrity. Oxford: Oxford University Press, 1998.
Gal, Susan and Kathryn Woolard. "Constructing Languages and Publics: Authority and Representation." In *Languages and Publics: The Making of Authority,* edited by Susan Gal and Kathryn Woolard. Manchester: St. Jerome Publishing, 2001.
Galíndez, Jesús de. *La era de Trujillo: un estudio casuístico de dictadura hispanoamericana.* Santo Domingo: Editora Taller, 1984.
García, José Gabriel. *Compendio de la historia dominicana.* Santo Domingo: Publicaciones Ahora, [1878] 1968.
García, Telesforo. "La raza: patria, raza y humanidad e iberoamericanismo." *Revista Positiva* 12 (Mexico) (1901): 492.
Garciadiego, Javier. *Rudos contra científicos: La Universidad Nacional durante la Revolución Mexicana.* Mexico: el Colegio de México, 1996.
Ghiano, Juan Carlos. "Pedro Henríquez Ureña, maestro de Nuestra América." In *Observaciones sobre el español en América y otros estudios filológicos,* edited by Juan Carlos Ghiano. Buenos Aires: Academia Argentina de Letras, 1976.
González Echevarría, Roberto. "Liminar." In *Pedro Henríquez Ureña: ensayos,* edited by José Luis Abellán and Ana María Barrenechea. Mexico: Fondo de Cultura Económica, 1998.
González, Raymundo et al., eds. *Política, identidad y pensamiento social en la República Dominicana (Siglos XIX y XX).* Madrid and Santo Domingo: Doce Calles and Academia de Ciencias de Dominicana, 1999.
González Stephan, Beatriz. "Las disciplinas escriturarias de la patria: constituciones, gramáticas y manuales." *Estudios. Revista de Investigaciones Literarias* 3, no. 5 (1995): 19–46.

González Tapia, Carlisle. *El pensamiento lingüístico de Pedro Henríquez Ureña.* Santo Domingo: Ciudad Universitaria, 1998.

———. *Habla campesina dominicana IV.* Santo Domingo: Editora Universitaria-UASD, 2001.

González Tirado, Rafael. *Lenguaje y nacionalismo.* Santo Domingo: Editorial Gente, 1987.

Gramsci, Antonio. *Selections from the Prison Notebooks of Antonio Gramsci,* edited by Quintin Hoare and Geoffrey Nowell Smith. New York: International Publishers, 1971.

Granados, Aimer and Carlos Marichal. *Construcción de la identidades latinoamericanas: ensayos de historia intelectual (siglos XIX y XX).* Mexico: El Colegio de México, 2004.

Guerra Sánchez, Ramiro. *Azúcar y población en las Antillas.* La Habana: Imprenta Nacional de Cuba, 1927.

Guerreiro, Leila. "Pedro Henríquez Ureña: el eterno extranjero," http://www.libresa.com/perspectiva_phu_sexta_entrega_20030616.htm (2003) (accessed July 14, 2007).

Guespin, Louis and Jean Baptiste Marcellesi. "Pour la glottopolitique." *Langages* 83 (1986): 5–34.

Guitarte, Guillermo. "El camino de Cuervo al español de América." In *Philologica Hispaniensia: in Honorem Manuel Álvar,* vol. 1, edited by Julio Fernández Sevilla et al. Madrid: Gredos, 1983.

———. "Cuervo, Henríquez Ureña y la polémica sobre el andalucismo de América." *Vox Románica* 17 (1958a): 363–416.

———. *Siete estudios sobre el español de América.* Mexico: Universidad Nacional Autónoma de México, [1958b] 1983.

———. "Un concepto de la filología hispanoamericana: la base del español en América." *La Torre* 3, no. 7–8 (1998): 417–434.

Gutiérrez Cuadrado, Juan. "El hispanismo lingüístico." *Ínsula* 725 (2007): 4–9.

Gutiérrez Girardot, Rafael. "El ensayo posmodernista: Pedro Henríquez Ureña." In *Presencia de Pedro Henríquez Ureña: escritos sobre el maestro,* edited by Jorge Tena Reyes and Tomás Castro Burdiez. Santo Domingo: Editorial Ciguapa, 2001a.

———. *El intelectual y la historia.* Caracas: Fondo Editorial La Nave Va, 2001b.

———. "La historiografía latinoamericana de Pedro Henríquez Ureña: promesa y desafío." In *Aproximaciones: ensayos,* edited by Rafael Gutiérrez Girardot. Bogotá: Nueva Biblioteca Colombiana de Cultura, 1986.

———. "Pedro Henríquez Ureña y la historiografía latinoamericana." In *Pedro Henríquez Ureña: ensayos,* edited by José Luis Abellán and Ana María Barrenechea. Madrid: Allca XX, 1998.

———. "Prólogo." In *La utopía de América,* edited by Rafael Gutiérrez Girardot and Ángel Rama. Caracas: Biblioteca Ayacucho, 1978.

Gumperz, John and Dell Hymes. *Directions in Sociolinguistics: The Ethnography of Communication.* New York: Holt, Rinehart and Winston, 1972.

Haiman, John. *Natural Syntax; Iconicity and Erosion.* New York: Cambridge University Press, 1985.

Halperín Donghi, Tulio. *Historia contemporánea de América Latina*. Madrid: Alianza Editorial, 1998.

———. *Vida y muerte de la república verdadera: 1910–1930*. Buenos Aires: Emecé, 1999.

Hanks, William. "Indexicality." In *Key Terms in Language and Culture*, edited by Alessandro Duranti. Malden, MA: Blackwell, 2001.

Harris, Roy. *Saussure and His Interpreters*. New York: New York University Press, 2001.

Hatzfeld, Helmut. "Hispanic Philology in Latin America." *The Americas* 3 (1947): 347–362.

Hawkins, Bruce. "The Social Dimension of a Cognitive Grammar." In *Discourse and Perspective in Cognitive Linguistics*, edited by W. A. Liebert et al. Amsterdam and Philadelphia: John Benjamins, 1997.

Henríquez Ureña, Max. "Hermano y maestro." In *Presencia de Pedro Henríquez Ureña: escritos sobre el maestro*, edited by Jorge Tena Reyes and Tomás Castro Burdiez. Santo Domingo: Editorial Ciguapa, 2001.

———. *Los Estados Unidos y la República Dominicana: la verdad de los hechos comprobada por datos y documentos oficiales*. La Habana: Imprenta el Siglo XX, 1919.

Henríquez Ureña, Pedro. "Ariel." In *Obras completas: escritos políticos, sociológicos y filosóficos*, vol. 4, edited by Manuel Núñez. Santo Domingo: Editora Nacional, [1904] 2004, 58.

———. "Ariel de Rodó." In *La utopía de América*, edited by Rafael Gutiérrez Girardot and Ángel Rama. Caracas: Biblioteca Ayacucho, [1900] 1978.

———. "Comienzos del español en América." In *Obras completas: estudios lingüísticos y filológicos*, vol. 4, edited by Irene Pérez Guerra. Santo Domingo: Editora Nacional, [1921a] 2004.

———. "El descontento y la promesa." In *La utopía de América*, edited by Rafael Gutiérrez Girardot and Ángel Rama. Caracas: Biblioteca Ayacucho, [1926] 1978, 38.

———. "El enigma del aje." In *Para la historia de los indigenismos*, edited by Pedro Henríquez Ureña. Buenos Aires: Biblioteca de Dialectología Hispanoamericana, 1938a.

———. *El español en Santo Domingo*. Santo Domingo: Taller, [1940] 1975.

———. "El idioma español y la historia política en Santo Domingo." In *Obras completas: estudios lingüísticos y filológicos*, vol. 4, edited by Irene Pérez Guerra. Santo Domingo: Editora Nacional, [1937] 2004.

———. "El lenguaje." In *Obras completas: estudios lingüísticos y filológicos*, vol. 4, edited by Irene Pérez Guerra. Santo Domingo: Editora Nacional, [1930a] 2004.

———. "El supuesto andalucismo de América." In *Obras completas: estudios lingüísticos y filológicos*, vol. 4, edited by Irene Pérez Guerra. Santo Domingo: Editora Nacional, [1925a] 2004.

———. "Ello." *Revista de Filología Hispánica* 1, no. 3 (1939): 209–229.

———. "En defensa de la Revista." In *Obras completas: estudios lingüísticos y filológicos*, vol. 4, edited by Irene Pérez Guerra. Santo Domingo: Editora Nacional, [1921b]: 2004.

———. *En la orilla: mi España*. Mexico: Cultura, 1922.

———. "Historia de palabras (batata)." *La Nación* (July 24, 1938b).

———. "Horas de estudio." Paris: Ollendorf, 1910.

———. "Hostos." In *Obras completas: escritos políticos, sociológicos y filosóficos*, vol. 4, edited by Manuel Núñez. Santo Domingo: Editora Nacional, [1903] 2004.

———. "Juan Ruiz de Alarcón." In *Estudios mexicanos*, edited by José Luis Martínez. Mexico: Fondo de Cultura Económica, [1913] 1984.

———. "La antigua sociedad patriarcal de las Antillas: modalidades arcaicas de la vida en Santo Domingo durante el siglo XIX." In *Obra dominicana*, edited by José Chez Checo. Santo Domingo: Sociedad Dominicana de Bibliófilos Inc., [1932c] 1988.

———. "La cultura y las letras coloniales en Santo Domingo." In *Obra dominicana*, edited by José Chez Checo. Santo Domingo: Sociedad Dominicana de Bibliófilos Inc., [1936] 1988.

———. "La influencia de la revolución en la vida intelectual de México." In *La utopía de América*, edited by Rafael Gutiérrez Girardot and Ángel Rama. Caracas: Biblioteca Ayacucho, [1925b] 1978.

———. "La intelectualidad hispanoamericana." *Revista Crítica* (1906): 1–9.

———. "La lengua en Santo Domingo." In *Obras completas: estudios lingüísticos y filológicos*, vol. 4, edited by Irene Pérez Guerra. Santo Domingo: Editora Nacional, [1919] 2004.

———. "La República Dominicana." In *Obras completas: escritos políticos, sociológicos y filosóficos*, vol. 4, edited by Manuel Núñez. Santo Domingo: Editora Nacional, [1917] 2004.

———. "La sociología de Hostos." In *Obras completas: escritos políticos, sociológicos y filosóficos*, vol. 4, edited by Manuel Núñez. Santo Domingo: Editora Nacional, [1905] 2004.

———. "La utopía en América." In *La utopía en América*, edited by Rafael Gutiérrez Girardot and Ángel Rama. Caracas: Biblioteca Ayacucho, [1933a] 1978.

———. *La versificación irregular en la poesía castellana*. Madrid: Publicaciones de la Revista de Filología Española, 1920.

———. *Literary Currents in Hispanic America*. Cambridge, MA: Harvard University Press, 1945.

———. *Memorias, diario, notas de viaje*, edited by Enrique Zuleta Álvarez. Mexico: Fondo de Cultura Económica, [1909] 2000.

———. *Obras completas*, volumes 1–4. Santo Domingo: Editora Nacional, 2004.

———. "Observaciones sobre el español en América I." In *Obras completas: estudios lingüísticos y filológicos*, vol. 4, edited by Irene Pérez Guerra. Santo Domingo: Editora Nacional, [1921c] 2004.

———. "Observaciones sobre el español en América II." In *Obras completas: estudios lingüísticos y filológicos*, vol. 4, edited by Irene Pérez Guerra. Santo Domingo: Editora Nacional, [1930b] 2004.

———. "Observaciones sobre el español en América III." In *Obras completas: estudios lingüísticos y filológicos*, vol. 4, ed. Irene Pérez Guerra. Santo Domingo: Editora Nacional, [1931] 2004.

———. "Observaciones II." *Revista de Filología Española* 17 (1932a): 227–284.
———. "Observaciones III." *Revista de Filología Española* 18 (1932b): 120–148.
———. "Papa y batata: historia de dos palabras." In *Para la historia de los indigenismos*, edited by Pedro Henríquez Ureña. Buenos Aires: Biblioteca de Dialectología Hispanoamericana, 1938c.
———. "Raza y cultura." In *La utopía de América*, edited by Rafael Gutiérrez Girardot and Ángel Rama. Caracas: Biblioteca Ayacucho, [1933b] 1978.
———. "Reseña de 'Vicisitudes de la lengua española en Santo Domingo' por Emilio Rodríguez Demorizi." In *Obra dominicana*, edited by José Chez Checo. Santo Domingo: Sociedad Dominicana de Bibliófilos Inc., [1944] 1988.
———. "Rufino José Cuervo." In *La utopía de América*, edited by Rafael Gutiérrez Girardot and Ángel Rama. Caracas: Biblioteca Ayacucho, 1978.
———. "Seis ensayos en busca de nuestra expresión." In *Obras completas: estudios lingüísticos y filológicos*, vol. 4, edited by Irene Pérez Guerra. Santo Domingo: Editora Nacional, [1928] 2004.
Henríquez Ureña, Pedro and Alfonso Reyes. *Epistolario íntimo, 1906–1946*, edited by Juan Jacobo de Lara. Santo Domingo: UNPHU, 1981.
Henríquez Ureña, Pedro and Narciso Binayan. *El libro del idioma*. Buenos Aires: Editorial A. Kapelusz y Cía., 1927.
———. *Guía para el uso de "El libro del idioma."* Buenos Aires: Editorial A. Kapelusz y Cía., 1928.
Henríquez Ureña de Hito, Sonia. *Pedro Henríquez Ureña: apuntes para una biografía*. Mexico: Siglo XXI Editores. 1993.
Hess, Steven. *Ramón Menéndez Pidal*. Boston: Twayne Publishers, 1982.
Hill, Jane. "'Today There is No Respect': Nostalgia, 'Respect' and Oppositional Discourse in Mexicano (Nahuatl) Language Ideology." In *Language Ideologies: Practice and Theory*, edited by B. Schieffelin, K. Woolard and P. Kroskrity. New York and Oxford: Oxford University Press, 1998.
Hinzelin, Marc-Olivier and Georg A. Kaiser. "El pronombre 'ello' en el léxico del español dominicano." In *Language Contact and Language Change in the Caribbean and Beyond*, edited by Wiltrud Mihatsch and Monika Sokol. Frankfurt: Peter Lang, 2007.
Hoetink, Harry. *The Dominican People 1850–1900: Notes for a Historical Sociology*. Baltimore and London: The Johns Hopkins University Press, 1982.
Hostos, Eugenio María de. "El cholo." http://www.ensayistas.org/antologia/XIXA/hostos/hostos2.htm (1870) (accessed April 4, 2007).
———. *Obras completas*. La Habana: Cultural S. A., 1939.
———. *Páginas dominicanas*, edited by Emilio Rodríguez Demorizi. Santo Domingo: Editora Taller, 1979.
Iordan, Iorgu. *An Introduction to Romance Linguistics: Its Schools and Scholars*. Oxford: Basil Blackwell, 1970.
Irvine, Judith. "Style as distinctiveness: The culture and ideology of linguistic differentiation." In *Style and Sociolinguistic Variation*, edited by Penelope Eckert and John Rickford. Cambridge: Cambridge University Press, 2001.
———. "When Talk Isn't Cheap: Language and Political Economy." *American Ethnologist* 16 (1989): 248–267.

Irvine, Judith and Susan Gal. "Language Ideology and Linguistic Differentiation." In *Regimes of Language: Ideologies, Polities and Identities,* edited by Paul V. Kroskrity. Santa Fe, NM: School of American Research Press, 2000.

Ives, Peter. *Language and Hegemony in Gramsci (Reading Gramsci).* London and Ann Arbor: Pluto Press, 2004.

Izzo, Herbert J. "Andalusia and America: The Regional Origins of New-World Spanish." *Romanistas: Studies in Romance Linguistics* 4 (1984): 109–131.

Jaime Julia, Julio. *El libro jubilar de Pedro Henríquez Ureña,* volumes 1 and 2. Santo Domingo: UNPHU, 1984.

Jimenes Grullón, Juan Isidro. *Pedro Henríquez Ureña, realidad y mito y otro ensayo.* Santo Domingo. Editorial Librería Dominicana, 1969.

Jiménez Sabater, Max. "Enfoques sociolingüísticos sobre el español dominicano." *Scriptura* II (1981): 85–92.

———. *Más datos sobre el español dominicano de la República Dominicana.* Santo Domingo: Intec, 1975.

Johansson, Troles Degn et al., eds. *Iconicity: A Fundamental Problem in Semiotics.* Denmark: NSU Press, 1999.

Joseph, John. *Language and Identity.* New York: Palgrave Macmillan, 2004.

Joseph, John and Talbot Taylor, *Ideologies of Language.* London: Routledge, 1990.

Kany, Charles. *American Spanish Syntax.* Chicago: Chicago University Press, 1951.

King, John. *Sur: A Study of the Argentine Literary Journal and its Role in the Development of a Culture (1931–1970).* Cambridge: Cambridge University Press, 1986.

Knight, Franklin. *The Caribbean: The Genesis of a Fragmented Nationalism.* New York and Oxford: Oxford University Press, 1990.

Koerner, Konrad. "Ideology in the 19th and 20th Century Linguistics." In *Language and Ideology: Theoretical Cognitive Approaches,* vol. 2, edited by René Dirven et al., Amsterdam: John Benjamins, 2001.

———. "Ideology, 'Resonanzbedarf,' and Linguistic-Philological Scholarship." In *Communicating Ideologies: Multidisciplinary Perspectives on Language, Discourse, and Social Practice,* edited by Martin Pütz, JoAnne Neff-van Aertselaer and Teun van Dijk. Frankfurt: Peter Lang, 2004.

———. *Professing Linguistic Historiography.* Amsterdam and Philadelphia: John Benjamins, 1995.

———. "Towards a Historiography of Linguistics: 19th and 20th Century Paradigms." In *Towards a Historiography of Linguistics: Selected Essays.* Amsterdam: John Benjamins, 1978.

Krauze, Enrique. "El crítico errante: Pedro Henríquez Ureña." *Vuelta* 100 (March 1985): 12–24.

Kroskrity, Paul V. "Regimenting Languages: Language Ideological Perspectives." In *Regimes of Language: Ideologies, Polities and Identities,* edited by Paul V. Kroskrity. Santa Fe, NM: School of American Research Press, 2000.

Lara, Juan Jacobo de. *Pedro Henríquez Ureña: su vida y su obra.* Santo Domingo: UNPHU, 1975.

———. *Sobre Pedro Henríquez Ureña y otros ensayos.* Santo Domingo: UNPHU, 1982.

Larrazábal Blanco, Carlos. *Los negros y la esclavitud en Santo Domingo*. Santo Domingo: La Trinitaria, [1967] 1998.

———. "Papeles de Familia." *Clio* 13 (1945).

Laurendeau, Paul. "Theory of Emergence: Towards a Historical-Materialistic Approach to the History of Linguistics." In *Ideologies of Language*, edited by John Joseph and Talbot Taylor. London: Routledge, 1990.

Leal, Luis. "Pedro Henríquez Ureña en México." In *Presencia de Pedro Henríquez Ureña: escritos sobre el maestro*, edited by Jorge Tena Reyes and Tomás Castro Burdiez. Santo Domingo: Editorial Ciguapa, 2001.

Lenz, Rudolph (Rodolfo). "Chilennische Studien." *Phonetische Studien* 5 (1892–1893): 272–292.

———. *El diccionario etimológico de las voces chilenas derivadas de lenguas indígenas americanas*. Santiago, Chile: Universidad de Chile, [1905–1910] 1980.

———. *El papiamento: la lengua criolla de Curazao*. Santiago: Los Anales de La Universidad de Chile, 1928.

———. *El español en Chile*, edited by Amado Alonso and Raimundo Lida. Buenos Aires: Biblioteca de Dialectología Hispanoamericana, [1891] 1940.

———. *La oración y sus partes*. Santiago, Chile: Nascimento, [1920] 1944.

Lipski, John. *A History of Afro-Hispanic Language*. Cambridge: Cambridge University Press, 2005.

———. "A New Perspective on Afro-Dominican Spanish: the Haitian Contribution," http//:www.personal.psu.edu/faculty/j/m/jml34/afrodom.pdf (1994) (accessed October 25, 2006).

Lope Blanch, Juan M. *Estudios de lingüística hispanoamericana*. Mexico: Universidad Nacional Autónoma de México, 1989.

López Morales, Humberto. "Introducción." In *Vocabulario de Puerto Rico*, edited by Humberto López Morales. Madrid: Arco Libros, 1999.

López Sánchez, José María. *Heterodoxos españoles: el Centro de Estudios Históricos, 1910-1936*. Madrid: Marcial Pons Ediciones de Historia, 2006.

Lugo, Américo. "Discurso inaugural del Ateneo Dominicano." In *Obras escogidas*, vol. 1. Santo Domingo: Ediciones de la Fundación Corripio, 1993.

———. *Historia de Santo Domingo desde el 1556 hasta 1608: edad media de la isla española*. Ciudad Trujillo: Editorial Librería Dominicana, 1952.

Luis, Carlos R. "Norma y nación: los galicismos en Salvá y Bello." In *El pensamiento ilustrado y el lenguaje*, edited by Elvira N. de Arnoux and Carlos R. Luis. Buenos Aires: Eudeba, 2003.

Malaret, Augusto. *Diccionario de americanismos*. Buenos Aires: Emecé, [1925] 1946.

———. *Diccionario de provincialismos de Puerto Rico*. San Juan: Tip. C. Fernández & Co., 1917.

———. *Por mi patria y por mi idioma*. San Juan: Establecimientos de Cerón, 1942.

———. *Vocabulario de Puerto Rico*, edited by Humberto López Morales. Madrid: Arco Libros, 1999.

Malkiel, Yakov. *Linguistics and Philology in Spanish America: A Survey (1925–1970)*. The Hague and Paris: Mouton, 1972.

———. "Filología española y lingüística general," http://cvc.cervantes.es/obref/aih/pdf/01/aih_01_009.pdf [1962] (accessed May 8, 2007).

Malmberg, Bertil. "L'espagnol dans le Noveau Monde." *Studia Linguistica* 1 (1947): 79–116.
Martí, José. "Nuestra América." *La Revista Ilustrada de Nueva York*, http://www.analitica.com/bitbiblioteca/jmarti/nuestra_america.asp [1891] (accessed January 15, 2007).
Martínez, Fernando Antonio. "Lexicography." In *Current Trends in Linguistics IV: Ibero-American and Caribbean Linguistics*, edited by Thomas Sebeok. The Hague and Paris: Mouton, 1968.
Martínez Valdez, Ciana. "El lenguaje elaborado y el lenguaje descuidado." In *Estado actual de los estudios lingüísticos y filológicos en la República Dominicana*, edited by Irene Pérez Guerra. Santo Domingo: Patronato de la Ciudad Colonial de Santo Domingo, 2000.
Martínez-Vergne, Teresita. *Nation and Citizen in the Dominican Republic, 1880–1916*. Chapel Hill: The University of North Carolina Press, 2005.
Marx, Karl and Frederick Engels. *The German Ideology*. Moscow: Progress Publishers, [1845] 1964.
Mateo, Andrés L. *Mito y cultura en la era de Trujillo*. Santo Domingo: Editora Manatí, 2004.
———. *Pedro Henríquez Ureña: errancia y creación*. Bogota: Taurus, 2001.
Matos Moquete, Manuel. *La cultura de la lengua*. Santo Domingo: Biblioteca Nacional, 1986.
Megenney, William. *África en Santo Domingo: su herencia lingüística*. Santo Domingo: Editorial Tiempo, 1990.
Membreño, Alberto. *Vocabulario de los provincialismos de Honduras*. Tegucigalpa, Honduras: Editorial Guaymuras, [1895] 1982.
Mendez, Danny. "In Zones of Contact (Combat): Dominican Narratives of Migration and Displacements in the United States and Puerto Rico," PhD diss., University of Texas at Austin, 2008.
Menéndez Pidal, Ramón. *La unidad del idioma*. Madrid: Instituto Nacional del Libro, 1944.
———. *Manual elemental de gramática histórica española*. Madrid: Librería General de Victoriano Suárez, [1904] 1925.
———. *Orígenes del español: estado lingüístico de la península ibérica hasta el siglo XI*. Madrid: Espasa-Calpe, [1926] 1964.
———. "Prólogo." La versificación irregular en la poesía castellana. Madrid: Centro de Estudios Históricos, 1920.
———. "Sevilla frente a Madrid: algunas precisiones sobre el español de América." In *Miscelánea homenaje a Andrés Martinet, Estructuralismo e Historia III"*, edited by Diego Catalán. Madrid: La Laguna, [1941] 1962.
Meyer-Lübke, Wilhelm. *Grammaire del langues romanes*. Paris: H. Welter, 1890.
———. Introducción al studio de la lingüística romance, translated by Américo Castro. Madrid: Tip. de la Revista de Arch., 1914.
Miller, Nicola. *In the Shadow of the State: Intellectuals and the Quest for National Identity in Twentieth-Century Spanish America*. London: Verso, 1999.
Mills, Sara. *Discourse*. London: Routledge, 2004.

Moré, Belford. "The Ideological Construction of an Empirical Base: Selection and Elaboration Andrés Bello's Grammar." In *The Battle over Spanish between 1800 and 2000: Language Ideologies and Hispanic Intellectuals,* edited by José Del Valle and Luis Gabriel-Stheeman. London and New York: Routledge, 2002.

Moreta Castillo, Américo. "La obra histórica del profesor Lic. Carlos Larrazábal Blanco." In *Coloquios* 2002, edited by Varios Autores. Santo Domingo: Comisión Permanente de la Feria del Libro, 2003.

Morris, Nancy. *Puerto Rico: Culture, Politics, and Identity.* Connecticut: Praeger Publishers, 1996.

Moscoso Puello, Francisco. *Cañas y bueyes.* Santo Domingo: La Nación, 1936.

Moya Pons, Frank. *The Dominican Republic: A National History.* New Rochelle, NY: Hispaniola Books, 1995.

Mühleisen, Susanne. "From Humboldt to Bickerton: Discourse on language contact and hybridity." In *The fuzzy logic of encounter: new perspectives on cultural contact,* edited by Sunne Juterczenka and Gesa Mackenthun. Germany: Waxmann Verlag, 2009.

Muller, Wolfgang and Olga Fischer. "Introduction: from Signing Back to Signs." In *From Sign to Signing: Iconicity in Language and Literature,* vol. 3, edited by Wolfgang Muller and Olga Fischer. Amsterdam: John Benjamins, 2003.

Muteba Rahier, Jean. "The Study of Latin-American 'Racial Formations': Different Approaches and Different Contexts." *Latin-American Research Review* 39, no. 3 (2004): 282–293.

Navarro Tomás, Tomás. *Manual de pronunciación española.* Madrid: Consejo Superior de Investigaciones Científicas, [1918] 1999.

Newmeyer, Frederick. The Politics of Linguistics. Chicago, University of Chicago Press, 1986.

Núñez Cedeño, Rafael. *La fonología moderna y el español de Santo Domingo.* Santo Domingo: Taller, 1980.

Núñez, Manuel. *El ocaso de la nación dominicana.* Santo Domingo: Alfa y Omega, 1990.

———. "La lengua española, compañera de la nación dominicana: discurso de ingreso." In *Boletín de la Academia Dominicana de la Lengua* 17 (2004a): 137–195.

———. "Las claves del pensamiento de Pedro Henríquez Ureña." In *Obras completas: escritos políticos, sociológicos y filosóficos,* vol. 4, edited by Manuel Núñez. Santo Domingo: Editora Nacional, 2004b.

———. "Uso del idioma en el periodismo dominicano." In *Estado actual de los estudios lingüísticos y filológicos en la República Dominicana,* edited by Irene Pérez Guerra. Santo Domingo: Patronato de la Ciudad Colonial de Santo Domingo, 2000.

Núñez, Victoria. "Unpacking the Suitcases They Carried: Narratives of Dominican and Puerto Rican Migrations to the Northeastern United States (Pura Belpre, Pedro Henríquez Ureña, Antonia Pantoja, Junot Diaz, Angie Cruz)." PhD diss., University of Massachusetts at Amherst, 2006.

Ochs, Elinor and Bambi Schieffelin. "Language Acquisition and Socialization: Three Developmental Stories and their Implications." In *Culture Theory: Essays on Mind, Self and Emotion*, edited by Richard Shweder and Robert Levine. Cambridge: Cambridge University Press, 1981.

Ortiz, Fernando. *El glosario de afronegrismos*. La Habana: Imprenta el Siglo XX, 1924.

———. "La cubanidad y los negros." *Estudios Afrocubanos* 3 (1939): 3–15.

———. "Los afronegrismos de nuestro lenguaje." In *Etnia y sociedad*, edited by Isaac Barreal. La Habana: Editorial de Ciencias Sociales, 1993.

———. *Un catauro de cubanismos*. La Habana: Editorial de Ciencias Sociales, 1975.

Otheguy, Ricardo and Naomi Lapidus. "Matización de la teoría de la simplificaciones en lenguas de contacto: el concepto de la adaptación en el español de Nueva York." In *Contactos y contextos lingüísticos: el español en Estado Unido y en contacto con otras lenguas*, edited by Luis Ortiz López and Manuel Lacorte. Madrid and Frankfurt: Iberoamericana and Vervuert, 2005.

Paulino, Alejandro and Aquiles Castro. *Diccionario de cultura y folklore dominicano*. Santo Domingo: ABC Editorial, 2005.

Patín Maceo, Manuel. *Dominicanismos*. Ciudad Trujillo: Editora Montalvo, 1940.

Peguero, Valentina. *The Militarization of Culture in the Dominican Republic: From Captains General to General Trujillo*. Lincoln: University of Nebraska Press, 2004.

Peirce, Charles Sanders. *The Essential Peirce: Selected Philosophical Writings*, volume 2. Bloomington and Indianapolis: Indiana University Press, 1998.

Peña Batlle, Manuel Arturo. "Ensayos históricos." In *Obras escogidas*, edited by J. D. Postigo. Santo Domingo: Santo Domingo: Fundación Peña Batlle, 1968.

Pérez Cabral, Pedro Andrés. *La comunidad mulata: el caso socio-político de la República Dominicana*. Caracas: Gráfica Americana, 1967.

Pérez, Odalís G. "Los intelectuales y el poder político en República Dominicana." In *Los Intelectuales y el Poder: Coloquio*, edited by Guillermo Piña-Contreras. Santo Domingo: Universidad Apec, 2005.

Pérez de la Cruz, Rosa Elena. "El concepto del hombre en el pensamiento de Pedro Henríquez Ureña." *Cuadernos Americanos* 5, no. 101 (2003): 72–88.

Pérez Guerra, Irene. "Africanismos lingüísticos en la República Dominicana: Notas metodológicas." In *Estudios sobre español de América y lingüística afroamericana*, edited by M. Ariza, R. Cano, J. M. Mendoza, and A. Narbona. Bogota: Instituto Caro y Cuervo, 1989.

———. "Aportación a un tema en debate en el Caribe hispánico: el arcaísmo del español dominicano." In *Actas del II Congreso Internacional de Historia de la Lengua Española 2*, edited by M. Ariza et al (1992).

———. "Introducción." In *Estado actual de los estudios lingüísticos y filológicos en la República Dominicana*, edited by Irene Pérez Guerra. Santo Domingo: Patronato de la Ciudad Colonial de Santo Domingo, 2000.

———. "La obra lingüística de Pedro Henríquez Ureña." In *Coloquios 2002*, edited by Varios Autores. Santo Domingo: Comisión Permanente de la Feria del Libro, 2003.

———. "La producción de tema lingüístico y filológico en la obra de Pedro Henríquez Ureña." *Obras completas: estudios lingüísticos y filológicos*, vol. 4, edited by Irene Pérez Guerra. Santo Domingo: Editora Nacional, 2004.

Pérez Pascual, José Ignacio. *Ramón Menéndez Pidal: ciencia y pasión*. Valladolid, Spain: Junta de Castilla y León, 1998.

Pérez y Pérez, Carlos Federíco. "Nacionalismo y americanismo en Pedro Henríquez Ureña." In *El libro jubilar de Pedro Henríquez Ureña*, volumes 1 and 2, edited by Julio Jaime Julia. Santo Domingo: UNPHU, 1984.

Pérez-Leroux, Ana Teresa. "Innovación sintáctica en el español del Caribe y los principios de la gramática general." In *El Caribe hispánico: perspectivas lingüísticas actuales*, edited by Luis Ortiz López. Frankfurt and Madrid: Vervuert and Iberoamericana, 1999.

Phillips, Susan. "Language Ideologies in Institutions of Power: A Commentary." In *Language Ideologies: Practice and Theory*, edited by B. Schieffelin, K. Woolard, and P. Kroskrity. New York and Oxford: Oxford University Press, 1998.

Pichardo, Esteban. *Diccionario provincial casi razonado de voces y frases cubanas*. La Habana: Editorial de Ciencias Sociales, [1836] 1985.

Pierre-Charles, Gérard. *El pensamiento sociopolítico moderno en el Caribe*. Mexico: Fondo de Cultura Económica, 1985.

Pike, Fredrick. *Hispanismo, 1898–1936: Spanish Conservatives and Liberals and Their Relations with Spanish America*. Notre Dame: University of Notre Dame Press, 1971.

Piña-Contreras, Guillermo. "El universo familiar en la formación intelectual de Pedro Henríquez Ureña." In *Presencia de Pedro Henríquez Ureña: escritos sobre el maestro*, edited by Jorge Tena Reyes and Tomás Castro Burdiez. Santo Domingo: Editorial Ciguapa, 2001.

Pitol, Sergio. *De la realidad a la literatura*. Mexico: Ariel and Editorial Planeta Mexicana, 2002.

Polo, José. *Epistemología del lenguaje e historia lingüística: momentos de su desarrollo bibliográfico en el ámbito hispanohablante*. Madrid: Gredos, 1986.

Portolés, José. *Medio siglo de filología española (1896–1952): Positivismo e idealismo*. Madrid: Cátedra, 1986.

Price-Mars, Jean. *La República de Haití y la República Dominicana*. Santo Domingo: Editora Taller, 2000.

Pucciarelli, Eugenio. *Pedro Henríquez Ureña, humanista*. Buenos Aires: Publicaciones del Centro de Estudios Filosóficos, 1984.

Rama, Ángel. *La ciudad letrada*. Hanover, NH: Ediciones del Norte, 1984.

Rama, Carlos. *Historia de las relaciones culturales entre España y la América Latina: Siglo XXI*. Mexico: Fondo de Cultura Económica, 1982.

Ramos, Julio. *Divergent Modernities: Culture and Politics in Nineteenth-Century Latin America*. Durham: Duke University Press, 2001.

Ramos, Samuel. "Pedro Henríquez Ureña." *Cuadernos Americanos* XXVIII, no. 4 (1946): 264–267.

Resina, Joan. "Whose hispanism?" In *Ideologies of Hispanism*, edited by Mabel Moraña. Nashville, Tennessee: Vanderbilt University Press, 2005.

Reyes, Alfonso. "El criticón." In *Obras completas III*. Mexico: Fondo de Cultura Económica, 1995.

Reyes, Alfonso and Pedro Henríquez Ureña. In *Correspondencia (1907–1914)*, edited by José Luis Martínez. Mexico: Fondo de Cultura Económica, 1986.

Roberge, Paul T. "The Ideological Profile of Afrikaans Historical Linguistics." In *Ideologies of Language*, edited by John Joseph and Talbot Taylor. London: Routledge, 1990.

Rodó, José Enrique. *Ariel*. Madrid: Espasa Calpe, [1900] 1991.

Rodríguez Demorizi, Emilio. *Breve panegírico de Pedro Henríquez Ureña*. Santo Domingo: Editora Taller, 1981.

———. "Dominicanidad de Pedro Henríquez Ureña." In *Presencia de Pedro Henríquez Ureña: escritos sobre el maestro*, edited by Jorge Tena Reyes and Tomás Castro Burdiez. Santo Domingo: Editorial Ciguapa, 2001.

———. *Hostos en Santo Domingo*. Ciudad Trujillo [Santo Domingo]: Impresora J. R. Viuda Gracía Sucs, 1939.

———. *Lengua y folklore de Santo Domingo*. Santo Domingo: Universidad Católica Madre y Maestra, 1975.

———. "Vicisitudes de la lengua española en Santo Domingo." In *Lengua y folklore de Santo Domingo*. Santo Domingo: Universidad Católica Madre y Maestra, 1975.

Rodríguez, Néstor. "Pedro Henríquez Ureña el militante," *Hoy*, November 24, 2007.

Rodríguez, Zorobabel. *Diccionario de chilenismos*. Valparaíso: Ediciones Universitarias de Valparaíso, 1875.

Roggiano, Alfredo. *Pedro Henríquez Ureña en los Estado Unidos*. Mexico: Editorial Cultura, 1961.

———. *Pedro Henríquez Ureña en México*. Mexico: Facultad de Filosofía y Letras de la Universidad Autónoma de México, 1989.

Rosario Candelier, Bruno. *El español en Santo Domingo: Ensayos lingüísticos*. Santo Domingo: PUCMM, 1990.

Rosenblat, Ángel. *La población indígena y el mestizaje en América*. Buenos Aires: Editorial Nova, 1954.

Said, Edward W. *Beginnings: Intention and Method*. New York: Columbia University Press, 1975.

———. *Orientalism*. New York: Vintage Books, 1979.

San Miguel, Pedro L. *The Imagined Island: History, Identity and Utopia in Hispaniola*. San Juan and Santo Domingo: Isla Negra and La Trinitaria, 2005.

Sánchez Valverde, Antonio. *La idea del valor de la Isla Española*, edited by Rodríguez Demorizi and Cipriano de Utrera. Santo Domingo: Editora Nacional, [1785] 1971.

Sang, Mu-kien A. *Ulises Heureaux: biografía de un dictador*. Santo Domingo: Instituto Tecnológico de Santo Domingo, 1987.

Sarlo, Beatriz. "Pedro Henríquez Ureña: lectura de una problemática." In *Pedro Henríquez Ureña: ensayos,* edited by José Luis Abellán and Ana María Barrenechea. Mexico: Fondo de Cultura Económica, 1998.

Sarmiento, Domingo Faustino. *Facundo: civilización y barbarie*. Madrid: Cátedra, 2005.

Saussure, Ferdinand de. *Course in General Linguistics*. New York: McGraw Hill, [1916] 1986.

Schieffelin, Bambi, Kathryn Woolard, and Paul V. Kroskrity, eds. *Language Ideologies: Practice and Theory*. New York and Oxford: Oxford University Press, 1998.

Schwartz, Lía. "De hispanismos, los siglos XVI y XVII, y el olvido de la historia," *Ciberletras* http://www.lehman.cuny.edu/ciberletras/v06/liaschwartz.html (2002) (accessed June 28, 2006).

Schwegler, Armin. "La doble negación dominicana y la génesis del español caribeño." *Lingüística Hispánica* 8 (1996): 247–317.

Sepúlveda Muñoz, Isidro. *El sueño de la Madre Patria: hispanoamericanismo y nacionalismo*. Madrid: Marcial Pons, 2005.

Silverstein, Michael. "Language Structure and Linguistic Ideology." In *The Elements: A Parasession on Linguistic Units and Levels*, edited by Paul Clyne et al. Chicago: Chicago Linguistic Society, 1979.

———. "Language Structure and the Culture of Gender: At the Intersection of Structure, Usage and Ideology." In *Semiotic Mediation*, edited by Elizabeth Mertz and Richard Parmetier. Orlando, Florida: Academic Press, 1985.

———. "Monoglot 'Standard' in American Standardization and Metaphors of Linguistic Hegemony." In *The Matrix of Language: Contemporary Linguistic Anthropology*, edited by D. Brenneis and R. Macaulay. Boulder, Colorado: Westview Press, 1998.

———. "Shifters, Linguistic Categories, and Cultural Description." In *Meaning in Anthropology*, edited by Keith Basso and Henry Selby. Albuquerque: University of New Mexico Press, 1976.

Simone, Raffaele. "Foreword: Under the Sign of Cratylus." In *Iconicity in Language*, edited by Raffaele Simone. Amsterdam: John Benjamins, 1995.

Sommer, Doris. *Foundational Fictions: The National Romances of Latin America*. Berkeley: University of California Press, 1991.

Taylor, Talbot. "Which is to be Master? The Institutionalization of Authority in the Science of Language." In *Ideologies of Language*, edited by John Joseph and Talbot Taylor. London: Routledge, 1990.

Tena Reyes, Jorge and Tomás Castro Burdiez, eds. *Presencia de Pedro Henríquez Ureña: escritos sobre el maestro*. Santo Domingo: Editorial Ciguapa, 2001.

Tolentino Dipp, Hugo. *Ensayos sobre la restauración*. Santo Domingo: Editora Universitaria, 2004.

Toribio, Jacqueline. "Language Variation and the Linguistic Enactment of Identity among Dominicans." *Linguistics* 38, no. 5 (2000a): 1133–1159.

———. "Linguistic Displays of Identity among Dominicans in National and Diasporic Settlements." In *English and Ethnicity*, edited by C. Davies and J. Brutt-Griffler. New York: Palgrave Macmillan, 2005.

———. "Nosotros Somos Dominicanos: Language and Self-Definition among Dominicans." In *Research on Spanish in the U.S.*, edited by Ana Roca. Somerville, MA: Cascadilla Press, 2000b.

Torres-Saillant, Silvio. "The Tribulations of Blackness: Stages in Dominican Racial Identity." *Callaloo* 23, no. 3 (2000): 1086–1111.

Urciuoli, Bonnie. *Exposing Prejudice: Puerto Rican Experiences of Language, Race, and Class.* Boulder, Colorado: Westview Press, 1996.

———. "The Political Topography of Spanish and English: The View from a New York Puerto Rican Neighborhood." *American Ethnologist* 18 (1991): 295–310.

Ureña, Salomé. *Poesías completas,* Ciudad Trujillo [Santo Domingo]: Impresora Dominicana, 1959.

Vann, Robert. "Language Exposure in Catalonia: an Example of Indoctrinating Linguistic Ideology." *Word* 50, no. 2 (1999): 191–209.

Van Dijk, Teun A. "Discourse Analysis as Ideology Analysis." In *Language and Peace,* edited by C. Shaffner and A. Wenden. Aldershot: Dartmouth, 1995.

———. "Discourse, Knowledge and Ideology: Reformulating Old Questions and Proposing Some New Solutions." In *Communicating Ideologies: Multidisciplinary Perspectives on Language, Discourse and Social Practice,* edited by Martín Putz et al. Frankfurt and Berlin: Peter Lang, 2002.

———. *Ideología y discurso: una introducción multidisciplinaria.* Barcelona: Ariel, 2003.

Valdez, Juan R. "The Iconization of Dominican Spanish in Pedro Henríquez Ureña's Linguistic Texts." *Spanish in Context* 6, no. 2 (2009): 176–98.

———. "Language, Race, and Identity in Pedro Henríquez Ureña's Dominican Oeuvre: A Study on Language Ideologies," PhD diss., The Graduate Center at The City University of New York, 2008.

———. "Language variation in a multilingual community: The Dominican Republic's Samaná peninsula." *Language and Literature (LL) Journal* http//:ojs.gc.cuny.edu/index.php/lljournal/article/view/valdez/228 (2007) (accessed January 23, 2010).

Valerio-Holguín, Fernando. "Pedro Henríquez Ureña: el mulato intelectual poscolonial." Paper presented at the II International Conference on Caribbean Studies. University of Cartagena, Cartagena, Colombia, March 15–19, 2010.

Van Name, Addison. *Contributions to Creole Grammar.* New Haven: Yale University Press, 1868.

Vaquero, María. "El español en América como problema en el siglo XX." *Revista de Estudios Hispánicos* 24, no. 1 (1997): 273–286.

Vargas, José Rafael. *El nacionalismo de Pedro Henríquez Ureña.* Santo Domingo: Editora de la UASD, 1984.

Vasconcelos, José. *La raza cósmica.* Costa Rica: Editorial Fundación-UNA, [1925] 1999.

Vellejo, Catharina. "Beautiful Lies: Legitimation of the National Identity in Two Series of Indianist Poems of the Dominican Republic." In *The Reordering of Culture: Latin America, the Caribbean and Canada in the Hood,* edited by Alvina Ruprecht and Cecilia Taiana. Canada: Carleton University Press, 1995.

Volosinov, V. N. *Marxism and the Philosophy of Language.* Cambridge, MA: Harvard University Press, 1986.

Wagner, Max Leopold. "El español de América y el latín vulgar." *Cuadernos del Instituto de Filología de la Universidad de Buenos Aires* 1 (1924): 45–110.

Weber de Kurlat, Frida. "Pedro Henríquez Ureña en el Instituto de Filología de Buenos Aires." In *El libro jubilar de Pedro Henríquez Ureña*, volumes 1 and 2, edited by Julio Jaime Julia. Santo Domingo: UNPHU, 1994.

Weinberg, Liliana. "Pedro Henríquez Ureña: exilio y ensayo." http://www.ccydel.unam.mx/ensayo/pdf/fragmento/PHU%20Exilio%20ensayo.pdf (2002) (accessed on June 12, 2007).

Weiner, Leo. *Africa and the Discovery of America*. Philadelphia: Innes & Sons, 1920.

Whitney, William Dwight. *The Life and Growth of Language: An Outline of Linguistic Science*. New York: Dover Publications, Inc., 1979.

Williams, Raymond. *Marxism and Literature*. Oxford and New York: Oxford University Press, 1977.

Williamson, Edwin. *The Penguin History of Latin America*. London: Penguin Books, 1992.

Woolard, Kathryn A. "Language Ideology as a Field of Inquiry." In *Language Ideologies: Practice and Theory*, edited by B. Schieffelin, K. Woolard and P. Kroskrity. New York and Oxford: Oxford University Press, 1998.

——. "La autoridad lingüística del español y las ideologías de la autenticidad y el anonimato." In *La lengua, ¿patria común? Ideas e ideologías del español*, edited by José Del Valle, Madrid and Frankfurt: Iberoamericana and Vervuert, 2007a.

——. "Why Dat Now? Linguistic Anthropological Contributions to the Explanation of Sociolinguistic Icons and Change." *Journal of Sociolinguistics* 12, no. 4 (2007b): 432–52.

Zea, Leopoldo. *El positivismo en México*. Mexico: El Colegio de México, 1943.

Zentella, Ana Celia. "Spanish in New York." In *The Multilingual Apple: Languages in New York City*, edited by Ofelia García and Joshua Fishman. New York and Berlin: Mouton de Gruyter, 2002.

Zuleta Álvarez, Enrique. "La recepción crítica de la obra de Pedro Henríquez Ureña." In *Pedro Henríquez Ureña: ensayos*, edited by José Luis Abellán and Ana María Barrenechea. Madrid: Allca XX, 1998.

——. *Literatura y sociedad: estudios sobre Pedro Henríquez Ureña*. Buenos Aires: Ediciones Atril, 1999.

——. *Pedro Henríquez Ureña y su tiempo*. Buenos Aires: Catálogo, 1996.

Index

Aesthetics, 13, 30, 45, 68, 89, 136, 168
Africa, 49, 125, 152, 155–6, 161
  African, 2, 22, 27, 48–9, 59–60, 85, 93, 100, 125, 131–5, 146–63, 166
  Africanism, 100, 155–7, 162
  African languages, 155, 161–2
  Afro-Dominican, 155, 161, 163
  Afro-Hispanic, 155, 157–9, 194
  Bozales, 148, 150
  South Africa, 49, 59–60
Alba, Orlando, 3, 24–6, 149, 154, 167
Alonso, Amado, 14, 28, 105–6, 108–10, 115–16, 118–21, 124, 126–30, 165
Álvarez, Soledad, 15–18, 29
Americanismo, 15–16, 87, 100
Andalucismo, 12–17, 15, 28, 30, 93, 120–3
  Andalusian, 15, 23, 93, 119–21, 123, 131, 133, 137, 146–7, 149–50, 161, 165, 193
  Antiandalucistas, 122–3
  polygenetic theory, 106, 119, 121, 127, 165
  Seseo, 121, 126
  Yeismo, 126, 146
Anderson Imbert, Enrique, 7, 17, 19, 165
Anglicsisms, 86
Anthropology, 4, 155, 163
  ethnography, 42, 48, 163
Archaism, 26–7, 113–14, 118, 132, 137, 140–1, 149, 161, 166
Archive, 54, 143, 165, 182

Argentina, 7, 14, 18, 28, 77, 80–1, 106, 115–18, 120, 126, 130, 141
  Buenos Aires, 14, 28, 64, 114–18, 120, 124, 126–7, 129, 130
Arnoux, Elvira N., 28–9, 31, 51–5, 118, 127
Ateneo de la Juventud de México, 13, 123

Bakhtin, Mikhail, 40–1, 58, 62
  Volosinov, V. N., 40
Balaguer, Joaquín, 3, 86
Bello, Andrés, 16, 54, 65, 95–9, 101–5, 108, 112–13, 118, 123, 126
  Gramática castellana, 28, 98
Betances, Ramón E., 8, 71
Borges, Jorge Luis, 80, 117, 126
Bourdieu, Pierre, 39–41, 62

Caribbean, 19–20, 25–6, 69, 76–7, 82–3, 86, 99–100, 112, 120, 131, 133, 135–41, 146–7, 155, 160
  Antilles, 2, 92, 160
  West Indies, 160
Carvajal, Federico Henríquez, 8, 68, 73–4, 77
Carvajal, Francisco Henríquez, 8–9, 68–70, 73, 77, 181
Caso, Antonio, 7, 13, 36
Cassá, Roberto, 72
Castile, 60, 97, 101, 108, 114, 122, 153, 156
  Castilian, 60, 89, 93, 97–8, 103, 107–9, 113–14, 131, 136–7, 146, 153, 161–2

Castro, Américo, 111–12, 115–20, 124, 129
Catalan, 44, 108–9, 120, 125
Center of Historical Studies, 108–12, 114, 124
Chile, 97–9, 104–6, 119
Climate of opinion, 4, 55–6, 95, 129–30
Colonialism, 63, 72–3, 78, 81, 87–8, 97, 102, 119, 122–3, 133–6, 138–9, 141–2, 151, 156
  Christopher Columbus, 1–3, 19, 162
  Las Casas, Bartolomé, 21, 134–5, 141, 150, 161
  neocolonialism, 64, 93, 101
  Oviedo, Fernando de, 135
Contact zone, 3, 12, 137, 158–9
Critical Linguistic Historiography, 55, 95, 131
  critique, 33, 57
  hermeneutics, 57
Criticism, 9, 23, 27, 29–30, 85, 101, 104, 111
Cuba, 8, 10, 14, 60, 64, 69–70, 74, 76–7, 84, 86, 89, 99–100, 132, 134, 146–8, 151, 155–6, 160
Cuervo, Rufino José, 21, 99, 101–5, 108, 112–13, 118–19, 121–4, 138
Culture, 1, 4, 9, 11, 13–14, 16–19, 21, 44, 50, 60–2, 64, 73, 78–9, 87–93, 99, 110–11, 113–14, 123, 125, 127–8, 133–4, 140, 143, 151–2, 155, 158–9, 166–8

Del Valle, José, 42–4, 50–3, 60–1, 88, 107–8, 114, 120
Deschamps, Enrique, 9, 75, 82, 163
Dialectology, 15, 21–3, 25, 31, 104, 107, 110, 115–16, 163
  Biblioteca de Dialectología Hispanoamericana, 116, 129
  dialectal zones, 93, 108, 127
  dialects, 22, 26, 60, 97–8, 102, 105, 108–9, 115–18, 121–2, 133, 137, 141–6, 148, 157, 168, 200
Díaz Quiñones, Arcadio, 1, 18, 20, 31
Discourse, 4, 7, 29, 34, 37–9, 41–4, 49, 51–5, 64–5, 67–71, 79, 83–5, 87, 90–3, 101, 127, 129, 137, 139, 142, 167–8
Dominican national identity, 3–4, 32, 44, 61, 82, 87, 92–3, 150
  Dominicanness, 1, 15, 17–18, 30–1, 79, 86, 132, 142, 166
Dominican Republic, the, 2–4, 7, 10, 17–19, 24–7, 49–51, 62–4, 67–77, 79–82, 85–7, 93–4, 114, 129–31, 133–8, 140, 142, 145, 146, 150, 152–5, 158, 160, 162, 164, 167–8
  Santo Domingo, 8–9, 11, 14, 18, 24, 67–8, 73, 76–7, 80–1, 84, 86–7, 93, 99–100, 124, 132–4, 136–42, 147, 151, 153, 157–8, 160–1, 164
Dominican Spanish, 2, 4, 15, 22, 24–6, 32, 93, 113, 124–5, 129, 134, 136–7, 140, 142–51, 154, 157, 161–3, 166–8
  double negation, 26, 154
  Ello, 143–5
  Gallicisms, 86, 126
  lexicon, 129, 131, 137, 140–1, 143, 146, 149–51
  loanwords, 167
  phonology, 146, 149–51
  syntax, 129, 132, 143, 145–6, 149–51, 154, 168
Durán, Diony, 7, 81

Eagleton, Terry, 33
Education, 8–9, 13–14, 36, 54–5, 64–5, 68–70, 73–4, 80–1, 97, 129, 151, 181
Enlightenment, 9, 34, 54–5, 65, 69–70, 84, 118
Erasure, 4, 48–9, 83, 89, 136, 149, 152–4, 161, 163

European, 2, 14, 20, 27, 48–9, 54, 59, 71–2, 78–9, 81, 87, 90–1, 96–7, 101–2, 104, 109–10, 112, 125, 134, 136, 152, 155, 160, 163, 166, 168, 170
Exile, 10, 15, 17–20, 70, 74, 97, 158

Fanon, Frantz, 136
Firstness theory, 2
Foucault, Michel, 38–9, 41, 62
Franco, Jean, 7, 30–1

Ghiano, Juan Carlos, 21
Glotopolítica, 51, 53
González Tapia, Carlisle, 21–4, 143
Gramsci, Antonio, 36–7, 39, 41, 62, 67, 129
Guitarte, Guillermo, 28–31, 98, 106, 109, 120, 122–3
Gutiérrez Girardot, Rafael, 7, 16, 65, 165

Haiti, 71–2, 79, 81–2, 85–6, 100, 124, 134, 136–9, 152, 156, 160, 162
  anti-Haitianism, 79, 85, 200
  Boyer, Jean Pierre, 71
  Haitian Creole, 51, 159
Halperín Donghi, Tulio, 19, 64, 165
Henríquez Ureña, Max, 9–10, 13, 24, 80, 84, 111
Henríquez Ureña, Pedro, 1–4, 7–32, 33, 37, 45, 58, 61–2, 63, 66–7, 69, 73–4, 76–7, 79–81, 84–94, 98–101, 104, 106, 111, 113, 116, 118–30, 131–64, 165–8
Hispanic linguistics, 14, 95, 116, 165
Hispaniola, 3, 71–2, 135, 138–9, 150–2, 162
Hispanism, 4, 27, 79, 87–8, 93, 100, 106–8, 110, 113, 132, 167–8
  Hispanic, 7, 11–16, 18, 20–5, 28, 32, 41, 51, 53–4, 60, 65, 67, 69, 72, 79–82, 84–91, 94–6, 101, 104, 106, 108, 110, 111–16, 119–20, 123, 125, 130, 135, 138–41, 143–4, 146, 150–3, 155, 158, 160, 162–5, 167
Hispanists, 11, 27, 110, 125, 168
Hispanoamericanism, 12, 31, 63, 84, 87–91, 93–5, 99, 102, 110, 112–13, 119, 124, 132
History, 1–4, 7–8, 11, 15–16, 19, 26–7, 33, 41, 49, 56–66, 68, 70–1, 77, 82–4, 86–7, 90, 96–7, 101–3, 106–8, 110, 113, 127–30, 134–5, 139–40, 144, 149, 156, 158–9, 162–3, 166
Hostos, Eugenio María, 10, 16, 65–71, 73, 75, 77–8, 83, 123, 158
Humanities, 81, 91

Iconicity
  icon, 17–18, 45–8, 60, 151
  iconist, 3
  iconization, 4, 47–9, 132, 134–6, 149, 152–3
  iconoclasts, 166
  iconographer, 166
  iconographic, 45–6
  indexicality, 47
Identity, 1, 4, 31–2, 42, 49, 50, 52–3, 52–3, 63, 72, 76, 78, 80, 82, 87–94, 104, 108, 132–3, 147, 149–51
  national, 20, 44, 51, 61, 65–6, 70, 77, 81–3, 87, 92–3, 132, 140, 150–1, 160, 163
Ideology, 9, 28, 30–1, 33–4, 47–51, 53–4, 57, 59, 67–8, 70–3, 75, 77, 79, 81–3, 88, 93, 128, 153, 158, 160, 164
  hegemony, 36–8, 41, 130
  linguistic, 42–3, 48–9, 51, 128, 153, 155, 164
Intellectuals, 2–3, 9–10, 12–13, 15–17, 20, 24, 44, 52, 62–71, 73–9, 82–3, 87–90, 94, 101, 104, 109–13, 117, 119, 123, 126, 139, 153, 165, 167
Irvine, Judith, 41–2, 47–9
  Gal, Susan, 41, 47–9, 53

Jimenes Grullón, Juan Isidro, 17, 26–31
Jiménez Sabater, Max, 3, 24, 143, 154

Knowledge, 4, 7, 14–16, 29–31, 33–5, 37–9, 41–2, 50, 57, 62, 68, 89, 99, 101, 120, 130, 157, 165
  epistemology, 56
Koerner, Konrad, 55–6, 59–60, 62

Language, 1, 3, 31, 37–42, 45–9, 54, 58–9, 86–7, 92–6
  standardization, 46, 50, 54, 97, 129
Latin America, 1, 4–12, 14–17, 20, 29, 32, 51, 60, 63–8, 75–9, 83–94, 123–4
Latinamericanism, 5, 7, 15–17, 27, 29–30, 81, 87, 132
Laurendeau, Paul, 56–7, 62
Lenz, Rudolph, 104–6, 116, 119–20, 125
Linguistics, 4, 23, 45, 51, 56–9, 96, 103, 110, 115–16, 126, 130
linguistic anthropology, 41, 46–9
Literature, 8, 15–16, 62, 64, 66, 74, 76, 83, 90–1, 97, 102–3, 108–9, 113, 118–19, 123, 126, 130, 133, 141, 162, 165
Letrados, 65–6, 82–3
Lope Blanch, Juan, 21, 23–4
Luperón, Gregorio, 67–9, 74

Martí, José, 8, 16, 64, 70, 78, 90–1
Mateo, Andrés L., 9, 11
Matos Moquete, Manuel, 82–3, 86–7
Menéndez Pelayo, Marcelino, 13, 91
Menéndez Pidal, Ramón, 21, 60–1, 90–2, 102–3, 106–15, 119, 121–2, 126, 165
  Center for Historical Studies, 108–9
  Madrid School of Philology, 91, 106, 111, 113, 126
Mexico, 7, 11–14, 18, 20, 64, 77, 113, 139
  Mexican Revolution, 13, 36
Meyer-Lübke, Wilhelm, 96, 109–10, 124–5, 132

Modernity, 10, 20, 65, 77–8, 85
Moscoso Puello, Francisco Eugenio, 154, 159–60
Moya Pons, Frank, 73

Nationalism, 17, 20, 30, 49–51, 63, 69, 71–2, 74–5, 80, 82, 84, 94, 101, 105–6, 117, 119, 165
  linguistic, 50–1, 106, 117
  national language, 50, 54, 82, 97–8, 103, 117, 120
  postnationalism, 168
Núñez de Cáceres, José, 71
Núñez, Manuel, 2, 49, 167

Ortiz, Fernando, 155–7, 159, 161
  transculturation, 159

Peirce, Charles Sanders, 3, 46–7, 131, 176
Pérez Guerra, Irene, 24–6, 149, 167
Philological Institute of Buenos Aires, 114, 124
Philology, 21–3, 59, 91, 95–7, 101–2, 104, 106, 108, 111, 113, 119, 125, 130, 165
  lexicography, 99, 101
  neogrammarians, 107
Pichardo, Esteban, 99, 132–3, 146–8, 155
Pierre-Charles, Gérard, 84
Positivism, 67–9, 81, 115
Power, 1, 4, 16, 21–2, 23, 28, 34, 36–41, 43, 61, 63, 66, 68, 72–74, 83, 88–9, 93, 97, 109, 114, 119, 128, 135–6, 138, 151, 153, 168
Price-Mars, Jean, 71–2
Puerto Rico, 26, 60, 64, 69, 77, 86, 99–100, 134, 147, 152, 160

Race, 3, 22, 49, 58–9, 71, 77–9, 83, 89, 91–2, 96, 125, 133–4, 140, 150, 153, 160, 164, 166, 168
  Blacks, 73, 83–4, 125, 132–3, 135, 146–8, 150–3, 156, 160–1, 163
  Cocolos, 159–60

Criollos, 73, 148, 152, 162
Indians, 78, 84, 105, 134, 153, 156, 166
Meztizo, 52, 73, 94, 105, 119
Mulatto, 14, 84, 93
Racism, 4, 59, 84–5, 91
Trigueña, 160
Whitening, 78, 83, 131, 149, 152
Whites, 72, 78–9, 84, 150
Rama, Carlos, 87–8, 93, 99
Ramos, Julio, 64, 78
Reyes, Alfonso, 7, 11–14, 17–18, 80, 123
Rodó, José Enrique, 10, 89–90
  Ariel, 89–90, 186
Rodríguez Demorizi, Emilio, 2, 17–18, 162
Roggiano, Alfredo, 10

Said, Edward, 1, 23, 96
Samaná, 74, 137
Sarlo, Beatriz, 15, 29
Sarmiento, Domingo Faustino, 16, 65, 92
Saussure, Ferdinand de, 56, 58–9, 96, 115, 126
Slavery, 64, 73, 156
Spaniards, 2–3, 64, 72–3, 79, 88, 98, 104–5, 117, 122, 134, 143, 152, 159, 162
Spanish reannexation, 162
Spanish language, the, 1–3, 24, 44, 51–4, 60, 71, 82, 88–9, 96–8, 103–4, 106–8, 114, 119, 130, 138–9, 145, 150, 153, 158, 162–3
  American Spanish, 15, 21, 23–4, 32, 63, 93, 98, 100–1, 103–6, 116, 119–22, 124, 127, 148–9, 156
  Buenos Aires speech, 116–17, 120, 126
  fragmentation, 97, 102, 116, 119–20, 165
  Golden Age Spanish, 81
  linguistic base, 28, 105–6, 137–8
  Peninsular norm, 97–8
  popular Spanish, 105
  regionalisms, 101–2

Toribio, Jacqueline, 3, 44, 51, 143, 167
Trujillo, Rafael L., 14, 80, 85–7, 158, 182

United States, 7, 10–12, 14, 18, 20, 44, 51, 53, 74–7, 88–9, 137, 139, 166
  Harvard University, 12, 124, 155
  Monroe Doctrine, the, 76
  New York, 10, 89
  Panamericanism, 10, 77
  Roosevelt, Franklin Delano, 76
  University of Minnesota, the, 11, 76, 112
  U.S. occupation, 76–7, 84, 138, 140
  Wilson, Woodrow, 10, 77
Ureña, Salomé, 8–9, 69, 75, 77, 81, 83

Vasconcelos, José, 7, 13, 78, 90–2
  La raza cósmica, 78
Venezuela, 77, 97, 158, 165

Whitney, William Dwight, 96
Woolard, Kathryn, 33, 41–2, 47, 53

Zuleta Álvarez, Emilio, 15–16, 111